ALL OR NOTHING AT ALL

The more you do, the better you get.

BILLY BLAND

By the same author

It's a Hill, Get Over It
The Round
Running Hard

ALL OR NOTHING AT ALL

The life of Billy Bland

Steve Chilton

Foreword by Kilian Jornet

First published by Sandstone Press Ltd
Suite 1, Willow House
Stoneyfield Business Park
Inverness
IV2 7PA
Scotland

www.sandstonepress.com

Editor: Robert Davidson

ISBN: 978-1-913207-22-9
ISBNe: 978-1-913207-23-6

Jack[illegible]urgh
Typ[illegible]more
P[illegible]d,

To Penelope and Kerena,
the next generation

CONTENTS

LIST OF CHAPTER ILLUSTRATIONS

All line drawings in the book were drawn specially for the book by Moira Chilton, and are not to be used without prior permission.

LIST OF RACE ROUTE MAPS

All maps in the book were compiled and drawn by the author. Map data is derived from the OpenStreetMap dataset which is available under an ODBL licence (http://www.openstreetmap.org/copyright). The contour data is derived from Andy Allan's reworking of the public domain SRTM data (http://opencyclemap.org/).

LIST OF PHOTOGRAPHIC PLATES

Photo Credits

All from the Billy Bland Collection, except:

Cover: Neil Shuttleworth
Plate 4: Robert Armstrong
Plate 7: V. B. Shaw
Plates 9, 10, 11, 12, 14, 31: Neil Shuttleworth
Plates 15, 16: Dave Woodhead
Plate 22: Lakeland Photographic
Plate 24: Steve Bateson
Plates 25, 26, 27, 28, 29, 30, 32, 41: Pete Hartley
Plates 33 and 35: Martin Stone
Plate 40: Allan Greenwood
Plate 42: Boff Whalley
Plate 43: David Woodthorpe
Plate 44: Martin Campbell
Plate 45: Mark Wilson
Plate 46: Danny Richardson
Plate 47: Pete Barron

ACKNOWLEDGEMENTS

There are always many people to thank when producing any book, and this is no exception. First and foremost, I must acknowledge Billy and Ann Bland, without whose cooperation the project would have remained just an idea. Billy Bland, whose very aura and reputation worried me at the start of this journey, proved to be a very charismatic subject. He was endlessly polite and honest, however personal my probing became. He always tried to say it like it was and has always produced great quotes when interviewed by myself or others. Ann Bland supported Billy, and myself, all the way. She prompted Billy if memory temporarily failed him, responded to my interminable follow-up queries, and proved herself to be the rock that she has been for him all their life together. My many visits to the top end of Borrowdale to talk with them both have been pivotal in telling this story, and it has always been a pleasure to discuss the old and recent times with them.

As well as Billy and Ann, I have also had some in depth conversations with several contemporaries, friends, family and rivals. To the following in particular I give my heartfelt thanks for finding the time to answer my sometimes naïve questions: Pete and Anne Bland, Pete Barron, Jan Darrall, Jon Broxap, Colin Donnelly, Howard Pattinson, Ross Brewster, Mark Wilson, Hugh Symonds, Kenny and

Pauline Stuart, Joe Ritson, Tony Cresswell, John Wild, Gavin Bland, Dave Hall, and Scoffer Schofield.

Help comes in many different ways. For finding and suggesting various reference sources I turned to Jeff Ford and Charlotte McCarthy (both from the Mountain Heritage Trust), the latter inviting me to look through material at the Trust library, where I also bagged some mountaineering book bargains as they were clearing out some unwanted stock. I also received some good leads from Julie Carter (author of *Running the Red Line*) and Joe Ritson, who followed a great chat at the Keswick Museum café with some really useful material from his own archive. Martin Stone was instrumental in connecting me to Kilian Jornet, who generously agreed to write the Foreword to the book.

That thing called the internet is also wonderful for finding contacts and resolving queries. So, thanks to diligent folk on the Fell Runners UK Facebook group and the FRA Forum for responding to my random requests for info, race results, or other trivia. For furnishing me with contact details for people that I wanted to speak to I am particularly grateful to Matt Bland, Chris Knox, Hugh Symonds, and Ann Bland. In a similar way I needed to refer to some *Fellrunner* magazines that I didn't have (and weren't on the brilliant FRA website archive) and both Marcus Covell and Simon Blease kindly offered to send me missing ones that they had and were prepared to donate to aid my research.

Let us not forgot the value of librarians. On several visits to the excellent Kendal Library Local History section Kate Holliday and Sylvia Kelly were invariably welcoming, and happy to search out my obscure reference requests from their stock. Equally valuable was the support I received from Vanessa Hill, of the Middlesex University Library, who tracked down (and sent me) some references when I was looking into re-wilding and specifically the Wild Ennerdale project. I have also done much reading around the subject as I have been writing the manuscript, and the main books and other resources referred to are listed in the references section.

Huge thanks are due to the following for help in sourcing photographs from their own collections and archives, and for giving permission to use them in the book: Pete Barron, Steve Bateson, Allan Greenwood, Denise Park, Neil Shuttleworth, Martin Stone, Boff Whalley, and Mark Wilson.

A writer always benefits from the support of friends, whom they can tire out with stories of how badly, or well sometimes, the manuscript is going. Among such friends one who stands out is Mike Cambray, who was always happy to accommodate me on dashes to the Lakes, and act as a sounding board for my ideas regarding this project. On one walk through his local Craggy Woods he came up with the brilliant suggestion of illustrating each chapter with a line drawing relevant to the part of the story within it. Moira Chilton somewhat nervously took on the task of providing the pen and ink illustrations which introduce each chapter. I hope you will agree that they are marvellous, helping set the scene and giving an excellent locational context to the journey.

On the many journeys to interview people for the manuscript Bruce Springsteen has many times been my companion. He has been the soundtrack to my writing and researching and is an inspiration to me on several levels. I once listed his 'Born to Run' in a blog on my favourite running books. It is actually the best written rock autobiography, in my opinion. The discerning reader/rock fan may detect his tangible presence in this tome.

At some point an author has to show their work to someone, ideally someone who is willing to read it and give constructive feedback. Massive thanks go to Ed Price for being my critical friend, despite having a very busy domestic and working life himself. He made some very sound suggestions regarding structure and style when reviewing the first draft of the manuscript for me, and I am sure the subsequent re-drafting has produced a better and more readable result. Any errors in the script are of course my responsibility.

Thanks to my editor Robert Davidson, proof-reader Joy Walton, cover designer Heather MacPherson of Raspberry Creative Type, indexer Roger Smith and all at Sandstone Press who, as always, have been a pleasure to work with.

FOREWORD

by

Kilian Jornet

When I came to England to consider doing the Bob Graham Round (BGR) I was very keen to meet Billy Bland, but also unsure about how a meeting would go. He is a legend and I had been told that he doesn't particularly like non-fell runners coming to run the fells.

Nervously I knocked on the door. I was somehow pleased when Ann, his wife, said that he wasn't at home. He was out for a ride on his bike and she wasn't expecting him to be home for a few hours. 'He likes biking now,' Ann explained. I could comprehend that for someone as compulsive and addicted to sport as Billy Bland that it didn't just mean that he'd take an hour bike ride twice a week, even in his 70s. I came back the day after, and Billy was home this time. We discussed me doing the BGR for a fair while, and early on he asked me, 'are you going to use poles?'. I said no. 'All right,' he said. Real fell runners don't use poles, apparently. We talked for ages, and he explained to me how he ran the Bob Graham Round nearly 40 years ago. It was in a time nobody has come close to since. He told me how much he likes cycling now that he can't run, mainly because of ankle problems. We also talked about some of his races and the training that he did in the past. A few days after that I ran the Round myself and Billy was at different locations on the route, with his bike, cheering for me.

Probably the first time I heard about Billy Bland was back in the early 2000s. At a race some fellow fell runners told me about races in the Lakes and Scotland which had records unbroken since the 80s. When I came to look up those races, the names of the winners were often the same; Kenny Stuart, Joss Naylor or Billy Bland. When the trail running scene was starting to develop in the rest of the world the UK scene (more often called fell running) had been around for years. With more than a hundred years of history, these races weren't something new with a few people running mountains. Fell running was already a sport with a long history, and the competition was fierce. Many of the best times for the fell races date from the period that Billy Bland was at his peak. The fell runners were pushing each other so hard that nobody has been able to beat some of those times since then. Billy Bland was outstanding among those runners. He dominated the classic fell races, even the short ones. But what was most inspirational was the strategy he used when taking on the longer races. He started sprinting and kept the pace up for as far as possible and used exactly the same strategy even up to the 60 or so miles of rounds like the Bob Graham.

Remember that this was a different time. Life was harder. They had no fancy shoes, or gels and training plans. But they just ran harder, with Billy perhaps being the hardest of all. His races and records have been inspiring generations of runners. His fame has spread from Borrowdale and the districts around the Lakes. It has crossed the seas to inspire the sky runners and trail runners in Europe, and even to America to show how to run ultras. But his legacy isn't in his performances, it is his generosity. He has helped many, many others to achieve their dreams, even down to pacing or advising them in their Bob Graham round attempts or fell race achievements.

In this book, Steve continues to explore the history of fell running in the brilliant style of his previous books, his in-depth analysis leading us to understand Billy Bland, whilst highlighting his achievements. Billy Bland is a legend, and he is a fine man. Steve takes us through Billy's life, to meet and know the man behind the legend.

Kilian Jornet
Champion mountain runner
Norway 2019

PREFACE

At odd times there is a need to tell the story of how my first book on fell running came about, about a decade ago. It goes something like this.

Having always loved fell running, my respect for Joss Naylor is no surprise. He has been a real hero to me. He is in many people's minds the greatest fell runner ever, perhaps the greatest endurance runner of all time. So, ages ago a thought crossed my mind, 'why is it that no-one has written a book about him and his exploits'. The germ of an idea formed somewhere in the far recesses of my mind, and I suddenly decided to be the one to right this wrong. I have no idea what made me think this was achievable, or how to make it happen, but there we are. Having just begun to give the thought some working space in my brain, lo and behold a biography of Joss came out. Keith Richardson's *Joss: The Life and Times of the Legendary Lake District Fell Runner and Shepherd Joss Naylor* was published in October 2009. Being in the Lakes when this news reached me, I ordered a signed copy of the book from *Fred Holdsworth Books* and read it with interest when it arrived. Good though the book is, it is certain that I would have told his story in a somewhat different way and dealt with some things that are glossed over in it.

This made me think that maybe there WAS a book in me, and so began the search for a different subject to apply myself to.

It soon became clear that another angle on fell running was my main interest, and that I should think about that. Having long admired the exploits of Billy Bland and Gavin Bland it seemed to me that the story of these two superb fell runners, and their extended families, might prove to be a rich subject. The various members of the family have both been involved in fell running and prominent in aspects of Cumbrian life, including farming and tourism. So, the idea of *The Blands of Borrowdale* was germinated. With no 'previous' in the area, and no real idea how to progress the idea, I did some research and compiled a synopsis, with a view to pitching to some publishers. Having looked for publishers who published in what seemed to be a niche genre it was easy to compile a list with details of contacts, and also their terms for submission of manuscripts. Having no manuscript to offer yet, the first choice was what looked like an interesting option, whose website suggested: 'An introductory email should outline the type of book being proposed and give a brief biography of the author, including their publishing history.

At this point what was fully expected was a rejection over that first application, and then a long round of further rejections. But to my huge surprise the commissioning editor at Sandstone Press said, 'we are interested, and my concern would be with the narrowness of the subject. I would hope to see it extended into more general fell running, its history, characters and events.' Even then it was not an acceptance. Swallowing any pride I might have had, I thought about it and decided to re-write the synopsis to encompass this change and re-submitted it to them. The response this time was, 'Thank you for such a thoughtful and positive response to my comments. Sandstone Press would indeed be interested in this book. Do it well and I am very confident that we will accept it.' So, a positive response but still no deal. With hope in my heart, and still no idea if I could deliver, a start was made on researching the revised manuscript idea. This was on 13 June 2011. In December 2012 the first draft of the manuscript went off to the publisher and was reviewed anonymously by their 'reader'. Three days before Christmas I received an acceptance email (with some suggestions from the review) and a draft contract. The rest as they say is history. The book was '*It's a Hill, Get Over It: Fell Running's History and Characters*'.

Having written what was nominally a history of the sport of fell running I was now inspired and over the next three years wrote a book about one particular running challenge (*The Round: In Bob Graham's Footsteps*), and another about a great running rivalry (*Running Hard: The Story of a Rivalry*).

Now this is book four, and I have gone back to the original idea, which has been itching at me ever since. It was decided that it should focus on just one person, Billy Bland, and the backdrop to his life, with other family members as supporting characters. So, it is a biography of Billy Bland, and also includes his extended family. There is also a parallel theme of the changes in the Borrowdale valley, the part of the Lake District that Billy has lived in for over seventy years.

Taken at face value Billy Bland seems to be a straightforward man who happened to be exceptionally good at running up and down hills. But look closer and there are a series of tensions and conflicts that moulded his character and have affected his life over the years. I have explored those conflicts and hope I have presented a fair picture of this extraordinary person.

Life is a journey. This is Billy Bland's journey.

Steve Chilton
Enfield
November 2019

GROWING UP

I don't do any running now. Knees are all right, ankles are the problem. Used to be 5 feet 10 and went for MOT and am now 5 feet 9. Got the shrinks. No spring in them ankles anymore. If I had to run to Seatoller, a few hundred yards, then my ankles would ache. To be quite honest I am not bothered. Took fell running as far as I could take it.

I did it my way or didn't do it at all. Be I right or be I wrong. Yes, you make mistakes, but if you have a head on your shoulders you will learn off them. There is an awful lot that gets printed that isn't right. There is one thing about me, if I said it I will stand by it.

These two connected comments from previous discussions with Billy Bland are swimming towards the front of my consciousness on the drive up the Borrowdale valley to talk to him about his upbringing. He has already told me that writing a book about him won't be an easy ride. This makes me more than somewhat nervous.

Clocking the bike collection in the back yard, there is a warm welcome from a still fit looking 70-something. Billy Bland certainly doesn't look his age, although sitting opposite him it is possible to see a discrete hearing aid as we start talking about his early life. Standing at 5 feet 10 inches tall, he weighed 10st 7lbs at his racing weight. He has certainly not let himself go, is still very fit from his cycling, and is what some might consider to be underweight.

Parked out the back are their Ford Fiesta and a Citroen Berlingo van. Billy's wife Ann joins us, often adding her perspective to the tales of early days. On this visit, and on the many other times we talked about his life, I notice Billy's relaxed way of talking. He answers my questions patiently and without hesitating, yet he defends his point rigorously if challenged.

Billy Bland has memories of having a pretty happy upbringing in Borrowdale. The family were not well off, but he had a good deal of freedom to enjoy his surroundings. He recalls that, 'as kids you might be asked to open a gate or run to round up a sheep if you happened to be with your father. But other than that, you were left to get on with your schooling and play with your mates.'

Billy was born at Nook Farm, which is just up the road from where he lives now. He was born in number five bedroom on 28 July 1947. His given name is William, as the church wouldn't christen anyone with shortened names. But he was called Billy right from when he was born. He has two brothers and a sister Kathleen, who is the eldest. All four children were born at the farm rather than going to hospital. Kathleen was born in 1943, Stuart was born in 1945, and David came along in 1949.

Life wasn't easy in the valley though. The Blands didn't get electricity at Nook Farm until 1960. That is when the mains arrived, after a long drawn out community campaign successfully lobbied for the installation of power. Watendlath had to wait another eighteen years and was only connected with electricity in 1978.

Billy spent the first thirteen years of life without the benefit of having electricity at the flick of a switch. They had had a generator for a year or two, and even ran a television off it. Billy can remember when they didn't have lights and they went about with a Tilley Lamp, and the cows being milked by hand.

It was very much a rural upbringing. Billy admits that he went bird nesting, adding that it, 'is a no-no these days, which is how it should be, but that is how it was then'. He says he came home from school and got changed and away out he went, to hang out with other lads from the village. Even then there were social divides in the valley, as Billy explains. 'It didn't tend to happen that we'd play with Grange kids. There was a thing with Grange kids on the school bus that they were different, and it is still there yet. There aren't many kids in Grange now. Grange always tended then to be more offcomers, and older people.'

In Billy's early days the kids used to enjoy playing hare and hounds, a catching game. The local children also had their own swimming spot, on a corner of Stonethwaite Beck, called Mill Close. That was where everybody south of Grange would go swimming. It was where Billy learnt to swim, not that he liked it. His parents weren't exactly happy about them swimming there without anyone being there to supervise them, but they did it anyway. When it snowed, they would go sledging on The How, 'where the Borrowdale race finishes, that bump there. There's about 250 yards maximum there, with a runout.' It was a very handy location near Nook Farm.

Billy Bland and his brothers certainly got a lot of freedom granted to them by their parents, as evidenced by something he tells me about attending the Wasdale Show, way over in the next valley. 'I'd go with my mother and father in a vehicle and Stuart, maybe David, and I would run home [*over Styhead Pass*] while they stayed for a drink. This was when I was at primary school mind! Which fathers and mothers would set their kids off like that now? I am sure I remembered this right, but I could do 46 minutes to Seathwaite yard from Burnthwaite which is by the church in Wasdale.'

Billy Bland was a healthy child, experiencing no particularly unusual illnesses. He did have his fair share of accidents, but no bones were broken as a kid. The Blands had two carthorses at Nook Farm, called Bonnie and Jewel. Billy remembers that he fell off one on his seventh birthday just messing about. His first broken bone was as a footballer with Keswick, breaking a small bone in his leg. He knew it was broken and came off the pitch and went to hospital and they said it wasn't broken. He was sure it was, but it wasn't until the following week that he was able to get it plastered.

Thinking back to childhood, Billy mentions two random fears that he can remember experiencing or being talked about. Borrowdale would not have been very diverse culturally in those days. 'There used to be a coloured/black person come to the door to sell cleaning and polishing stuff', Billy recalls. 'If mother answered the door we used to get fatha to come and talk to him and send him on his way.' The other was that Ann's great grandmother, who used to live at Longthwaite Farm, used to have to hide in a cupboard if there was thunder and lightning, as she was so scared.

Billy can't recall ever having pets when he was a youngster. There were four children on the farm and having a pet each wouldn't have worked, is how he puts it. Reflecting recently on the good and bad aspects of growing up on a farm, Billy recalls that, 'if you had asked me as a teenager there wouldn't have been any negativity at all. It was completely different to what it is now. We used to help in the fields at hay time.'

He continues. 'Now looking back, I can see many good parts of it, because you learnt to stand on your own two feet. There was no question you had to make your own way in life. No handouts whatsoever, which is good.' He says he could do his football and running, although not all of the family agreed they were a good use of his time. 'I know Uncle Noble up at Seatoller Farm didn't approve of me. He would be saying, "no wonder he can't do much during the day as he's running about them fells. He would be far better helping us." That is how they saw it. I was just wasting my time, according to some. Work was all-important, as was making a bob or two. My father was not like that. He used to say if I came home from a race, "well, why didn't you win?" But life had been hard for that generation and it was going to be hard for us.'

Billy was brought up in an environment that was neither especially religious nor political. His parents were not religious at all. But the Bland children had to go to Sunday

School. Most people did then. Ann Bland had to go too. She adds, 'it was to get us out of the road!' They would set off in their clogs, which were a cheap shoe option. Politics was no real concern for the family either. Billy's parents were only interested in farming really. They might talk about subsidies for ship workers and miners, but as long as they were able to get on with the farming that was all they were interested in. Billy points out that, 'farmers are the ones that get subsidies now.'

The mention of clogs surprised me, and resulted in a roundabout discussion of footwear, starting with the man next door to them that used to make clogs in his shed. Ann giggles, as she comments that, 'our kids had clogs too, cute little red ones, made at Caldbeck.' She reckoned that going back ten years or more from them everyone locally would have clogs. Billy adds that, 'farmers like my father would get their boots made up at Rydal, by a man called Ottaway. Studded at the bottom and one short leather lace. Up at Honister quarry it was either clogs or steel toe-capped boots – *strang boots* they were called'.

In an historical exhibition at Grange Church, in Borrowdale, there are several panels that detail family life in the valley. One of them has some memories contributed by Billy Bland's sister Kathleen, who was the eldest child, four years older than Billy (who was the third child). The following extract sheds light, literally, on bedtimes for the four Bland children, who Kathleen remembers all having to share one bed sometimes:

> She was the tomboy with bright orange hair and exaggerated by the 'clashy' green twin sets her mum would knit her. And she helped look after her little brothers, recalling the tin bath where they bathed in front of the

> fire and helped to keep their antics in order. 'Going upstairs to bed,' she says, 'I'd carry the candle so carefully.' Yet the flickering flame might blow out in the draughty old farmhouse. 'Mother would scold me for dripping candle fat on the carpet.'

Hot water from the kitchen range filled the tin bath. Cold water from a bucket cooled it off and green Fairy soap worked up a lather. That kitchen range was kept black-leaded, prepared by using a kind of liquid shoe polish – and elbow grease. The paraffin lamp had to be watched too. If the wick went untrimmed, the flame rose and blackened the ceiling with soot.

Kathleen also recalls two aspects of the cleanliness that the family typically sought:

> She remembers laboriously scrubbing the farmhouse flagstones on her hands and knees – with a drop of milk in the water 'to bring out the blue' of the slate. Because there was no television to watch in the evenings, the family would sit round and make 'proddy' mats to cover the flagstones, using pegs from bones. Using these, you pushed pieces of old clothes and rags cut up into strips through a hessian base that was stretched on a frame.

When it was time for him to go to school Billy had about a kilometre to go to get to Borrowdale School. At the time that he started school it was next to the church in Stonethwaite. Both Billy and Ann Bland went to the primary school there, with Billy being two years ahead of Ann, and both took the eleven-plus exam. The school has been replaced by six houses, with a new school being built just along the road in 1968. This new school was built by the grandsons of the builder of the old school, all from the Hodgson family, a long-established firm from Keswick.

Between 20 and 45 pupils attended Borrowdale School for the years Billy was there. He freely admits he was not a good scholar and didn't want to be there, but he had to be there by law, 'so that was that', he says. He recalls that he once hid in the coalhouse so he could nip away and watch the sheep dipping. He got caught and was given a hiding. 'My fatha was a lovely gentle man who wasn't bothered, but I got plenty from my mother. She lost it quite easily with all of us lads. We were young buggers who thought we knew it all.'

After primary school children from the valley went onwards to Keswick Grammar School or Lairthwaite Secondary Modern (also in Keswick), depending on their eleven-plus results. These two schools are now combined as a comprehensive school (Keswick School). There was a special school bus to take pupils to Keswick from Borrowdale. Ann lived half a mile up the road from Billy, so they got to know each other well early in life, meeting every day virtually, going to school together for instance. But things weren't that simple. Ann was at Keswick Grammar, and says that pupils at Lairthwaite School, where Billy was, had 'no regard' for those at the Grammar. Ann notes that pupils from the Grammar School used to sit at the front of the bus and pupils from Billy's school sat at the back, by tradition.

Billy reckons that they didn't get out of the valley much. 'We had a Morecambe trip every year that my mother was one of the organisers of. We went on two buses and that was our almost yearly trip. My uncle Nat would also take us in the Land Rover to Allonby [*on the NW Cumbrian coast*] for a day out but that was it. But we were happy enough.'

At Lairthwaite School Billy Bland met Howard Pattinson. He is 72 years old, 6 months older than Billy, and they were in the same class at the school. Howard Pattinson was born in Keswick and lived there from 1946 till he was 23 years old, when he left to move down to Hertfordshire. In Keswick he worked at the Keswick Reminder newspaper and went to college in Carlisle and realised there was more to print and design than he was ever going to get in Keswick. He says that one strong catalyst for change for him was that being in the town centre going to work indoors when everybody else is on holiday in Keswick isn't a good thing. 'I thought if I can get a job in a college and get the holidays then I would have more time in Keswick to explore the fells than when I was living there.' He says he ended up working at a great college, West Herts College (in Watford), and then stayed there for 38 years. Ironically his own fell running started after he moved south.

Howard Pattinson and I recently had a long chat after I drove round the M25 to meet him in Rickmansworth, at his partner's house. He has a good memory of his early life in the Lakes, where he still has a house.

He first went through some school experiences that he and Billy shared. 'I have a picture of a football team at school and Billy is in there and so am I, I think he was only a reserve. He was quite small. Billy and I were just like any other kids at school. We didn't necessarily have great natural talent for running or football, but we worked at it.'

Pattinson didn't really know Billy before Lairthwaite Secondary School, as they lived at opposite ends of the Borrowdale valley from each other. But he has an interesting perspective on their two differing upbringings. 'I envied him living in a house in Borrowdale. He was in a farm and I was in a council house in Keswick. As a child I visited his house [*Nook Farm*] a couple of times I suppose, nothing more than that. It seemed heavenly, beautiful. I would have liked to have been a farmer if I could.'

Pattinson recalls that everyone ran a little when they were at school. 'I got some fitness from doing a milk round. I am not sure what Billy would have been doing at the time. I didn't knock about with Billy really, because he went back up Borrowdale after school.'

It was practical things and sport that Billy liked when he was younger. He liked woodwork as it was working with his hands. He notes wryly that he got the woodwork prize at school. 'I have never had any issues in my head about myself from school. I have always had a mind that thought for itself and if someone didn't agree then they were wrong!', he says disarmingly.

There had been no school trips at their primary school, but from secondary school Billy remembers going to the steelworks at Workington, and also to the coalmine at Haig Pit, under the sea at Whitehaven. 'That was interesting, and there has been some talk of opening it up again. School was more practical-based in my time, but now it is all university-based. You were not looked on as a failure then if you wanted to take an apprenticeship in something.'

Howard Pattinson is very scathing about the school system at the time, as he had experienced it. 'I was at Crosthwaite [Primary] School, my dad had died, and my mother was disabled and had no money. I was second in everything at school, but the headteacher (Mr Slee) said, "you are not going to go to Keswick School because they will ask for money your mother can't afford. You are going to Lairthwaite regardless of your eleven-plus results". They were a lot of us like that. I never did any

GCSEs, none of us did. I left school with no qualifications whatsoever. The wasted potential in our era was criminal.'

The teachers couldn't have cared less, Pattinson reckons. 'If someone asks you, do you want to work in the garden or sit in a maths lesson, you'll go in the garden won't you? One or two teachers were half interested, but most were not. Two of us left at Christmas and there were two jobs available. Dennis Cartwright got first choice and he went to the Gasworks, and I was left with the printers. However, I finished up as a Senior Lecturer and Course Director of a BA (Hons) Degree in Graphic Design.'

He concludes, 'at school we were never introduced to the countryside or anything. But it was just beginning to be considered. There was a man called Clarke came there who was keen on the outdoors, and he started to take groups walking, but that must have been after Billy and I had left. Basically, we both went through school then left and got whatever jobs we could. It was shocking really.'

Billy Bland does remember collecting wildflowers as a kid and pressing them in a book. It speaks volumes about Billy that he even made this competitive. 'It is a no-no now to pick wildflowers, but that was how it was then. You put the name beside them, and it was a competition to see who could collect the most.' Everyone did it, and it helped them learn their names and also to be able to recognise the flora. It was the start of Billy's enduring love, and understanding, of the countryside. Billy Bland's record of the wildflower species he'd identified during his school days is now famous locally – it was highlighted in the September 2017 issue of *Borrowdale News*.

At school, as a farmer's son you just thought that by instincts you could soon be a farmer, but Billy never really got the opportunity. His older brother Stuart was already there before him to take on the family farm and so Billy had to get a job. When Stuart left the farm, David was just leaving school, so he went on to the farm, with Billy getting bypassed in a way, which he says he wasn't that bothered about. 'It was just something that happened, you didn't kick up a fuss about it.'

Recently Billy has been a very keen cyclist, but there were no new bikes for Christmas in his household when he was young. 'We had bikes on the farm but who knows where they came from. There were certainly no brand-new bikes that I can remember. We used to double up, using the crossbar a lot too as kids.' The first year of his working life he cycled to work, and then he got a motorbike. It was second-hand bike, described by Billy as 'a rubbish bike.' He went on to get a bigger and better one, a Velocette.

In the bad winter of 1963 Derwentwater got iced over and they rode their bikes on it to take a short cut home. 'There was a lad from Keswick used to come across the ice on his bike. It was that thick someone drove a bus on it once.' Ann recalls that she was at school and they couldn't have games lessons, so they used to go and skate on the lake.

Both Ann and Billy point out that you just knew everybody locally when they were young. Billy's youngest brother David is the same age as Ann and was in the same class as her in Borrowdale school. There were only six pupils that took the eleven-plus exam that year, and three went to Keswick School and three to Lairthwaite School. Both David and Stuart Bland also went to Lairthwaite School, like Billy. The little Bland boys all had to go to school with the same things on when at primary school. Their mother used to knit them the same tank tops. She was an expert at knitting, and all the grandchildren had beautiful knitted cardigans and jumpers.

Billy and Ann began courting as teenagers. Ann recalls that she was still at Keswick School, so says she was just sixteen. 'We had to go to school on Saturday mornings. I took my O Levels and the night before the English Literature exam Billy took me dancing.' She adds that her school results were nothing to be proud of. On leaving school she worked as an audit clerk in an accountant's office in Keswick for five years.

On being asked how much of a romancer Billy had been, Ann immediately came back with, 'he must have had something!' Billy sagely responds, 'what you see is what you get. I don't think I have changed in any way.' He goes on to explain that there was a cinema in Keswick and a dancehall there too. 'It was opposite Fitz Park, where the Youth Hostel is now, by the bridge. You went downstairs into the dancehall. The Kinks played there once, when they were on their way up in the world.' They also used to go out with Billy's brother Stuart and the girl who became his wife, and another couple. They used to go to the Coledale Inn, in Braithwaite, to have a drink or two, although Ann wasn't old enough to drink yet. They then went on to the Pavilion for a dance.

Ann and Billy were married at the ages of 20 and 22 respectively. But their parents didn't know it was happening, as they just took off and did it. They were married at Cockermouth Registry Office on 21 February 1970 in what Ann describes as a 'seven-minute wonder', as people in the valley saw it. After the event, Billy played football in the afternoon. 'Our parents just accepted it, even though we had nowhere to live. So, we lived with Ann's mum and dad', says Billy now.

Ann tops it with the *coup de grace*. 'In a small valley like this everyone is thinking, "well she must be pregnant then". [*Laughs*] Well, she was.'

Billy Bland had an interesting route from Nook Farm to Mountain View (where he now lives). After he married Ann in 1970, they both lived with Ann's parents for three years, from 1970 to 1973. This was half a mile down the road at a hamlet called Peat Howe, in the end cottage. When he retired from farming in 1964 Ann's grandfather had wanted to live next door to Ann's parents. Dick Richardson, who was in that next-door cottage already had two children and it was too small for the family. In the meantime, Ann's grandfather had bought a house at Mountain View for £1,800 (in 1964). It was intended for Dick really, so he could move there and leave the Peat Howe one for the grandfather. For a while then, Dick Richardson lived at Mountain View and worked up at Honister. But then he put in for a farm because he had a farming background, and he secured Watendlath Farm through the National Trust.

While they lived with Ann's parents in that tiny two-bedroom end cottage Billy and Ann had two children, Andrea (born 1970) and Shaun (1972). Then they moved to the Mountain View in 1973, as it had become available after Dick Richardson's move. When they had lived in the house for just one month, suddenly Ann's father died at the age of 55. Ann's mother was in an awful state, so they moved back in with her for a while. Twelve days later Ann's grandfather died. Ann's mother had lost her husband and her father within a fortnight. Ann's grandmother lived on in the house and died about 3 years later. Ann's mother died four years ago.

Ann confirms that they got on well with her parents

when they lived with them, and subsequently too. Billy's take is that both pairs of parents knew what they were dealing with, with Ann and himself. 'We are what we are. Don't pretend to be something you are not. I have never believed in that and I never will.' Ann added, 'I don't think we ever had a wrong word with my parents. His mother I could fall out with though.' Billy added with some feeling in his voice that, 'really my parents should have supported us more than they did. It is what it is, you can't change it.'

Childhood and upbringing can shed light on a person's future life, but we must also look at how their family background has influenced that development process. To do this we will step back through a couple of generations of the Blands.

MY HOMETOWN

Borrowdale has the character of a cul-de-sac valley, even though the road over Honister Pass can take you across into Buttermere. It famously includes the narrow section near Castle Crag that Alfred Wainwright described in his guidebook thus: 'No high mountain, no lake, no famous crag, no tarn. But in the author's humble submission, it encloses the loveliest square mile in Lakeland – the Jaws of Borrowdale.'

There was a time when you couldn't move around in the top end of Borrowdale without tripping over someone from the extended Bland clan. Over the years members of the family have owned or been tenants at many of the farms in Seatoller, Stonethwaite and Rosthwaite. Billy

Bland's family background is fundamental to his development as an individual.

Billy Bland's grandfather Willie was not from Borrowdale but from over the fells. Willie Bland had been born in Patterdale in 1883, to James and Esther Bland, a farming family. The family moved when he was seven to Brotherilkeld Farm, Eskdale. James Bland then moved the family to Scar Green (Calder Bridge) at the turn of the century. By now Willie was a teenager with seven brothers and sisters. Around 1910 Willie married Elizabeth and had had his first three children when they all moved to a hamlet called Nannycatch (near Cleator Moor).

Here Willie was a tenant farmer with lands between Dent and the Cold Fell Road. Willie Bland eventually had a family of six boys and one girl, who all had to walk to school two or three miles away in Ennerdale Bridge. He then took the step of moving into Borrowdale to take on a tenancy at Nook Farm in Rosthwaite in the 1920s with all the children: Jim, Jack, Billy, Joe, Nathan and Noble, and their sister Esther. Nook Farm was eventually one of many farms that the National Trust bought up, a trend spear-headed by one Mrs Heelis (Beatrix Potter as was), before she died in 1943.

The details of the National Trust purchase of Nook Farm, made on 3 Apr 1947, are shown on their website archive as:

> Nook Farm, Rosthwaite – 58.97 hectares (145.72 acres) Land comprised of fields and farmland. Purchased in 1947 from Lt Col. E. S. Jones, in memory of Capt. John Diver, of the Royal Army Medical Corps. Farm buildings (and 2.40 hectares of land (inclusive)) were also bought with a bequest from Mrs S. J. Tomlinson.

When Willie Bland retired from Nook Farm he moved to Cleator Moor, close to where he had previously lived (at Nannycatch), and Billy's father Joe took over the farm tenancy in Rosthwaite. Farmers often find it hard to stop living the farming life, so Willie used to look after some of Joe's hoggs (sheep up to their second shearing) when they were sent over to him to winter, as they do better away from the fells. They would take the sheep to Cleator Moor in October, having been born in the Spring. The grandfather would look after them, going the rounds to see they weren't stuck in briar and that the fences were OK. When it came to bringing them home at the end of March, they walked them from Cleator Moor to Buttermere (over the pass by Floutern Tarn, north of Great Borne) and they over-nighted there. Billy's father's mate was at Wilkinsyke Farm (at Buttermere) where they would be penned overnight. They would go back the next day and walk them over Honister Pass. 'Too tight to pay for transporting them, I would say', says Billy now. 'They would be one of the last one's that drove their hoggs, rather than transporting them.' Before grandfather Willie went to Cleator Moor they used to winter the hoggs at Isel, between Bassenthwaite and Cockermouth, as well as at Cleator Moor. A family called Nicholson used to mind them.

Billy's father Joe and his uncle Nathan (or Nat), who was a single man who never married, ran Nook Farm between them. They were involved in sheep farming predominantly. In those days all farms in the valley had a cow and their own potato fields. You collected the bedding for your calves, by cutting bracken.

Billy's mother's Lily (nee Stuart) was brought up by her Auntie Hannah, and they lived at several different locations in Borrowdale. The trail is a little too vague to identify the exact locations involved. Lily did live at Cragg Cottage in Rosthwaite for a while just before she married, which is just across from Nook Farm, and that is how she met Billy's father Joe. Lily and Joe were married in 1942, on 20 February, at Borrowdale Church.

Joe Bland was a farmer for all his working life, not always on his own farm though. He worked at Gatesgarth Farm before his own father retired, while waiting to take over Nook Farm. Joe's brothers were all farmers, who all spread their wings to take on a range of positions in the area. Nat shared the running of Nook Farm with Joe, Jim was up at Watendlath (via a spell at Stonethwaite), Noble was at Seatoller Farm, Billy (Billy Bland's uncle Billy) at Croft Farm in Stonethwaite (which isn't a farm anymore). Finally, Jack worked for Billy's wife Ann Bland's grandfather at Longthwaite, but never had a farm of his own. This was the first of several connections between the Billy Bland and the Ann Bland family branches. None of the Bland brothers owned their own farm until Jim went on to Ravenstonedale.

Fell runner Dave Hall both trained and worked with Billy Bland at times. He has memories of camping in the early days up at Seatoller Farm on a basic campsite there. He says, 'I think Billy's uncle used to own it. He used to come round and accurately predict what time it would start raining. If he was wrong, he would say his watch was wrong.' Billy confirms that it would be his uncle Noble, adding, 'he would say that, he was a bloody old blowfat, as I would describe him'. A classic Bland expression, apparently meaning, 'think you know everything'.

Lily Bland was no more or less than a farmer's wife. Women at that time rarely went out to work. She had to work when living with Auntie Hannah though, who was very hard on her as a young girl. They were very poor, and Lily was made to go out and do various cleaning jobs. She didn't have a very good upbringing, as she was born out of wedlock. It was many years later that Lily found out that Hannah wasn't actually her mother.

When Joe and Lily Bland were there, Nook Farm and Yew Tree Farm (which are next door to each other) encompassed most of the fields in that part of Borrowdale. Nearly all the intakes to the south of Castle Crag went with Nook Farm, including Castle Intake and Lingy Bank. Being called 'Lingy' suggests a prevalence of heather, but when Billy was young it was full of stumps of trees which had been felled in the First World War, and they had scythed the bracken down for years and years to keep it good and grassy. But it had all been wooded at one time. At this time a tenancy would have a patch of land right where the farm was. Farms now are all more spread about because they have bought grounds further afield, for better grazing or growing.

There are many Edmondsons in the history of Borrowdale, and Ann Bland's grandmother was an Edmondson before she married. But for a while the Blands were pretty dominant, what with all the brothers working the various farms. 'There wasn't much room for anybody else!', recalls Billy. In writing about Thorneythwaite Farm, Ian Hall commented that, 'if all the [Bland] children had been the same age they would have filled Borrowdale School unaided.'

Contemporary photos show a typical farm scene – workers down on their knees tending the turnip crop, real backbreaking work. Billy points out that, 'in those days farmers wore a shirt with no collar, and never EVER took that shirt off when working in the fields. They had really brown arms though.' Joe and Nat used to clip the sheep by hand at Nook Farm.

Ann Bland's family are also from Borrowdale. Her maiden name is Horsley, and her given names are Margaret Ann. Her father, Maurice Horsley, was from Braithwaite, and ended up working at forestry for Lord Rochdale on the Lingholm Estate, near Keswick. This was after Billy had left his job there, as her father did not go there till he was fifty years old. Earlier he worked for a timber merchant at Greenodd, over near Ulverston, and he travelled there every day in an old van. Then they made him redundant, and he went to Lingholm after that. Ann's mother, Peggy, was brought up down at Longthwaite Farm.

Big families were the norm then, and Ann's father had seven sisters. Ann's mother was bridesmaid when Billy Bland's mother and father got married, and her mother was also his sister Kathleen's godmother. Billy and Ann knew each other at primary school, although they were separated by two school years because of the age difference.

Billy's mother Lily used to take in visitors for bed and breakfast in the summer and all the children then used to have to sleep outside in a wooden hut, as their bedrooms had been let out. You could hear the rain pattering on the roof, but the money helped to keep the family afloat. This happened from when Billy was quite little until he was about sixteen. Times were harder than they are now. There were no other farm workers, but as oldest son Stuart Bland had to start working on the farm as soon as he left school.

Billy's parents were farmers who lived the contemporary

farmer's life, which is much different from life now. Billy remembers, 'we still had carthorses when I was young, and there was no electricity in Borrowdale. Farming was hard graft. Farm lads these days, all they want to do is sit on their arse on a tractor, it is as if they haven't any legs.'

His parents were not especially sporty, they just worked at raising a family, having very little spare time. If you read a profile of Billy Bland one of the first things it will say is that he is the son of a Guides racer, but this is not as significant and important a fact as it might seem. Joe Bland did do a bit of running for a while, but not much, and it is a mistaken characterisation to imply that this particularly influenced Billy, or any of his brothers for that matter. Joe Bland was a farmer and he would just turn up and run occasionally. 'He didn't do many, but he certainly ran at Grasmere, as he worked at Grasmere for a bit. He would be running in his boots, and probably didn't have any shorts or t-shirts', says Billy.

Billy certainly inherited something from his father though, as part of his physiological makeup. 'He had a remarkably slow pulse rate,' he says. 'Mine maybe is now in the 40s, but I've had it down to 32. But fatha's pulse was always in the 30s.'

Although Billy claims his father didn't influence him particularly as he grew up, they have similar characters. Billy comments that he did instill in him a strong work ethic. 'You were brought up in that you would have to make your own way in life. Nobody was going to make it for you. It wasn't a choice you were given. That is how it was.' Neither Billy's father or mother ever showed emotion or affection. Ann Bland notes that, 'they just didn't. It was a different generation, and ours is a different generation to this generation.' There wasn't any favouritism with the children, although possibly the youngest (David) was favoured in some ways. Billy adds, 'I didn't think there was any favouritism, it never registered with me (although David did get the farm). But if I had really wanted to be a farmer then they would have backed us up by putting in for another farm.'

Billy Bland's father Joe and mother Lily both died of old age, in 1995 and 2005 respectively.

Billy's younger brother David is married to Ann's cousin Elizabeth, and they lived for a while in a caravan at Nook Farm, with their sons Gavin and Peter, as they were taking over the farm shortly. Billy's mother and father retired and moved into one of the six houses where Borrowdale School used to be in Stonethwaite. That allowed David and Elizabeth to move into Nook Farm. It was a family toss-up between Ann or Elizabeth as to who got Mountain View. Elizabeth and David moved into the farm. Thus, Ann and Billy moved to Mountain View. Billy says they were lucky to be able to stay in Borrowdale because they couldn't have afforded a house otherwise.

Billy's brother Stuart had moved down to live in Braithwaite before moving back to Thorneythwaite Farm, which he farmed for 35 years (1975 to 2010), before Stuart's son Jonny Bland took over. Jonny lived with his parents at Thorneythwaite till he was about 18 and then Stuart and Shirley Bland bought a house at Rosthwaite for Jonny and his girlfriend of the time. They then split up and Jonny met Joanne and they lived there and brought their kids up there. Eventually Stuart and Jonny swapped houses, basically so Jonny could farm. Jonny lived there from 2010 to 2016, then he got the tenancy of Yew Tree Farm.

Billy and Ann Bland's two children have long since fled the nest. Andrea lives in Penrith and has been a teacher at a local primary school there for 25 years. When the children were young their weekends were spent going to fell races to support their father. Neither fully realised the extent of his achievements until later in life. Andrea is very proud of what her father has achieved throughout his running career. She says to maintain that amount of self-discipline and drive for so long is amazing.

According to Ann, 'people are also picking up on Billy's running more than they did at the time. People have only just started asking for talks and Q and As and all that. For ages Billy has tried to keep a lid on that too.' He has opened up to talking about his running life a lot more recently though.

Their son Shaun is a self-employed builder. He has been with his partner for about 14 years, and she has two sons of 16 and 17 from a previous marriage. They live in Keswick. Shaun's partner, Hayley Hodgson, is a full time school teacher, and does triathlons and is a keen runner. According to Ann, 'she is always running, exercise is like a drug to her'. Shaun never really ran much, just kids sports at school. As soon as he was old enough not to go to races with his parents that was it. Ann reckons he would have had a lot to live up to if he had taken up running. Billy doesn't think it was really that. 'He just wasn't interested. I am happy as long as he is happy doing what he wants. You can't push string, as I have often said. It has got to come from within. He could have been all right, but he weren't bothered.'

Shaun is currently into motorbiking. He and Billy don't get on so well these days, because according to Ann they are, 'too much alike. Shaun's labourers haven't lasted five minutes, because like Billy he is fussy.' Billy gets defensive, saying, 'it is not fussy, it has to be done right. For me, I'd go, "I'll say this only once, and if you are not taking any notice then I am not wasting my breath on you." The right sort of self-employed person is self-motivated. You have to be responsible for the finished product', is his conclusion. We drop the subject.

We did come back to it on another occasion, which produced the following exchange between Billy and Ann. Billy started us off. 'I don't really see him now. That is the way it is. We worked together and fell out like.' Ann concedes that Shaun did come to her 70th birthday dinner. The photo shows he and Billy at opposite ends of the dinner table. Billy continues, 'if it had carried on it was only going to get worse. By distancing ourselves from each other it deals with it. If he walked in now and wanted to say something to me then I would speak to him. I think it is best left as it is though.' Ann comes back with, 'his girlfriend has been out bike riding with Billy. I meet up with them as well.' Billy carries on. 'You need your space. That is how our family has always been. We don't go visiting each other much. You just get on with doing stuff, that is how it has been. If I had nothing in my life I might be visiting more, but I've got plenty in my life.' Ann concludes with, 'we are a pretty dysfunctional family. To be honest a lot of families round here are like that. It may be us Cumbrians!'

We leave the Bland family with a story about Joe Bland that was recounted in Sheila Richardson's book *Borrowdale*, but which turned out to not be as heroic as it at first seemed, and slightly inaccurately recorded. As the book recounted it:

> In 1942 there was a flood that almost claimed the life of a visitor to Rosthwaite. There used to be wooden chalets that served as an annexe to the Scafell Hotel, and on the night of a tremendous storm, the heavy downpour of rain caused flooding to sweep through the chalets. While

> the inhabitants were attempting to reach the safety of the main hotel, a Mrs Forsythe was swept away. [*According to an eyewitness*] “It went with her, right down through the village; an’ she caught on some barbed wire. If she hadn’t o’ caught on that barbed wire, she would ha’ drowned. Joe Bland, and maybe one or two more got a rope and they went down. It was dark you know, but Joe went down on this rope and they found her, catched on to this barbed wire in a bit of a hedge”.

Discussion of this event with David Woodthorpe (organiser of the Borrowdale Story), and later with Billy Bland himself, produced a further strand to the story, if you will. Woodthorpe recently re-told the story in *The Borrowdale Story Newsletter* (of Oct–Nov 2018) after confirming the details with Billy.

> Billy told me that the event had actually happened in 1966 because he remembers it and of course he wasn’t around in 1942.
>
> As with our more recent floods, the floods of 1966 followed a prolonged period of heavy rain, but on this occasion the flooding was not only of much longer duration; almost three weeks but was exacerbated by a large land slip off the side of Eagle Crag which avalanched into the Langstrath Beck about half a mile upstream from Stonethwaite village. The resultant wash travelled downstream and created a tsunami-like effect in the valley.
>
> In addition to the traditional hotel rooms within the main building, the Scafell Hotel also had a number of chalets in its grounds which people hired for weeks at a time for their holidays. As the floodwater surged down the valley the occupants of the chalets were evacuated onto the first

floor of the main building. Soon the water was deeper than waist high and running so powerfully as it sped through the narrows in Rosthwaite that it upended cars and washed them away. You can imagine the blind panic as people clung on to fences and walls as they tried to navigate from the chalets into the hotel. Apparently Mrs Forsythe, one of the chalet evacuees, was quite stout and as she waded she clung on to the wall. The wall collapsed through the combined weight of the water and Mrs Forsythe! So, along with the cars she also got washed down.

Billy and his wife to be, Ann, were enjoying Saturday night dancing at The Pavilion on Station Road in Keswick at the time. They were oblivious to the drama unfolding, but Billy's Dad, Joe, was in the thick of it. Joe witnessed the trouble that Mrs Forsythe was in and went to her aid. He had a shepherd's crook with him and he grabbed Mrs Forsythe in an effort to save her.

But the current was too strong and her weight was too much. My fatha couldn't swim. A touch of self-preservation took hold. So, he let go of the crook and off she went! Mrs Forsythe was recovered safely hanging on to a hedge a bit farther down the valley. Some say she got snagged on barbed wire, but I don't think that was true. I don't remember any barbed wire down there.

Joe was going to try and rescue some sheep when he heard Mrs Forsythe's scream, and tried to help her. Billy and Ann and couldn't get home that night in 1966 because of the flood.

Such was life in rural Cumbria at the time. Billy Bland threw himself into that life, particularly the sporting branch. The two sports of football and running became a massive part of Billy's life from his late teenage years onwards.

SEEDS

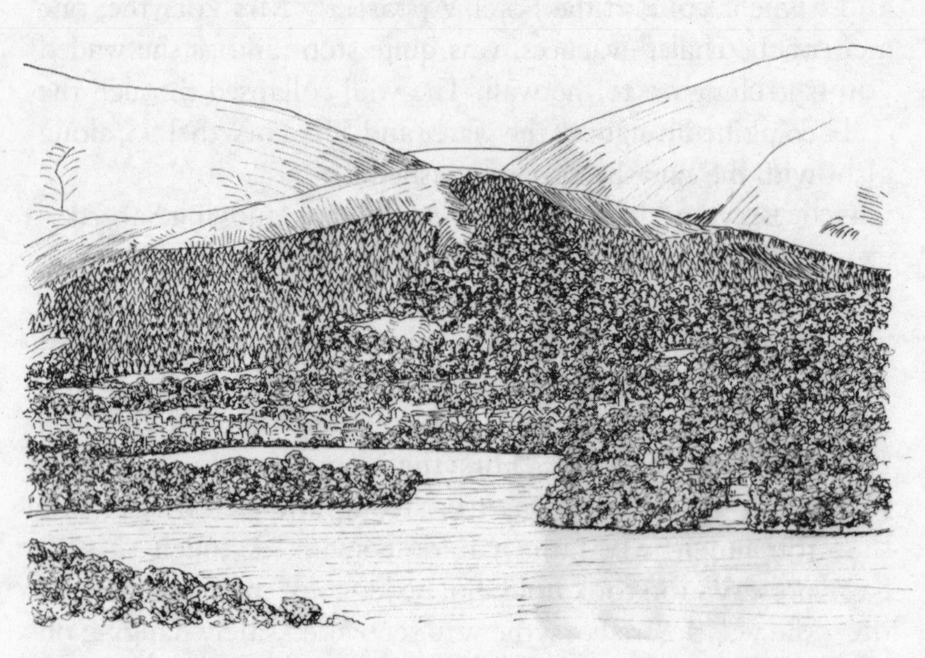

Sport has always played an important part in Billy Bland's life, but perhaps surprisingly it was not running initially that caught his interest. It was not until he was a teenager that Billy first started running. Football was very much his first love, from a much earlier age. He says, 'all the lads would get together and play football, so we were always knocking a ball about as youngsters.'

Then Billy got in the school football team and it just followed on from that. He started playing for Keswick football club when he was 17. His brother Stuart was already in the team. Stuart was a good header of the ball, mostly playing at centre half. Billy played as a midfielder as he could run about, but readily admits he was no good at heading the ball. He muses, 'was it [Ferenc] Puskas that said, "your head is for thinking with". Puskas also played with only one foot, saying "the other is for standing on". That was me too really, I was right-footed. I was all right, and I was a competitor. It is a bit like running. If you are a competitor and you want to be better at something and you try to be better, you will be.'

The high point for Billy was playing for Westmorland, although he was already in a team in Braithwaite that was better than the Westmorland team. 'We had some ex-professionals who still liked to play. I was playing for Keswick and thought when Braithwaite asked me to join that I wouldn't get in that team. My sister's husband was playing over there, and he said, "I think I will get in their first team, but don't think you will". It ended up the other way around!', Billy chuckles now. He reckons it was much easier playing with the ex-pros at Braithwaite than it was with the Keswick lads. 'Not wishing to do the Keswick lads down, but these boys knew where to be on the field. Gus Alexander, I think he played for Rangers, he was one of them.' In fact, Gus Alexander played for Burnley (where he was understudy for Jimmy McIlroy, who was a regular in the Northern Ireland team), and then Southport, Workington and York. Maybe there was somebody else at the club from Rangers.

Billy loved playing football, especially 5-a-side. Although he played for the Westmorland County team, he reckons he probably wouldn't have got into any other county team. 'I was from Cumberland at the time, but whatever. I played for Keswick FC. I started as a centre forward, then played as winger, anywhere really as I was fit and could run about.'

Whilst playing football Billy was only dabbling with running as he was very much into his football. He did a bit of running in the summer and played football in the winter. By the time he was 27 he was starting to really fall in love with running, and he soon packed in football, thinking that he had taken it as far as he could anyway. Billy's football career paralleled his professional running career, both starting in 1964 and both lasting for ten years.

Billy concludes that he ended up preferring an individual sport, 'as if anyone lets you down it is yourself. I have been a Manchester United fan since I was that high, but I cannot watch a football match right through now. Shuffling the ball sideways, and there will never ever be another George Best. It is coached out of them now.'

I wondered what his disciplinary record was like as a footballer. 'A bloody good record I had. Never got booked in my career, and not many players could say that. I wanted to play the game fairly. If a referee had said you were off, I am not sure I would have gone, because it would have been wrong.' As always, both assertive and certain of himself.

Billy's first ever race was up Latrigg, as part of Keswick Sports when he was 17. This was in 1964. Billy recalls, 'Keswick Sports would be something we had gone to and paid to go into, in Fitz Park. There was a real good quarter mile grass track there then, pan flat. They used to have bike races on it. It was maybe an even bigger show than Ambleside. It stopped quite soon after that, as the gatekeepers were said to be fiddling', Billy reckoned. There would be something like 10,000 people there. It also attracted some impressive guest stars. Shot putter Geoff Capes came one year, and the Olympic middle distance runner Gordon Pirie another time. They tried to bring celebrities in (celebrity culture is nothing new), but the cost of paying them accelerated the event's demise.

In that first race Billy was last on to the summit but had the pleasure, on the way up, of passing another runner who promptly retired to leave Billy last into the field – an ignominy which would never be repeated. Running became inter-twined with football for the next ten years, culminating in a spell of three years as a Westmorland County mid-fielder, during which time, as he puts it, 'the running got better'.

Having started running races at 17, Billy soon had a motorbike to get himself about. This was useful as Billy's father never drove a car. But Chris Bland's father (Billy's uncle Billy) followed them at races a fair bit. He also used to take Ann and the children around too.

After the local sports came the professional Guides races: at venues like Ambleside, Grasmere and Patterdale. In professional events the distances were short and there were fewer competitors – only about half a dozen usually, except for Grasmere and Ambleside which attracted 20 to 30. In the smaller races the prize money would be something like £8, whereas the Grasmere victor received £75 (in 1977).

Billy didn't really take his pro career seriously enough to do himself justice. He was just playing at it in those days. However, he did manage wins at Patterdale in both 1967 and 1968, and also placed well at both Grasmere and Ambleside. In Bill Smith's chapter on pro racing in *Stud Marks on the Summits* the only mention of Billy Bland is from a Grasmere event: 'Tommy Garside won at Grasmere in 1968, his best season as a fell runner, with Joe Richardson of Lamplugh second, Billy Bland third and Pete Bland fourth.'

Billy recollects that first race win at Patterdale, when he was only in his late teens. Apart from winning and beating pro legend Bill Teasdale into the bargain, he was shrewd enough to have left money with some local lads under instructions to place a bet on himself if he was well-placed at the summit. He won, and they did too, at 5 to 1.

Similarly, Billy Bland hardly gets a mention in *See the Conquering Hero Comes* – the book by Michael Miller and Denis Bland (who is not related to Billy, but is Pete Bland's brother) on the Guides races at the Grasmere Sports. He is listed as an entrant in the 1967 race (in a replica start list); is shown as 'W Bland, Rosthwaite' when coming third in 1968; and is shown as third finisher in 1972, behind winner Tommy Sedgwick and Fred Reeves. He will have won £7 10s for that podium position.

Some of the pro races had been going for many years. Grasmere had been run annually since 1868, except for the war years. From 1919 it has been on the current route to and from Castle Rock, adjoining Butter Crag. Winning the race, 'was sure to bring several offers of a luxury ride home in a well-to-do patron's coach.' A scan of the Grasmere results shows Billy Bland in fifth in 1966, third in 1968, sixth in 1969 and third in 1972.

In *Feet in the Clouds*, Richard Askwith quoted Bill Teasdale as saying that Billy Bland, 'never won the races he should have done when he ran with us'. Teasdale added that he suspects that, 'local supporters' hunger for gambling coups may have added to the pressure', and Askwith speculated that, 'Billy drifted away from running towards football'.

Billy doesn't deny that he didn't win much, but says it is not surprising with the low mileage he was doing at the time. 'Bill always had more talent for that stuff than me anyway. But he never trained hard either. He was a shepherd-cum-gamekeeper over Caldbeck way. He was a hard old bugger.'

However, Billy reckons that he was under no external pressure. 'It was me that was putting pressure on myself which made me nervous', he says. It was all too much for him at the time. Ann chuckles, 'can you imagine him being nervous?' Rising to the bait, Billy explains his situation and his priorities. 'I was just dipping into the scene. I wasn't running a full season of pro races. I might run three in a year. Football was more important at that time. I was 12 and half stone then. You couldn't run much of a race with that weight, knowing that I was 10-10 at my fittest! Most of them years I didn't race at all you know. I used to run for my football.'

Someone who knows Billy quite well from his pro racing days is Pete Bland (of sports shop fame), and who better than him to add his thoughts and fill out the picture, with some stories from those days. So, I had a long chat with him recently.

I walked from my friend's house, where I was staying at the time, down the back alley of a row of neat terraced houses in Staveley, in the southern Lakes. Past Rob Jebb's house, and in through Pete Bland's 'yard' to their comfortable and well-appointed house, to have what I thought would be a short chat with him. An hour and half later we had put the fell running world to rights, chatting about way more than is presented here. He also very kindly loaned me two books relevant to my research.

Pete Bland was born in 1941, so is six years older than Billy Bland. Like many others, Pete Bland went from school to pro races as that was pretty much all there was if you wanted to run in those days. He ran as a pro until

1972, when at the age of 31 he changed to the amateur code. He says now that he, 'was getting bored with the pro scene because I had been going to the same places for twenty years virtually to run a short fifteen-minute run.'

He adds that he knew Billy as a competitor, but he wasn't running that regularly then. 'I well remember running against him a few times. In particular one time at Mungrisdale, where the race went up the side of Souther Fell. I came in first and he was second. I can just remember the headline. It was a really thick cloudy day and it said something like, 'Blands running in the clouds', or some such. With it being a Guides race it was only a fifteen minute run through the bracken and straight back down again. I think it was connected to the sheepdog trials.'

Pete Bland remembers as a thirteen-year-old coming second at Ambleside. He won a table lamp, which is still going strong in this house. As a junior you usually didn't get money, but you might win a cutlery set or something like that, with money occasionally at bigger events. There were certainly some unusual prizes to be won. Pete says he remembers one in particular. 'It was at Mungrisdale and it was a pound, split three ways. Something like 6s 8d each for fourth, fifth and sixth or some such. But an Ambleside Senior win in those days was worth about £20.'

Pete Bland didn't ever win at Grasmere, but he got a second and three thirds. He was always the bridesmaid really. He says his biggest and best achievement was winning at Ambleside Sports in 1968. Ambleside was almost on a par with Grasmere then, and if you couldn't win Grasmere, then Ambleside was the one to win.

Pete Bland knew Billy Bland's father in the early days and his mother. 'The one that I knew best was Uncle

Billy, who was his dad's brother. Even I called him Uncle Billy and he was the one that used to turn up to support Billy. Uncle Billy always told me that we were related very distantly. You know what old people are like about families. He'd say there's so and so and that we were related. He is probably the only one who knew, and nobody would know now, so I don't really know if I am properly related to Billy.' Myth or reality? We are none the wiser.

In 1972 the amateur fell race scene was expanding in the Lakes, with Wasdale being run for the first time that year, and the Langdale, Latrigg and Wansfell races all being inaugurated in 1973. Pete Bland started running some of these while he was still a professional, unofficially. He did quite well and really enjoyed doing the longer distances. Pete went along to the first Wasdale race in 1972 and when he went to enter, he says:

'The people on registration said, "can we have a quiet word?". We went around the back of the climbing hut at Wasdale. They said they couldn't allow me to run officially, because they had had a complaint, as I was a professional and this was an amateur race. They said, "it is not us; it is somebody who has complained, and we have to uphold it. You can run but unofficially with no number. We will keep track of you, take your time through every checkpoint, and we will put your name at the bottom of the results sheet with your time". It was Joss that got me to do this long race. In this first Wasdale race Joss never ran because he had an iron bar drop on his foot, so he couldn't run. We were into the race and Joss was up a fell in the bracken and he knew what had happened, and I am going up through the bracken and he says, "go on Pete, give it some welly". He told me then and there who it was who had complained, and it was a guy who is still around, I think. He is older than me, and he was a runner. The ironic thing is that when I got to Sty Head stretcher box this same guy was there giving drinks out. He offered me a drink – but I won't tell you what I said to him.'

Billy Bland also ran unofficially sometimes when he was a pro. At the end of 1972 Pete Bland wrote to the AAAs and asked to be re-instated as an amateur. He had to sign a declaration that he wouldn't accept any more money prizes. 'If I did, then I would be banned for life. I had to pay £2 to the Northern Counties AAA and I have still got the letter. It came through fairly quick. It was November when I wrote the letter and I was running as an amateur for Kendal AC in the new year of 1973.'

Pete says, 'I may be wrong, but Billy never did change codes formally. Because he hadn't run that many races as a pro. He may have done, but I don't remember it [*this is not correct, as we shall see later*]. I ran the first Borrowdale race and also the second one with Billy. We were coming off Scafell Pike, about six of us including Billy and myself. Billy said, "hey Pete, just hang back here, I know a short cut, and they won't know it". When you come off Scafell Pike you come right down to the col and drop down onto the Corridor Route. But Billy knew a short cut down through the scree, and we nipped down it. We let them go, and Billy and I shot down this scree. I don't know what happened to Billy, he seemed to die as he wasn't as fit in those days. When we got to Sty Head stretcher box to go up Great Gable I was in the lead. But I got awful blisters. Check this with Billy, but I am pretty sure he dropped out.' Speaking with Billy recently he confirmed the drop-out. 'I didn't finish through lack of fitness. That's it in a nutshell. I had not ever done a long race really. But to run in those races was the reason for wanting to get re-instated.'

Pete continues, 'I was thinking of dropping out too, but I carried on up Great Gable and I was dying. I had obviously gone too fast. I got to Honister Pass, sat down, took my shoes off, and someone gave me a couple of plasters. I stuck these on my heels and set off, finishing about twentieth.'

It is a continual fascination to consider the pro and amateur code runners racing against each other. Billy Bland is well placed to say how the leading pros like Fred Reeves and Tommy Sedgwick would compare with the top amateurs. 'I think Fred would have done very well in the Pendle, Latrigg, Kentmere type of races as he was a very good track runner before turning to fell racing. However, in some of the longer events, with their rough descents, he would probably not fare so well. I think the opposite would apply to Tommy Sedgwick as he was a strong climber and very good on rough descents.'

There wasn't a huge number of professionals seeking to be reinstated as amateurs, when it became possible. By 1986 only seven pros had been officially reinstated – Pete Bland, Billy Bland, Tommy Robertshaw, Fred Reeves, Kenny Stuart, Graham Moffat and Mick Hawkins.

When he was re-instated as an amateur, in 1974, Billy reflected on the two codes in place at the time. 'The main difference I find now as an amateur is a friendly and more relaxed atmosphere at a race, where before a professional race I used to be very tense and nervous as they are more like a sprint and it's all over in 10 to 20 minutes. In the early days there were too many expectations from family and stuff, so I didn't like racing so much.'

He also admitted that although he used to like going out

training he never really competed regularly. He used to get very nervous before races. He used to do the training and go to meetings, but because he got so nervous and often didn't run, he'd end up running about three races a year. It has been estimated that Billy won a total of about £40 as a pro before he got re-instated as an amateur.

Billy has never mentioned being nervous before football games, but as he changed from football to running he managed those pre-race nerves and became more interested in competing. He admits that he loved racing later and competed very frequently.

Billy's early nervousness didn't really stop him from winning as he progressed. He just needed to train and race more. Billy outlined more details of this period at one of the talks he gave recently on his running life. 'I was 17 when I first ran at Keswick Sports but had never ran as a kid, not competitively. It was all new then. I was just a boy out of Borrowdale Valley who turned up amongst a lot of people. I did my training, something like twenty miles a week, which I thought was enough at the time. I would get there [*at a race*] and it would just spoil my day, so I said to my brother I am not going to do it. Then I got some confidence later as I got better, but I couldn't have seen myself sitting here spouting out, but you get more confident as you get older, in what you say and do, and couldn't give a toss what people think of you anyway.'

Pete Bland has a few tales of underhand tactics on the pro scene. They used to hold a sports gala at Kendal on the old rugby field. It was called Kendal Gala and it was always on a Tuesday after Keswick Gala had been on the August Bank Holiday Monday. Pete re-tells a story he was told about the event. 'The fell race went up Benson Knott. A very high-profile pro racer got the fell race stopped there once. He was leading coming back down off Benson Knott and he blatantly sat on a wall and let someone win, whoever it was, because he had backed him. He had to have a police escort off the field because the crowd weren't happy.'

Hard to believe, but Pete swears it is true. They never had a pro fell race up Benson Knott again, only a Junior one

While Billy Bland was finding his way, in both football and running, he also had to find his feet in life. He had to earn a living. He left school at an earlier age than would be the case nowadays and had to join the world of work in his early teenage years.

MAN'S JOB

Leaving school at fourteen, with limited qualifications, Billy Bland had to find a job. Billy's parents couldn't keep him or give him work, so he had to find work somewhere. Having worked throughout his life for others and for himself, he is still working manually in his seventies.

After school, Billy managed somehow to get a job at Lord Rochdale's estate at Newlands and Lingholm and was there for two years doing forestry work. He is not altogether sure how he got that first job now, looking back.

His father had no connection with the estate, so Billy must have just applied for a job there. He thinks that someone at school might have told him there was a job there. Lord Rochdale had a lot of farms at the time and required a large workforce. There were manual jobs in the maintenance department, the forestry department, and the gardening department. When Billy started worked it was five days a week for eight hours a day.

Billy worked in the forestry department, using a chainsaw and brashing trees. That is taking out the lower branches. As the tree gets bigger and the canopy closes in the bottom branches die. They used to take them off up to man height, so you could walk through. The estate included pretty much all of the bottom end of Newlands, including several farms. The garden work was where Lingholm is now. There was a team of four or five of them in the forestry department. Surprisingly perhaps, Billy got to work with a chainsaw right from when he started, at fifteen years old.

The main house of the Lingholm estate is on the west bank of Derwentwater and was built by Alfred Waterhouse, one of the Victorian period's most prominent and prolific architects. Waterhouse went on to build many notable public buildings and private houses, including the Natural History Museum in London, and Manchester Town Hall. His style was described as 'modern' Gothic. Beatrix Potter often holidayed there with her family and made sketches of the old kitchen garden and referred to it as her original inspiration for Mr McGregor's garden in *The Tale of Peter Rabbit*. The estate is now concentrated in the one location, based around the main house which is a listed building. It is popular with tourists, with its Kitchen Café, Walled Garden and upmarket holiday accommodation in a variety of surrounding buildings.

Billy changed to working at Honister Quarry when he

was seventeen years old, where he stayed for ten and a half years. There were about fifty men working at Honister when he started work there. At that time, it was desirable employment, as it was the best paid manual job in the area, paying £20 a week. Billy doesn't consider that it was particularly dangerous work. 'In my job you were sitting on a 6-inch stool with your legs out [*he demos it*] with a bit of sack over your leg, with a metal bar for a brake, and you were shaping slates. That is called being a dresser. Shaping and scraping, chippings all over your legs. Then after a while I started thinking I needed my bloody head tested!' After three or four years he learnt to use a dressing machine and he says, 'that was just standing there really. But initially I was an apprentice, and I went from £5 6s at Lingholm down to £5 at Honister.'

Although the work may have not been too dangerous it could be life-threatening just getting home from work in the wintertime, when there was snow and ice about. When he worked at Honister you would go back down to the valley after work in the back of a wagon and there might be three or four inches of snow in winter, and you were under a canopy at the back and sitting there with about 25 or 30 fellow workers. 'You can't see the driver, who is in the cab with two sitting beside him. You set off down and you were just in his hands, we knew he was a good driver. Some of the long-standing fellas who worked up there would want to be snug in the cab. Then all of a sudden you were sat in the middle seat and they would all be sliding along over you with their hands trying to hang on as the lorry slipped on the snow. Then there would be a great laugh go up as they went back to their seats, having shown their colours.' He also remembers coming down when he was 19 on his motorbike. Him and another lad were seeing how fast they could do it.'I recall getting up to 70 m.p.h. coming down there and then shutting off after a split second. Bloody crazy. If a sheep had come across the front of you, you would have been in the next county. But that is youth, isn't it?'

Talking about it another time, Billy agrees though that Honister could in fact be a dangerous place to work. He very nearly lost his life there once. 'I had big bushy hair and there was a big terex machine backing on to a drilling machine, and they had this boom and a drawbar to fasten it on the back. I was waving it back to put the pin in. This boom just brushed the side of my head and that was so nearly my head squashed. I still think about it occasionally', he shudders.

When they were blasting you had to go outside. 'It was misty up there many a time and there would be a shout to get out, so you went what you thought was a reasonable distance. Then sometimes there was lumps coming at you, and one of them might have nailed you, but it didn't. There is more health and safety in place now, I am sure.'

He also drove a face shovel, which he says you need to be, 'nearly an octopus to drive, using your knees and elbows. It wasn't in the best condition, maintenance wise. You would also put chains round lumps and swing them on to the wagon and take the chain off with the machine.'

The Duke of Edinburgh came to visit the quarry when Billy was an apprentice and came around to have a look. Billy says he has a picture of him and the Duke somewhere. He bent over to ask Billy a question. Performing a reasonable impression of the Duke, he recounts that he said, "Do they dig you out at night?" Billy has no time for the royalty, whom he calls spongers. 'I was a young 'un and thinking don't be so bloody soft. Everybody was brought down out of the quarry and pretending to have a job in the sheds. Prince Philip wanted to go up into the mine, but everyone had been brought down to the sheds. The job I was doing was my job, but not all the others. The mine bosses had an office up in Keswick and they were there like performing monkeys that day.' Ann Bland adds that Prince Philip also came back later to look at the mine again, when Mark Weir was in charge.

Shaping slates shaped Billy. Working there certainly influenced him and taught him, even more than his early family life had, that he had to stand up for himself. It was hard work and was part of a toughening-up process that he went through that stood him in good stead. He reckons there was a fair bit of camaraderie up at the quarry as well. It was tough, character-building work. 'There was one heater high up in a huge airy shed space. You could hear the wind rattling the tin building and on really wild days the wind would be picking up chippings and throwing them against the shed walls.'

He tells a story of starting work there, and the reception he received as a novice, as I suspect every new employee would have received in those days. 'I remember the first day I started, and there was a fella out of Rosthwaite village who had known me all my life. There was a wagon with seats in that used to pick you up to take you to work. I got on the wagon at Rosthwaite and I heard old Jont Hind, who couldn't whisper to save his life, sounding off like a trumpet. I had long curly hair down to my shoulders and as I sat down, I heard him say (in Cumbrian dialect), "a heed o hair like a lyad o brackins, what ivver can be amang aw that" – (a head of hair like a load of bracken, whatever can be amongst all that). He was just making a point at me. It was the time of the Beatles and all that.

I remember my uncle Nat saying "Mick Jagger, what is that" once, talking about his long hair', Billy laughs.

In a subconscious Beatles reference, Billy tells a quarrymen story. They would have half an hour for lunch and play football alongside the sheds, with loads of slates all over the place. With strong boots on mind you, but with a tennis ball. Sometimes there were fights that broke out over the games. The ball would go out the gate and start down the hill, and it would be either Billy or Mick Taylor who would go for it as they were fastest and would be back soonest. They were savage games. They would go back in, sweating buckets and carry on working.

There would be darts games on a Friday night at the Scafell Hotel. There would be maybe four or five quarrymen out of the six playing. Billy reminisces on a particularly special social event from his quarrying days. 'I remember going to London with Chris [Bland] and a couple of others. We went to see a two football matches, at Tottenham and West Ham, and that was a big thing for a teenager like me. Henry Cooper was boxing someone that day elsewhere in London, I can't remember who, and Mick Taylor thought it would be quiet because they would all be at the boxing match. All of London! Mick got his leg pulled about coming out with that statement.'

As an indication of the work conditions, Billy remembers once being laid off at Honister for weeks as it was so cold that year. It was that icy that they had to walk up [*from Seatoller*] as vehicles couldn't make it. All the pipes were frozen up and it was too cold to work, so they were sent home.

There was an old road up to Honister from Seatoller, which you can still see many parts of, that had to carry all the heavy stuff as it came down into Borrowdale as its route out of the quarry. The old road was zigzagged to make it possible for the traction engine to use it.

Billy Bland's current house was built by the Honister quarry company, as were some at Seatoller, to attract the workers to come there. This was in the very late 1890s, and the houses were probably finished in about 1902. The row of eight houses were called Leconfield Terrace originally. Leconfield Estate, based in Cockermouth, had the mineral rights for the Honister quarry company. Lord Leconfield then took over the quarry, when the Buttermere and Westmorland Slate Company ceased to exist. Later he bought in a manager who by all accounts did little work, except take a big wage out, perhaps starting the decline in the quarry's fortunes.

In Billy's view the quarry was being badly run, so after over ten years he left. Expanding on this point, he reckoned the management couldn't see the potential that it has achieved now, with tourists paying to go around and watch them work the slate. 'It is still the same process it has always been. Bring it in to the sheds, the rivers work it, they split them and then dress and stack them. It is all there to be seen. Admittedly there wasn't so much tourism then anyway.'

He continues explaining his feelings about the quarry being run down. 'I will give you an instance. The slates were all stacked up and weren't selling, for whatever reason I don't know. I said to the fellas, "we should buy this slate, collectively". It was something like £70 a ton. We should have bought that stock and we would have been quids in after ten years or so.' Wanting a change, he asked for a move out of the sheds and he got to do machine driving and then driving diggers, so got a bit of variety. But the wages were no longer the best in the area and were going down relatively, until they were similar to agricultural workers' wages. 'I was having great difficulty living off it, with a young family and that. There were pressures and arguments at home. They wanted volunteers for redundancy, and I put both hands up. I got the princely sum of £370 pay off.'

He was pleased to get out, and initially went off to work on the Keswick bypass as a labourer with Tarmac. Not happy with that, he looked for something more rewarding. He says he always knew he could 'wall' because he had done a bit on the farm. There were some new walls needed, down by Bassenthwaite Lake, and he thought he could do that. The pay was so much a metre for the wall. 'They said they will give me a start and if I can do it and pass the overseer then I am away. If you can't you are out. I was fine, and in.' His cousin Chris had left the quarry as well, having been there more years than Billy. He had got into walling and building, and he was getting jobs and so Billy started working alongside him but was self-employed. That was the year when he won the British Fell Championship, in 1980.

Billy Bland taught himself walling, as he explains. 'If there was a wall gap when I was a teenager then you just went and mended it. My fatha taught me the principles, through stones and filling and that. After that it was just a case of getting better. I wanted to do it to the best of my ability and better than anyone else if I am honest. Well, not really better than you but the best I can. I have seen walls that Joss [Naylor] has put up, but he is what I call a farm waller. "Rough and strang, and don't be lang", as the saying goes. There are certain stones, especially when you are facing a house, that are just not suitable. They are not good enough to make a real tidy job of it. There are also a lot of field walls that have been put up with stone that isn't right. Round rubbish stones with no depth in them either. If a lot of these walls had been put up with better stone, then they would have stood a lot longer than they have.'

Dave Hall did a bit of work with Billy Bland, as he was a plasterer, Billy was a waller and builder and Chris Bland was also a builder. He says they made a good team. Dave Hall ran for a Hertfordshire club, but started coming up to the Lakes for races. He was a very good standard runner, pacing Joss Naylor on his Wainwrights Round at one point. He met Billy initially through fell running, as he recalls. 'I was big friends with Pete Barron, and I used to stay with him a lot. I plastered Pete's house at one point. Then I did some work for Billy and the friendship grew from that. It would be around the late 1970s when I started running up there.'

Dave Hall sheds some light on Billy's dismissal of fear and also his work ethic. 'I remember at Dave Spedding's shop we did an extension, and Billy was taking down a chimney stack. He was like some kind of Fred Dibnah, swinging about on a rope. Health and safety would slaughter him now. He was very much the perfectionist with his work though. So much so that if he was having an off day he would decide to go home, as he couldn't face building a rubbish wall.' Billy doesn't remember that chimney, but he was happy enough working on a roof or other exposed situations. As he puts it, 'I am quite weak in the upper body, but was good for building work. I always thought me head and me legs were my strongest points.' Ann comes back straightaway, 'he's certainly headstrong'.

Dave also had a go at stonewalling, and chuckles at the memory. Billy had a load of stone dumped at his house and he was going to build a wall to separate two gardens. Dave continues, 'he said to me, "do you want to have a go at drystone walling?" So, me and Pete Barron went round there. Billy said, "here's the job. I'll have a bite to eat and come back to see how you are getting on". About forty minutes later he comes back and looks at it and says, "when you gonna start?" I said, "we have", so he comes straight back with, "it don't look any different to when the lorry dumped it". Then he showed us how to do it. It is a real art. He was an artist.'

One less artistic piece of work Billy Bland was asked to do was to straighten up the memorial to Bob Graham that is sited on the side of the road up to Ashness Bridge. It was tilting and Billy was asked if he could do something with it. He went to see, thinking it would just be a case of putting an iron bar under it and pulling it straight. 'It wasn't that easy. There were metal bars going right down in it. It took some tilting I can tell you. I don't know what it is like now. It is surrounded by bracken and sometimes not even visible.'

Billy thinks that the outdoor working environment he had (as did his nephew Gavin, as a shepherd) was a real benefit in terms of being fit as a runner. To him it was core training. 'As a stonewaller you didn't need core training, because you were bending down picking stones up all day. It hardens you up. I can't see how looking at a computer all day is going to help you as a runner, but that is what some people do nowadays. I wouldn't have been any good at it anyway as I am just a practical person.'

A strong work ethic is so ingrained in Billy that even in his early seventies he is still doing manual work. His work ethic has always been exemplary. He would go to work to do eight hours work and do that and then go home.

Billy did, and still does, take great pride in the quality of his work. His current job when I first spoke to him was stone-facing a house down at Bassenthwaite. He explains. 'I now go and do five or six hours and come home again, and then get on the bike. My days are running out, but I don't mind doing a bit because physically I am perfectly all right. If you can ride a bike for 200 miles a week and find that nae bother, well a day's work is no problem. That was how it was when you were walling. Instead of having half an hour for your dinner you would have ten minutes and you were away again, as that is how you were paid. I always thought that if you couldn't make a living in 40 hours (a week) then the job wasn't worth having. I had other things to do with my life.'

In my research I came across an article about a 76-year-old Cumbrian stone waller and former wrestler Bill Bland, from Yorkshire, who was quoted in the Farmers Guardian as saying of his job:

> It definitely keeps you fit and helps keep the weight down. My claim to fame was being able to wall a walking yard in an hour. 'I do not think I am that fast now though,' he jokes, adding a good waller 'never has a bad stone'. With two of us, we could take down and put back up between eight and 10 yards of wall a day. This depended on what the foundations were like though.

Billy Bland listens to the tale and then chunders, 'he wouldn't have won any competitions if he was putting up eight yards in a day with his mate. I doubt very much. That is too fast to be any good. That will be one of them lot of wrestler Blands that come from Silverdale.

They are vaguely related to us.' Billy then qualifies his previous comment by repeating the phrase he used before in describing farmers doing field walls, 'rough and strang, and don't be lang' [*rough and strong, and don't be long*].

Referring to the related wrestlers, Billy adds, 'Gilpin Bland is related to my grandfather. They were down Silverdale way. He was a farmer too. They were big boys – for wrestling. They wouldn't have been big boys if they had trained with Billy Bland, would they!'

Rather than training wrestlers Billy Bland moved from the pro racing scene to run as an amateur, began to get fitter for the longer races, and to make his mark in the sport.

THE RISING

Moving to the amateur ranks in 1974, Billy Bland began to race more frequently. He overcame his early nerves and came to like racing even more than training. He eventually became a very frequent racer, sometimes competing twice in a weekend.

The amateur races blossomed around this time, particularly some of the Lake District Classics, like the Wasdale and Langdale races, being inaugurated in the early 1970s. Ennerdale was one of the first horseshoe races in the Lakes, being run first in 1968, with Fairfield having started two years earlier.

Billy reckons that, 'with Joss running, and Dave Cannon

and the lads coming from Lancashire and Yorkshire it kind of exploded and started getting in the papers. Then Chris [Bland] started the Borrowdale race in 1974.' Chris Bland made the trophy for the first local to finish the Borrowdale race. It is a slate one and is still presented each year. The main trophy is a silver one.

Billy had to go through the process of re-instatement as an amateur, even though he had only meagre winnings as a professional runner. That was how it was then. Billy doesn't think there was any time penalty when you changed codes then. When he applied for re-instatement (via the Northern Counties AAA) Ross Brewster of Keswick AC wrote a letter in support of him changing codes.

Billy Bland joined the Keswick club only a year or so after it had been established. The story of its founding, which incidentally was half a dozen years after the Skiddaw race was established in 1966 by Des Oliver (and promoted by the Lake District Mountain Trial Association), is recorded in an amusing piece by Ross Brewster, who is a journalist, on the Keswick club's website. Its genesis was due to the enthusiasm of another local footballer, as this edited down version of the piece shows:

> Keswick AC made its first appearance before an eager public in a drizzly, grey Lancashire mist at the Musbury Tor Relay race one afternoon in 1974. So recently formed was the club that its yellow and green kit had still not been delivered and it was a rag, tag bunch of hopefuls in t-shirts, old jumpers, shorts of varying length and colour and totally unsuitable footwear, that turned up that day to face the cream of British fell running talent. The top fell running clubs all had a team out for the race. Bolton United even had Ron Hill, the

European and Commonwealth marathon champion, in their ranks. There were at least two Fell Runners of the Year in the other teams.

Totally unprepared in mind, body and running kit, it all went wrong for Keswick at the start of the second leg. It turned out the club's runner had forgotten his gear and had to race in a pair of clumping great hiking boots, while his 'tracksuit' was actually a voluminous brown raincoat appropriated from his dad's wardrobe.

In the confusion, he had still not removed the overcoat when the first runner came in to hand over. It got stuck over his head, both arms were now unaccountably thrust down the same sleeve, and, like a scene from a TV comedy classic, several runners from rival teams joined in the struggle, tugging and wrestling, to divest the Keswick man of his coat. In the end he set off up the lane, miles behind, still battling with the recalcitrant garment which he eventually cast off and left hanging over a wire fence, to be reunited with it on the return journey.

Hopelessly last of course. Lesser mortals would have quit there and then. But a couple of weeks later, lessons learnt, the same four Keswick runners toed the line for the Skiddaw race where, this time, they did not return in such disgrace. This was truly the birth of the new club.

But really it all began by accident. A local footballer was looking for some training companions, a few friends joined him on his twice-a-week runs, and from such simple beginnings they began to hold Sunday afternoon eyeballs-out races over a four-mile road course.

David Ellison had been a runner, knew a few people in the sport, persuaded Ron Hill to come up one weekend and take the lads out round one of the lakes, had ideas for raising a few quid, entered people for races they never knew existed and, in their right minds, would never have considered taking part in. Perfect. That's the secretary appointed. Plus, the hospitable Ellison family flat, above the town centre shop, was a perfect base for runners to come and go, be fed and watered and kip down overnight.

The foursome who ran in that first embarrassing relay, Ellison himself, Ken Cartmell (the man with the raincoat), Kenneth Clark and Ross Brewster, were to form the basis of the Keswick club in the early days. The fun-running boom was as yet unheard of and it was not easy to recruit more members.

Having had a long discussion with founder member Ross Brewster, there is still some uncertainty about exact dates. Some evidence points to a late 1972 date, rather than 1974, as suggested above. In *Stud Marks on the Summits*, Bill Smith claims that Keswick AC re-started the Latrigg fell race as an amateur event in 1973. Furthermore, an athlete named Ian Kellie (a master at St Bees School) appears in the result for Fairfield on 20 May 1973, with Keswick as his affiliation, and subsequently in several other races in months to come. Ross remembers running Skiddaw in 1972 but is not sure if Keswick AC were affiliated or not [*he is not listed in first few runners that appear in the Fellrunner report, but presumably was further down the field*].

Alan Lowis, the footballer who was the instigator of the club, never actually became a member of the club. He preferred his first sport. Brewster can't recall which team he played for at that time. 'It may have been Braithwaite, possibly Shap, but definitely not Keswick', he says. Billy recalls that he did play for Keswick FC and also Shap, which was where he was from. Lowis worked for Barclays Bank, and was a very good striker. Sadly, he died in his forties. They used to meet up at his house at Portinscale every Thursday evening and on Sundays and have eyeballs out races round a 4-mile road course.

Harking back to those early days, Brewster adds that on another occasion Ron Hill needed someone to show him around the fells. 'He asked us to turn up at 8a.m., and then took us on a 25-mile run, rather more than we had expected!' Keswick was very small club at first, having only four members for ages. But the club gradually developed. David Ellison was the man who galvanised them into more formal action. Sadly, he passed away a couple of years ago, with his ashes being spread halfway up Latrigg.

At the time they started up they had to persuade the organiser of the Skiddaw race that they were a proper club, as he said he didn't think they were. Soon though, Billy Bland was one of those recruited and was part of an early small group of runners at the fledgling Keswick AC. Billy Bland later became a committee member, but Ross Brewster says it was initially all very low key, no real elections, and that Billy had no formal role.

Racing as an amateur brought Billy to the attention of the wider fell racing community. He also started getting mentioned in dispatches, although not initially setting the scene on fire. The first mention of Billy Bland in *The Fellrunner* was from the Kentmere Horseshoe race, where he came seventeenth in the inaugural race on 12 April 1975, which was won by Jeff Norman. Billy dabbled at racing in the remaining months of that year, and his best finish was fourth at Langdale on 20 September.

He started but did not finish his first Borrowdale race in August 1975. 'I remember Pete [Bland] squawking as me and David [Bland] went around the back of Allen Crags, where they all go now. The first three or four had gone over the top of Allen Crags and Pete was following them. David was in front of me then, but he and I knew the way. Next year they all went that way', Billy recalls. The results show that Billy was in the lead bunch early on but was beginning to lose time by Scafell Pike. By Honister he was 20 minutes down on winner Mike Short, and duly dropped out.

In 1976 Billy started making his mark in the longer races, where he seemed to find his feet best. The reporter on the Ennerdale race on 12 June, where Billy came fifth, noted the performance of, 'Billy Bland, of Seatoller in Borrowdale, an ex-professional who has only lately started to come through on the long ones.' Either side of that, Billy had come fifteenth in two Medium category races, at Kentmere and Skiddaw.

Then on 9 August 1976 the third running of the Borrowdale race took place, which was the first time Joss Naylor had run it. Joss had promised that, 'the record would be lowered under three hours if not by him, then by the man that beats him.' Joss came in second in 2:59:56, but Billy had pulled away to finish over six minutes earlier, in a new record that five years later he absolutely slaughtered. Billy Bland had managed the first of his 100 or so career race wins. The report summarises this monumental event. 'Joss [Naylor] and Billy Bland arrived at checkpoint one in 29 minutes with eleven chasing [them] at 30 minutes. By Scafell Pike Joss and Billy had 5 minutes on Mike Nicholson and Duncan Overton. By Honister, Billy was 4 minutes up on Joss having broken away on the ascent of Gable, with Stuart Bland moving up to third.

The order was unchanged over Dale Head to the finish and the time of 2:53:30 broke Dave Halstead's record by almost 12 minutes.'

At the time Billy said that he was delighted to win and beat Joss Naylor because he thought that on previous form he would do well to finish in the first six. It was certainly a breakthrough for Billy. He now adds an intriguing vignette from the race. 'Old Joss [*as Billy thought of him, compared to himself*] and I were climbing Gable together and he said, "how you garn, Billy?" and I said, "all right so far", and shortly after that I went away from him. It would have been a bit of a shock for the old lad then, as he wouldn't be expecting to be beat by me.'

The next weekend Billy Bland ran his first Bob Graham Round, but more of that later.

Billy now started getting out of the Lakes to race more often and travelled to Scotland to compete in the prestigious Ben Nevis race for the first time on 4 September 1976. Billy came sixth, making his debut over the course and continuing to maintain the generally high standard of his other performances so far that year. Race conditions were ideal, and Dave Cannon won for the fifth time, despite having taken up marathon running. His record time was 1:26:55.

The Mountain Trial, on 12 September, was held from The Old Dungeon Ghyll Hotel. Billy and David Bland, making their debut in the Mountain Trial, both put up tremendous performances in finishing third and sixth respectively. Mountain Trial specialist Joss Naylor took his sixth consecutive win, from Pete Walkington.

At the end of the year the 1976 Fellrunner of the Year was Martin Weeks, with Mike Short second, and Billy Bland eighth, having not really committed to enough of

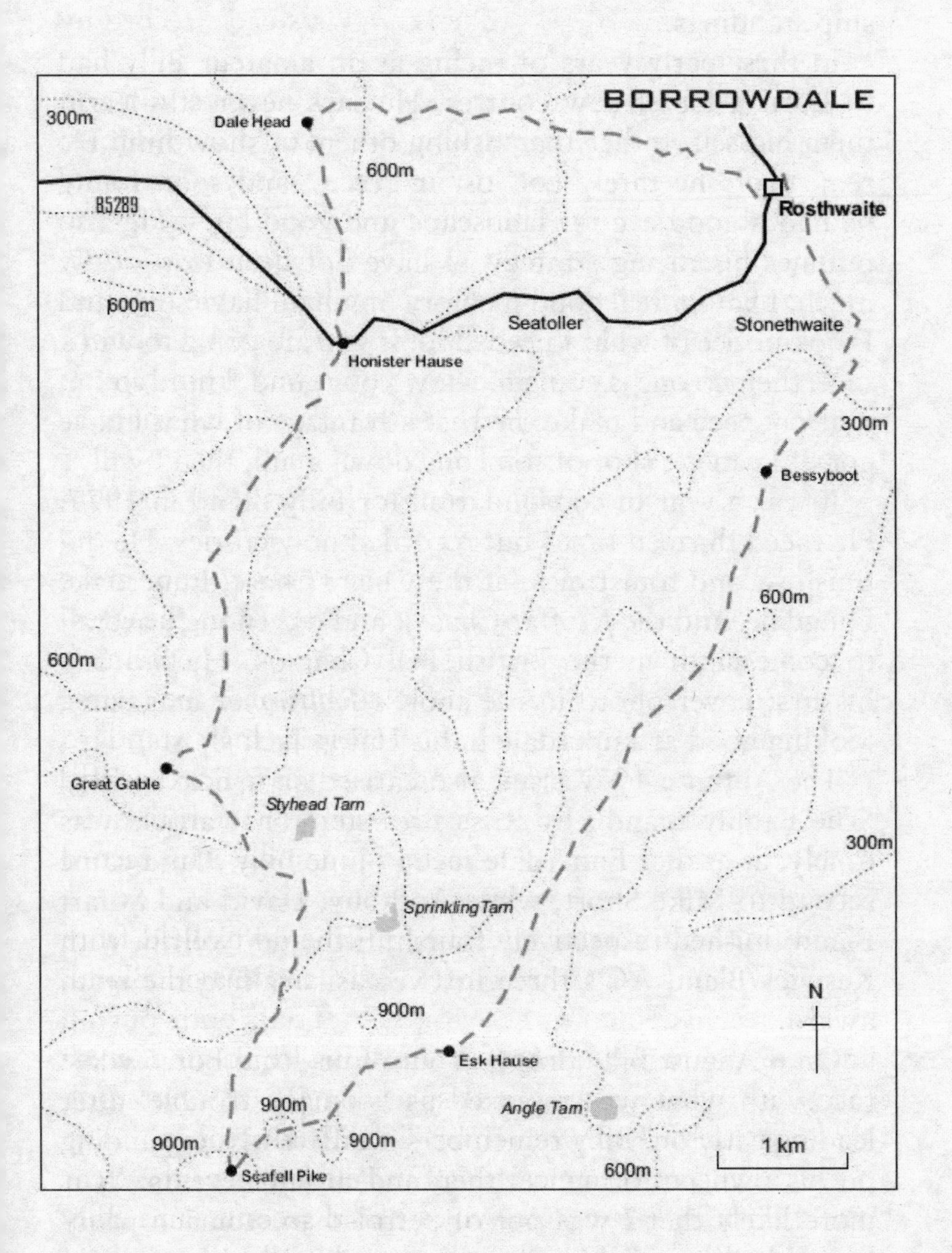
BORROWDALE
300m
Dale Head
600m
B5289
Rosthwaite
600m
Seatoller
Stonethwaite
Honister Hause
300m
Bessyboot
600m
600m
Great Gable
Styhead Tarn
300m
Sprinkling Tarn
N
900m
Esk Hause
900m
Angle Tarn
900m
900m
1 km
Scafell Pike
600m

the races, and thus stand a real chance in the championship standings.

In these early years of racing as an amateur Billy had to learn a lot of new courses. He says he mostly learnt them himself, rather than asking others to show him. He remembers he rarely got lost in recces, and soon found he had a good eye for landscape and good lines. He also outlines his racing strategy. 'I have not been lost locally much. I have a real good memory of what I have seen, and I took notice of what I needed to. If you are going to win a race, then no one is going to show you round. I need to run it at my pace and make the best advantage of what I have got. If I can get shot of someone down a hill, then I will.'

It was a year of consolidation for Billy Bland in 1977. He raced thirteen times but recorded no victories. He did finish second four times (at the Chevy Chase, Ennerdale, Langdale, and the Moffat Chase), and did enough overall to come sixth in the British Fell Champs. He did bag his first cover photo in the sport's *Fellrunner* magazine, looking good at Ennerdale in his Union Jack shorts.

The Autumn 1977 issue also carried an article entitled 'The Family Bland', by Ross Brewster. That article was timely, as at that Ennerdale race in June Billy Bland came second to Mike Short, while Anthony, David and Stuart Bland finished respectively fourth, fifth and twelfth, with Keswick/Bland AC's three in five easily taking the team award.

On 6 August Billy dropped out of his local Borrowdale race with what was reported as 'stomach trouble' after leading early on. Billy remembers it differently, expanding on his own performance, then and in later events. 'It is more likely that I was out of petrol than stomach problems. I had given all I had got and couldn't see the sense in going further and slipping further back. For that particular race I always said, "first is first and second is last" as far as I was concerned, especially once you had won it.' That expression was used by someone else when describing Billy Bland's attitude. At different times it has been attributed to Bill Shankly (the iconic Liverpool FC manager) and to Ian Stewart (the tough Scottish 5,000 metre runner).

Billy continued. 'There is only one thing that will satisfy you and that is winning it again. You don't drop out because you are sulking. It is because you are not achieving what you set out to do on that day. What is the point in slipping away back down the field? I have never had the mentality that finishing is all important. If you are not right on the day, then pull out and come back another day when you are right. I might have had a few more dropouts later in life too. I definitely dropped out of one Mountain Trial when I got lost, at Mungrisdale. I knew I had blown it, so that was that.'

On this occasion, and on several others where he dropped out of events, Billy showed no fear of failure. He was not affected by it and usually came back stronger from it, which is surely the mark of a champion.

Completing a poor late summer, by his own increasingly high standards, in September he came fourth at the Ben. This was also Dave Hall's first ever fell race. He gives a Southerner's perspective of that milestone. 'I was running for Stevenage and North Herts and I put a notice up in the clubhouse, "anyone want to share petrol for a 10-mile race in Scotland". Someone said, "knowing you it is the Ben Nevis race". We got a team out though, and went up on the Wednesday to recce, just following the path. Just as we pulled up to the top one of our lads collapsed. He blacked out for 20 seconds. We came down and about 2 or 3 years later he had to have a pacemaker fitted. That day on the Ben they reckoned was the beginning of the trouble. I finished twenty-fourth in the race a couple of days later. Coming down I ran round to the burn then saw most of the others going straight over the steep side. I ran down that last bit of road like I'd had ten pints. My legs had gone.' Dave became a very competent fell runner though after that.

Then a week later Billy Bland finished eighth in the Mountain Trial, held that year from Kirkstone Foot. That was Billy's lowest ever position in the Trial. He never finished outside the first three in his remaining thirteen Mountain Trials.

The same year the Autumn 1977 *Fellrunner* magazine carried this brief note of a race that took place on 17 September. 'New course record set in the Langdale race by Andy Styan (1:55:03) with Billy Bland, Alan McGee and Mike Short all inside Mike's previous course record.' Hiding behind that short note is a course record that is at the time of writing the longest standing fell race record. Thirty years on the Summer 2007 *Fellrunner* carried an article entitled *THAT Langdale Record*, with some more details from Styan himself, who admitted that he had been on, 'an extensive weight loss programme, and increased mileage'.

Styan described the running battle during the race in some detail. 'Every uphill, Mike and Alan would pull away, and every downhill or bit of rough ground, Billy and I would catch them up. At the top of Blisco I knew it was between Billy and myself. I followed Billy on the descent, because I didn't know the route, and left him as soon as I reached familiar ground at the cattle grid.'

He added the reason why they had produced such fast times that day. 'Perfect conditions and four determined

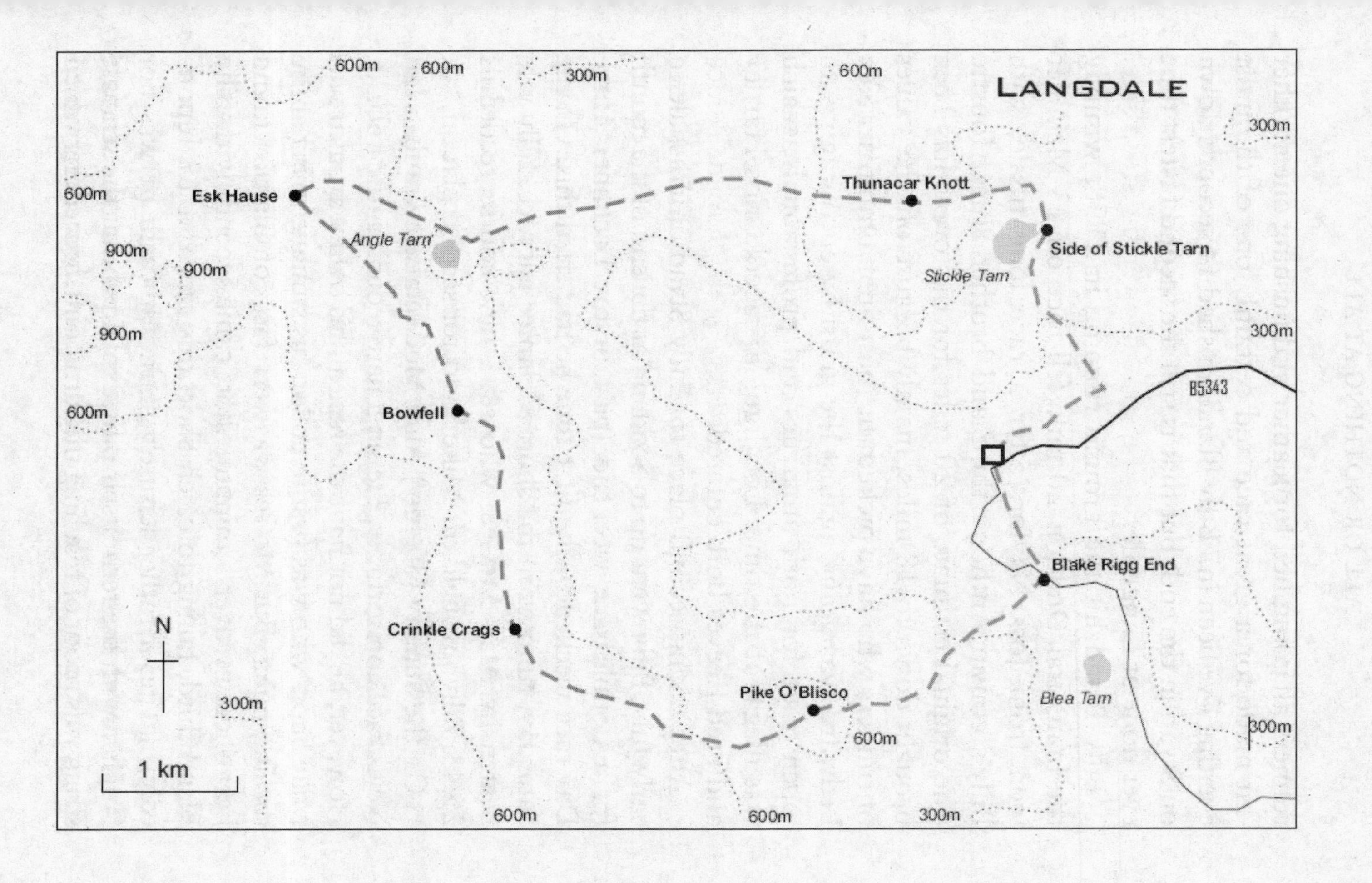

LANGDALE
Esk Hause
Angle Tarn
Thunacar Knott
Side of Stickle Tarn
Stickle Tarn
Bowfell
Crinkle Crags
Pike O'Blisco
Blake Rigg End
Blea Tam
B5343
N
1 km
300m
600m
900m

runners all going hell for leather and pushing one another – it made for a great race and certainly one of the most exciting I've been in.' Billy Bland finished 14 seconds down on Styan in the end, but that is still the second fastest time ever done at Langdale.

Billy Bland hit the ground running in 1978, winning the inaugural Duddon 20 mile fell race on 13 May. He won from Joss Naylor, after a race long tussle, with Billy's cousin Anthony third and brother Stuart fourth. The original estimate of 20 miles for this event has been brought down to 18 miles, mainly because of GPS values of runners who have picked the 'best line'. Organiser Ken Ledward was going against the grain by encouraging an 'open' race for both amateurs and professionals, which was illegal at the time. Local guides racers Chris Hartley and Fred Reeves both entered.

After taking second place to Andy Styan at Wasdale in early July, Billy went up to Scotland at the end of the month for a double race weekend (part of the Lochaber Three Day race weekend), the first time he had tried this. On the Saturday, running in the short Melantee fell race, Billy was beaten by Alan McGee, who set a new course record of 29:43. Billy just held off Mike Short for second place.

On the Sunday (30 July) Alan McGee also won the Half Nevis race comfortably. He set a new record time of 60:33. However, he did not have the race all his own way, as it was Mike Short who was first to collect his strangle string at the turning point. But McGee was very fast coming down and beat Short by over a minute. Short came second; with Billy Bland third, failing to catch Short this time due to (reportedly) having a rather leisurely start. Although he was not familiar with the term itself Billy explained that the strangle string was proof of reaching the turn point, something which you put round your neck. He also bridled at the suggestion that he had made a leisurely start, as he explained, in passing delving further into his racing strategy. 'I would be further back as you run out on the road, as I wouldn't be able to keep up. Once I got on to the fells I'd start. I didn't run leisurely; it was to suit the conditions. There is no point in going eyeballs out at first if you can't maintain it. Saying that, that is exactly what happened at some of the early Borrowdale races where I struggled later. You don't want to be pulled about by someone else's pace. You need to run the pace that is best for you on that day and course.'

The next weekend Billy Bland only went and did the double race thing again. At Borrowdale on the Saturday Mike Short knocked 4:11 off Billy's record, in a race run in mist and rain. Billy Bland was his main rival. After a close battle over Bessyboot, Scafell Pike and the Gables, Billy was first down to Honister, only for Short's tremendous climbing ability to assert itself on the way up Dale Head. He outpaced Billy by seven minutes on the ascent and stretched it to over nine minutes on the descent.

The next day it was the short Latrigg race. Alan McGee, who had not run Borrowdale the day before, won in 17:14, despite the heavy rain making it a very slippery course. Billy Bland came a solid fourth and was said to be looking remarkably fresh after his Borrowdale exertions the previous day.

In September Billy finally hit a rich streak of form, gaining his only Ben Nevis win, and the first of his Mountain Trial wins. In *Stud Marks* Bill Smith reported on the Ben Nevis race:

> Billy Bland came within one second of Cannon's record with a splendid run in 1:26:56, and it is thought that

> if he had been informed on the run-in of how close he was, it may have provided the extra spur necessary for him to break it. After three second placings, Mike Short knew that to be in with a chance, he must utilise his awesome climbing prowess to the full, for Billy is one of the swiftest and most fearless descenders in the sport. The mountain's higher slopes were shrouded in mist, and at the summit Mike held a slender 15 second lead over Billy, which the latter reduced to shreds on the descent, finally winning by 1:47.

Billy has mixed feelings about the Ben race, pleased though he obviously was with this particular result. He was beaten at the end of the Ben Nevis race where it flattened out a couple of times. Reminiscing, he tries to explain. 'If you talk about regrets then I regret that I didn't learn how to run the Ben Nevis race properly. When I first went up, I think I was sixth, and then I won it. I thought I could win half a dozen of these, because I was good downhill runner. When I was sixth, I didn't expect to be sixth, and when I won it I didn't expect to either. After that I was going up there thinking I could win it and trying to get to the top too fast. Then coming down the legs were going to jelly, and I was also out of petrol again. Year after year, I led over the bridge near the bottom, probably five times, and I never won it again.'

Looking back on coming so close to the record he comments, 'I always thought I could get it. Even though I missed it by a second, I certainly became a better runner after that, but I never got it. If I had got it right, I could have broken the record as it is now.'

The next weekend the Mountain Trial was held from Gatesgarth Farm, Buttermere. The weather was dreadfull and the course had to be shortened. Joss Naylor and Billy Bland took it out, with Billy establishing a lead of eight minutes by Haystacks, which was pulled back a bit before Billy pulled away again to win by ten minutes in 3:46:04, denying Joss his tenth victory in the event.

The Mountain Trial was not run under AAAs Laws. There was a feeling amongst officials of Keswick AC that their runners could not compete as a team in the Trial without dire consequences. Therefore, a group of runners from the club competed in that year's Trial as Borrowdale Fell Runners. Billy Bland, who won, was amongst them. Pete Barron adds that they, 'ran as Borrowdale possibly twice before the club was formed. There was a bit of a kerfuffle going on about AAAs status and myself, Billy and Jon Broxap did the Mountain Trial as Borrowdale. How ridiculous does that seem now?'

Billy Bland rounded off his season with second places in the Blisco Dash, where he was beaten on the road run-in, and the Wansfell race. In the Fell Runner of the Year championships Billy was placed third behind winner Mike Short and second-placed Andy Styan. He may not have won the fell championships but winning the Ben race and the Mountain Trial on successive weekends was something of a statement from Billy Bland, it being an impressive show of both strength and recovery, and a precursor to great things to come.

In 1979 Billy Bland started racing in February with a second place at Benson Knott, being beaten on the long run in, and a third at Carnethy. Rather surprisingly, Billy now thinks that Benson Knott was one of his best ever races, even though he didn't win. 'I absolutely amazed myself. I had probably done my thousand training miles by about 20 March and had done a good winter's training. I went there as a fitness test, like I used to go down to Chew Valley. It is really a cross country course, that is all it is. To lead that back down on to the road, I couldn't believe it. There is no good downhill in it really. The quality of runners that I beat was significant too, including Alan McGee and Dave Edge. If I had to look back, I would be thinking well Billy Bland has been on something! I surprised even myself.'

Billy came first in the 'Long' Duddon race on 12 May, followed by a second at Goat Fell a week later, where the race report noted that, 'Styan, Overton and Billy Bland shot past [Roger Boswell] spraying scree in all directions ... Bland was well pleased to finish second, as he had only recently got back into full training following a nasty bout of shin splint trouble.'

The next day Billy was ninth at Fairfield, followed a week later with second at the Northern Counties race. The report, by Danny Hughes, shows a typical ding-dong battle between Mike Short and Billy Bland, and highlights their individual strengths:

> Spectators had thrilling views of the battle for ascendency between Mike Short, Billy Bland and Harry Jarrett as they led the long thin line of colourful club vests strung across the steep slopes. Billy Bland was first to the top [*of Causey Pike*]. However, the sharp up and downs of the ridge to Wandope enabled Short to take a comfortable lead. The wily Short hesitated at Wandope just long enough for the local Keswick men to catch him and together they made an economical descent of the Wandope screes. Short was 50 yards or so behind Bland crossing the road at Newlands Hause, but once onto the climb up Robinson he closed in. The straightforward ridge run over Littledale and Hindscarth to the final checkpoint on Dale Head enabled

Short to establish a four-minute lead and he swept down to Honister [*to win*].

In June Billy ran at Ennerdale (coming third), Muncaster Luck (fourth), and Eildon Two Hills (third), and also set a record of 7:35 for the 46-mile Lake District Four 3000s 'Walk', which has never been beaten. In early July Billy came third at Skiddaw, and then second to Andy Styan at Wasdale. In a report in *The Fellrunner* (written by Styan himself) Andy is quoted as saying, 'I set off this year with one thing in mind – breaking the record. It felt to be going effortlessly until the top of Seatallan and it was a struggle crossing to Pillar as Billy Bland began to catch me .... I got the record all right, but all I could think about afterwards was wishing that the second half of the race could have been as comfortable as the first.'

It is interesting to contrast this with Billy's memory of the event which came back to him vividly when we discussed the race recently. 'I remember that Styan went clear in the Wasdale race up on to Whin Rigg and we were running along the tops alongside Ian Roberts, and he said, "nobody will catch him today". I remember turning to him and saying, "well, I have got plans to catch him". I did actually get to him on Gable, but the effort of getting there was likely making me start to fade and he did us by about four minutes in the end. I got him the next year though, and then I won nine on the trot.' Ian Roberts finished in a lowly (for him) fourty-fifth place that day, so must have suffered an injury of some sort to drift back through the pack like that.

The week after the Wasdale race Billy Bland travelled to Wales to run his only Snowdon race. He finished fifth, four minutes behind the winner, Jeff Norman. Ann Bland recalls that she had got mumps, along with their children Shaun and Andrea. Ann was ill at that Snowdon race and was really grumpy. 'It was a hot day, and I got blistered feet', says Billy. 'Not my race really, a bit like Skiddaw, which also nailed your feet. Not a brilliant day.'

Then came five tough races in three weeks. Billy only failed to come out on top in one of them.

Firstly, two of the Lochaber Three. On the Saturday winning the rough and tough Melantee race from what Roger Boswell described as, 'fell running's latest bombshell, Colin Donnelly'. The next day Billy won the Half Nevis race, breaking Alan McGee's course record from the year before by over two minutes.

The very next Saturday Billy excelled on his home course on a sunny day. He reduced Mike Short's Borrowdale race record from the year before by a massive 7:41. Billy showed the form he was in by leading all the way, being five minutes up by Scafell Pike, seven on Great Gable, twelve at Honister, twelve at Dale Head, and almost sixteen minutes at the end. Billy couldn't quite sustain the streak the next day, but managed third place at Latrigg, as Brian Robinson set a new course record. Two weeks later he won the inaugural 16-mile Sedbergh Hills race in the Howgills. A week later Billy came third in the short Burnsall Classic fell race.

On the first weekend in September it was the Ben Nevis race which was won by Colin Donnelly, at his first attempt. Billy was fourth to the summit and going well on the descent, taking the lead after Red Burn. Unfortunately, Billy took a tumble and badly gashed his arm. He finished (according to the race report), 'a brave third, bleeding profusely, and was smartly carted off to the Belford Hospital where some say it took fourteen stitches to patch up his arm.'

Reminiscing with Colin Donnelly recently, he told me the story from his perspective, as very much a novice fell runner at the time. 'It was an adventure really. I took the bike on the train and got off at Corrour Station and pushed the bike over the rough stuff to Glen Nevis, to get to the hostel. I did the race the following day. I was just lucky because Billy Bland, who was ahead of me on the descent, pranged himself on one of the bridges. I found myself in second place on the road. The guy ahead of me, Brian Robinson, his legs went, and fortunately with the Ben it is a tough race and even though you have done the training, the body may find it difficult to cope with it. I steamed past him in disbelief. I can never forget the moment when I crossed that finish line, with the pipes blazing, and I am thinking, "what am I doing, I have won the legendary Ben race". Sometimes in life we just get handed a piece of luck on a plate.'

Three more September and October races resulted in Billy being fourth at Langdale and Thieveley Pike, and third at the Moffat Chase. In the middle of November Billy completed another double race weekend of non-championship events. In poor visibility, and with snow on the tops, he won the Blisco Dash from Bob Whitfield, and the next day the orienteering-type Copeland Chase from Joss Naylor, again in poor weather.

Very late in the year, the last Championship race took place at Wansfell (on 29 December). Billy Bland needed a win to possibly force a tie in the Championship. He was only able to manage third, so came an excellent second overall at the end of a tough year, in which he had raced 24 times altogether.

The Fell Champs report noted that, 'Billy Bland came through gradually after a winter injury setback and brought himself back into contention in the autumn.' This was written by the then editor of *The Fellrunner* (Andy Styan), who had just won the title.

The progress that Billy Bland had made in his first five years as an amateur was down to an increased training regime, and a high commitment to his sport. The detail of that training shows him to be one of the most single-minded athletes the sport of fell running has ever seen.

REASON TO BELIEVE

One of the first things people seem to want to know about Billy Bland is exactly how he trained, and more specifically was it REALLY hard training that took him to the level he reached. I have had the opportunity to delve into the subject with him on a number of occasions and will try to explain what training he did, how it differed from other fell runners, and how it made him the athlete he was.

A starting point might be to consider how much of what he achieved was down to natural ability and how much was a result of his training.

His early results suggest he was certainly not an athletic prodigy. What he was though was a natural at downhill running. In an interview once Ricky Lightfoot quoted Billy Bland as saying, 'If you can't walk to the edge of a roof without being comfortable, you'll never be good at running downhill.' Very apt, as I am sure Billy has walked a good few roofs in his working life.

I quoted the 'brakes off, brain off' maxim to Billy and asked if that applied to his descending. 'Absolutely not!', he snorted. 'I look after myself and wouldn't do anything that would endanger myself. You are in control. You could have asked Stuart [Bland] the same question. They called him kamikaze and that. But I bet we were both more in control than those chasing us. If you run downhill out of control, then you will end up in hospital.'

However, Billy Bland did have a basic lack of pure speed, which was part of the hand he was dealt. Billy's own view is that he could have done loads of sprint training and still been poor ('useless' as he bluntly put it) at that aspect of running. He also admits that he had to work on his ascending once he got more serious about running on the fells.

For him it wasn't long before he realised that there was a training and lifestyle choice to be made. Initially he would, 'just go out, say to Scafell Pike and back, or Gable, this that and t'other, and the more I did the better I got.' And as he progressed, he still kept things pretty simple.

There was a lovely exchange reported in the Daily Express article that was published shortly after his record Bob Graham Round. After interviewing Billy and Ann Bland, the reporter recorded them reflecting on his frequent trips to run to the highest peak in the Lakes and back.

'It's so quiet up there. And there's nothing but scenery.

Sometimes I come home, and I have been messed about at work, I have got a temper up, and all I need to do is go up there to all that peace. I come back down again. So placid.' Said his wife: 'Well, let's just say he's in a better mood.' Her husband went on: 'I really like to be by myself ...' 'Thanks', retorted Ann.

However, there were several things that Billy Bland didn't do, as we will see. When in serious training, he was all for getting to bed, getting recovered and going again the next day. 'If you wanna go to a nightclub and that, you probably won't want to go out the next day', he said to me once.

His training was all self-determined, and he had no time for coaches, preferring to be his own man, a characteristic that carried through into other aspects of his life. 'I am a serious bad hand at doing what I am told. My mother thought I was stupid because I wouldn't do as I was told, but I think she was wrong! A coach wouldn't have had a chance with me. He would have said, "Billy you should be doing this", and Billy would have done something else. You don't tell me what to do. You have to be your own man and make your own mistakes. You learn better from making mistakes. I got enjoyment out of doing it my way', is how he puts it.

He certainly wasn't a fan of track sessions. 'I just cannot get it into my head to do two laps of anything. Reps? I tried repetitions a few odd times, but I didn't like it.'

When they became rivals, Billy used to argue about training with Kenny Stuart. Billy felt Kenny didn't put in enough miles. Kenny's response is that Billy, 'was a beast when it came to training. But there is no way I could have coped with what he was doing – two or three hours on the fells every night.'

Billy also strangely didn't have much time for rest and recovery, saying it was 'bloody rubbish'. He also didn't really recognise the concept of over-racing, a point he emphasised by once winning the Mountain Trial, and the Langdale and Ben Nevis races on consecutive weekends.

On the positive side then, what did his training look like?

We have already seen how he didn't train especially hard when he was racing as a pro. Initially, as a newly re-instated amateur, he was doing just forty miles a week in training. However, he was putting a lot into it when he went out and thinking that he was doing enough. Looking back from today's perspective, he says it obviously wasn't. Over the years he progressed training-wise and results-wise.

By the first six months of 1980, his championship year, he was up to eighty miles a week in training. But when racing often it would come down to the middle sixties. Mischievously, he says, 'I've made a point of never doing more than 99 miles in a week just to say I've never done 100 – but maybe I was telling lies!' This was all done on the fells when it was light enough, but when the dark nights came in it was mostly on roads in the week and on the fells at weekends.

The normal training pattern for Billy would be that virtually every day he would be out running. For him there was no such thing as days off. There had to be a reason to have a rest day. He would just get out and run, anything from 70 to 100 miles a week. Now the truth comes out. 'I didn't often top a 100, but I did sometimes, and I did average seventy right through the year. It doesn't sound a lot, but it was nearly all on the fells.' They weren't cheap miles, and they weren't soft miles. He would be running at 90% of race pace a lot of the time. Re-emphasising his life choices, he would get himself off to bed at night, get plenty of sleep and recover for the next day. He didn't go down the pub, and he wanted to wake up ready to go again. He emphasises that work had to come first, mind. 'I wouldn't have wanted it any other way, actually. That is amateur sport isn't it? I was doing what I liked doing, working and running.'

Mind you, he could combine his work and running by doing the latter straight after the former, sometimes to quite an extreme level. 'Once me and Chris [Bland] were working on a job at Ambleside and I ran home over the tops at the end of the working day from there once a week - via Red Bank and up to Sergeant Man and then via Angle Tarn and Sprinkling and come back in here just to make it a bit longer.' That is something like 17 miles. Just training, he says quietly.

I once suggested to Billy that one of the keys to being successful at any endeavour is to be enjoying what you are doing and wondered if that applied to him and his training. 'Absolutely, for me', he replied. 'I am the sort of person that if I didn't want to do it, then I wouldn't do it. You have got to mean what you do. But you have also got to do it because you like it. You have come home from work and instead of sitting on your arse watching TV, then you have got to go out and run for two or three hours on the fells. You do that because you like it, not because you necessarily want to win some particular race. You mebbe had a bad day at work and someone annoyed you, and you get your shorts on, get up on the fells and you are on your own and your mind floats away. By the time you come back, what was bothering you doesn't matter anymore. It is a great stress buster.'

With this regime in place, he kept getting better. The better he got, the more he felt he could train.

However, in a moment of reflection he admitted that he had made mistakes on the way. Asked what the mistakes might have been, he chuckled and just said, 'Well, it would take too long to tell you them all! I made plenty. Maybe I over-trained sometimes. Not resting up enough. I ran out of petrol in races, done that plenty of times. But you learn how to pace yourself and find what you are capable of.'

Being the self-determining person that he is, Billy didn't have too many fruitful training partnerships. There was nobody really that he would train with regularly. He recalls that people would call and say, "can I train with you?", and he would say, "aye you can come but I am not waiting on yer. You either keep up or I'll see you when we get back". The training had to be what Billy wanted to do. He wanted to run as he felt most of the time. Not selfish, just focussed.

Billy does admit that he wasn't always out on his own. There was the odd occasion when someone would go with him, but mostly they wouldn't do it. 'People tend to burn one another off if they go together, but there were occasions when I ran with my brother Stuart, Ian Charlton, and Jon Broxap, when he lived in the valley. But it's almost all been on my own. Runs were never social. I would say I am not waiting on you. As for club runs, well, no thank you.'

Jon Broxap moved to the Lakes in 1976, to live in Borrowdale as he went to work at the YHA hostel there, which is half a mile down the road from where Billy Bland lives. He didn't know Billy before he moved to the valley. Jon ran at University and had a hill walking background, and the YHA had an active informal race setup amongst the wardens and assistants. He remembers that he met

Pete Barron at one of those, and that he got Jon into the local running scene, and the first race that they did was Kentmere in 1978. 'We joined the local club, Keswick AC, and the Blands were all running by then, and were famous as well', says Jon.

I met Jon recently for a chat about these days. As a venue he chose the café in the Brewery Arts Centre, in Kendal. Unfortunately, we had only a little time then as the café was closing in 20 minutes or so. Still fighting fit, he arrived on his bike, and diplomatically answered my questions (showing the skills that allowed him to navigate the tricky job of Secretary of the FRA for a good while). He knows the fell scene well, having been a high standard racer and having worked a long time in Pete Bland's shop. We had another conversation over the phone, mostly dealing with his part in pacing Billy Bland's record BGR.

At the time Jon arrived in the Borrowdale valley Keswick AC were a very strong club and their teams were winning races, and Jon recalls that, 'the winning team was often comprised of Bland, Bland and Bland. I think Pete Barron was the first one to break that hegemony. I was very much a novice compared with them at the time.' Pete Barron was an exceptionally good runner, and Jon notes that, 'Pete still teases [his son] Martin that he has a faster time than him for the Ben race, coming in about tenth to Martin's third, or whatever'.

Once established, Jon did do some running with Billy. He didn't go out with him much on the fells, but they trained regularly on the road. 'Stuart Bland was training seriously then, so he would come as well. Stuart lived at Thorneythwaite Farm up the valley a bit, so he would pick Billy up and I would meet them at the road end at Rosthwaite, and we'd run to Keswick and back or round

Derwentwater and back, often running the white line in the dark.'

The YHA hostels were quite often closed in winter so Jon could go out training after work with Billy. Jon expands on the situation, giving an insight into training with Billy. 'It was quite often we did that, and they were proper runs! Occasionally I ran with him in the daytime too. I remember once we went down to do the Edale Skyline race on the Sunday and on the Tuesday we went round Derwentwater and over Watendlath on the country on tracks and stuff and I didn't know that he had taken a day off on the Monday, and I had been out training. On the way back with Billy the wheels fell off. I was left for dead to find my own way home.'

Pete Barron also suffered from Billy's competitive attitude in training with others, recalling one particular instance. 'One day we went running on a long one out to Keswick and back from Honister. Running back up towards Honister we were going up the old mine track. Billy was ahead of me and he suddenly stopped. He says, "what are you doing?" I said, "what do you mean?" He goes, "are you saving yourself for a sprint finish". If I could have caught him, I would have killed him.'

Howard Pattinson didn't train with Billy, as he says Billy was always fitter than him, and more dedicated. 'One of the training runs I enjoyed was the annual Four Passes run from Longthwaite Youth Hostel. Billy would give everyone a half hour start and I would see how far I could get before he passed me. One year I can remember thinking "I've beat the bugger", but on the final climb to Honister he passed me. I did a run with him from the Wasdale over the other side of Shap, to Wasdale in the west. It was just a case of doing it for a bit of training. We stopped at David's (Billy's brothers) for tea and cake, and then went on.' Pattinson added a note of caution about the problems obsessive trainers can have. 'I was not quite as dedicated to running as Billy was, I only trained once a day, seven days a week. On reflection, I think that even my mild obsession may have contributed to my marriage breakup.' A counter to that view of obsession is given by cyclist Geraint Thomas in his autobiography, where he says, 'obsession gets a bad name in the ordinary world. In sport, it's what turns you from outstanding to unbeatable'. I believe Billy Bland was treading a fine line, but it made him the athlete he was.

One other person who trained with Billy has subsequently become a close friend, and that is Andrew Schofield – who henceforth in this volume will be referred to, as everyone does, as Scoffer. How it all started is rather unusual as well, as I recently found out when talking with him.

Scoffer was born in Rochdale in 1967 and is a painter and decorator by trade. He ran first for Rochdale, and then for Rossendale. 'Dave Lewis was the main man there. But also Ken Taylor, Pete Irwin and Bob Ashworth, I used to look up to them all', Scoffer recalls.

He is a bit younger than Billy and it was all going pear-shaped between the professional and amateur sides of the sport when Scoffer got into it. There wasn't really a pro scene in Lancashire. It was all in the Lakes really. Scoffer was up a lot at weekends with friends and decided he might as well move up and live in the Lakes.

In 1983–4 Scoffer started doing the Junior fell races, and progressed to longer Senior races, like Wasdale and Borrowdale. 'I was OK, but not brilliant', he says. 'Gary Devine and Robin Bergstrand were the top Juniors, and they could also do well as Seniors. I might be fourth or fifth maybe, never winning.'

Once he knew Billy, he would sometimes stay with him and they would go out training. He just got to know Billy by going to races and knowing who he was. 'He was The Man, and I watched him and then introduced myself. If you show an interest, he will give you as much time as you want. I used to come up for weekends and go for a run with Billy. I used to sleep on his settee, or camp in his garden. "You are welcome to come with me, but I am not waiting", he would say.' So, the same treatment as all other training partners, even though Scoffer was really young then, being 17 or 18. Scoffer does say that Billy didn't used to rub him into the ground too much. He used to come up to Borrowdale by bike and public transport, or cadge lifts off people.

But Scoffer didn't train regularly with Billy much really, apart from those times when he used to come up for weekends. Billy was tailing off really as Scoffer was getting going. But that early training with Billy certainly helped his progress. 'The advice I got off Billy was in showing us where to go in fell races. It is just common sense with running really isn't it. You train and you get better. I was a good trainer, and I still go running every day. I wouldn't call it training. It is just going for a run now. If you have no natural ability you have got to run harder to keep up with those that have.'

Although still running, Scoffer reckons that the highlight of his career was winning Wasdale in 2002. There was no hesitation in that response. He also did a Bob Graham Round in 17:01. 'Billy clapped me through at the top of Honister', he laughs. 'No that is not right, he did the last leg with me. It was OK for ten hours, then it was a walk.'

One story that I wasn't sure whether to believe or not was confirmed by Scoffer, who was there. It concerned Gary Devine at the Ben Nevis race one year. 'The lads were in the chip shop the night before the race and the guy in the chip shop the night before said to Gary, "if you win I will give you all free pie and chips". Gary had bright pink hair and to look at him you would think he would not be able to run a bath, never mind up and down Ben Nevis. But we knew he could win, like. He did, and we got free pies and chips all round.'

Scoffer is proud of Borrowdale winning the Hodgson Relay twenty times in a row, although he may have missed many of them as he was the race organiser. He organises several races, including Steel Fell and Glaramara, and Borrowdale since 2005. 'For Borrowdale it is me and Ann Bland, and used to be Len I'Anson as well. Also, the Hodgson Relay since 2005, with two others.' He finished with his take on race organiser responsibilities. 'The rules are there to protect us, but more of an onus should be on the runner. I say no GPS. It isn't really the spirit of things otherwise. But if it is misty and GPS got runners back safe, I would be happy about that.' He adds that his own navigation is good. 'But I don't practice. It is just knowing where you are. Do the recces', is his final advice.

In several ways then, Billy Bland was something of a trailbreaker, although he himself fully acknowledges that his actual training regime was very unscientific. No room for a coach, track sessions, repetitions, or even tapering down for races with him. Just hard training. Billy also says he was no good in a fell race unless he was 'passing clear water before the off', having drunk enough water previously in preparation to stave off the ill-effects of dehydration. I am not sure how that would be received by nutritionists today, but doubt if what they say would change his view.

His training arena of Borrowdale has plenty of steep fells nearby and he developed into a fearless descender, particularly over rough terrain.

So, what detail of the training? How much running time was involved?

It could be as much as thirteen hours a week sometimes, but more often an average of ten hours a week. That is a fair bit of training time. All the long session stuff was after he finished work – from six o'clock onwards. But he didn't like pounding the roads in the dark. That was no fun, having to contend with the dazzle of headlights and the splashing from passing cars.

Billy has some memories of running in the dark. He recalls that he once ran into Colin Valentine running in the opposite direction along the same white line in the middle of the road. 'What a crash,' he says. 'It was pitch black, and it floored us and Colin.'

By mid-February each year he would have his first opportunity to go back on the fells in the week for training after the road work he had to do throughout the winter. He would get home from work, change into his running kit, go out of the back door and up the fell and it would still be daylight. In the early part of the year the first stop might be Watendlath, twenty minutes away over the hill, and then he'd run along the tarmac via Ashness Bridge and back home by the road.

Later as the evenings drew out, his favourite was the five tarns route, which he would take at a fair lick. It meant climbing from his home up to Styhead Tarn, then going via Sprinkling Tarn, Angle Tarn, Blea Tarn and Watendlath Tarn. A decent distance, done in two and a half hours. 'Maybe fifteen miles', he adds in a matter of fact sort of way.

There wasn't really a training plan, as such. Mostly, it was just instinctive. 'First off, I knew I wasn't the best, and secondly, I knew if someone else was out training then you weren't gonna beat them. So, kick yourself in the backside and get out there running, then you had a bit of a chance. If the other guy is sitting on his backside three days a week then you will get him. That is preparation.'

He also commented on race judgement. 'On race day you have got to pace yourself and know what you are capable of. No good turning up and in the first two miles trying to compete with someone who is a better starter, let them go. No need to beat them in the first part of the race, you need to beat them at the end. Don't get drawn into blowing it in the first few miles. If you are good enough then you will catch them, if you are not good enough then you won't. Your confidence in this aspect should build over the years. You are learning what you are doing.'

Although Billy says he was not over-endowed with talent and accepts his failings on flat ground, he certainly made up for it on the fells by his assiduous training.

There was no fuss, he just headed out the door. 'If Ann said, "where are you going tonight?", I couldn't say, because I didn't know myself. Or if I did then many a time, I'd change my mind. I just did what I felt like. Sometimes it would be around ten miles, sometimes way more. I had no real structure.' It is worth noting that it is reckoned that one mile on the fells takes out of you as much as two miles on roads.

Another popular training route was to go up Glaramara, contour round Allen Crags and go past Esk Hause, then down the tourist path to Angle Tarn, and on to the boggy link to High Raise, finishing down Greenup, all in two or three hours. A standard training run, after a hard day's work.

In a way, dark nights and winter training helped bring about the end of his fell running career, as he began to hate it and it started eating away at him and his enthusiasm. He tried as hard as he could. Yet it was winter training that finished him. He started pulling muscles.

Preparation is a word he uses a lot, as befits a man with his race record. It is that gruelling winter roadwork that counted during the summer months, when most of the competitions take place. This was when his preparation paid off.

I wondered if when it was rainy, dark and cold, whether he might sometimes say, 'I am not going out there', and go to the pub instead. He says it was never a problem with him about the pub, but he used to look at it that if he didn't go out training he would not be prepared well. 'I didn't mind running the white line in the dark, and you went to other side of the road if a car came along. But I was doing it to prepare for what I was going to do, or hope to do, in the summer.'

I posited that running 70 to 100 miles a week, and not cheap miles either, that he might suffer from overtraining. He responded with a longish explanation of how his fitness and recovery ability might see him through.

'Yes, quite possibly on certain occasions I can accept that I over-cooked it', he conceded. 'One Duddon race in particular I can think of when I was only two miles into it, and I was kicking stones. I wasn't picking my feet up, and my brain wasn't sending messages fast enough, and that was from fatigue. I didn't know it at the time. I got around, but I was obviously tired when I set off. That is what happens to you when you are fatigued. Funny thing is I ran myself legless that day and then the next day I was bloody flying. I am not kidding. I could run the Borrowdale race and then the [short] Latrigg race the next day faster than when it was on an individual day with no race before. Isn't that strange? My brother Stuart and I used to say that you could clean out your body and it be empty, and as long as you got a good sleep and plenty to eat, and you needed to be fit mind, then you could recover. We both commented that our breathing would be fantastic after a long race. Next day your legs might feel a bit shit, but your breathing was bang on, really good. There was something there, maybe because we are the same breed, I dunno.'

The only training-induced injury he can pinpoint was the shin splints he experienced worst in the spring of 1979, which all came about from training on the road. Although he avoided any major injuries, Billy used to get shin soreness after coming off the roads in winter. He reckons that it happened when transferring from road to fell and was caused by the two different running actions. 'Come March you could get up on the fells for part of your runs, say up over Watendlath and back down the road, without a headtorch. I was either too tight to buy one or there weren't any. I used to get sore shins from running on the flat then doing more on my toes on the fell. So, I had to watch that, once I sussed out what was causing it. But actually, I was very lucky with injuries, as I didn't get a lot, probably because I didn't do any sprint work. I just went out and ran.'

Complex in many ways, in training terms Billy was a simple man, and never used the more complex training methods that Kenny Stuart did. Kenny's training more closely resembled that of a cross country runner than a traditional fell runner. He tended to have a lower overall mileage than most top fell racers; limiting his running on fells to one third of total mileage in order to maintain leg speed; and he regularly included interval and fartlek sessions on road and grass. Conversely, Billy Bland would spend 2 to 3 hours every night on the high fells, pushing himself.

Even Joss Naylor, the master of pain, noted that Billy could be self-destructive with his training. Quoted in *Feet in the Clouds*, Joss reflected on Billy's training. 'There was no bugger trained harder than Billy. He put the miles in, and he put them in hard. He was so self-centred, so self-destructive – he put himself through a hell of a regime. But I'll tell you what: he had a lot of bloody guts and determination in his training.' Joss also made an interesting comparison in one of the videos of his endurance events when in commentary as he runs across some seriously rocky ground. He says, 'you have to concentrate and read the stones. You gotta be able to read the stones. It is like making a (stone) wall.' Billy Bland could make a good stone wall and was a recognised master at running well on really rough ground. He could certainly read the stones.

As well as working with Billy Bland, Dave Hall also at times trained with him. He told me a story from their training together. 'I was up there training for my Bob Graham and called in on Billy. He said, "I am doing a leg of the Cumbria Way Relay, do you want to come with us?". I said, "yeh, go on". Part of it was going around Derwentwater and over to Keswick. Billy didn't train with many people, but if he did, he would try to find out something about you, maybe find your weaknesses. I was going really well that day. He was desperately trying to drop me on the fells. We got to Rosthwaite and his wife Ann was there to give us water and a Mars bar. I was about five metres behind him and she said, "are you struggling?". I said "no, I am shutting these gates behind him". Billy just looked across and said, "you should be opening the bloody things as well". That is Billy', said Dave, with a laugh.

Dave Hall pointed out that Billy was both a hard trainer and tough racer, and that he used to gauge his fitness by how many times he went up Scafell Pike in a week. Illustrating the hard racing, he points out that he had never beaten Billy in a race. 'The nearest I got was at Blisco when it was a championship race in 1983 [*when he was sixth to Billy's fifth*]. Again, at Coniston the following year when it was a championship race again. We were going flat out when we got down to the cattle grid and he hurdled it and I had to step on it, and that was enough for him to beat me.' Billy admits he certainly would have jumped the cattle grid, and that probably did see him through to the finish ahead.

On another occasion I was discussing endurance running with Mark Hartell, who still holds the record of 77 Lakeland peaks in 24 hours (the extended Bob Graham Record). In the conversation Mark commented on topics he has ruminated on with Billy Bland over the years. 'Billy and I have had good chats at Bob Graham Club dinners. He has said to me that his wasn't some kind of genetic natural ability. He firmly believes that he simply worked harder than anyone in training at the time. "If the weather was bad then I would run on the spot in the kitchen for three hours". I am sure that is an exaggeration, but the point being made is that there are many ways to train hard.' When I passed that story by Billy for confirmation, he laughed and said he just might have done it, but only once!

Jim Mann is another athlete who knows how to train and race hard. He held the record for a Winter Bob Graham Round, and in 2017 did all three main UK rounds in winter, each within 24 hours and within a total of four weeks. He explained his own philosophy to me. 'When you go up there [*on the fells*] in snow, gales and blizzards, it makes you *fell hard*,' he explained. 'That is something that I know Billy Bland talks about. *Fell hard* is what you get off that kind of training.'

I took the opportunity to ask Gavin Bland about his own training, as it seemed like a worthwhile comparison with Billy's. He started by emphasising what it was like as a young athlete, before describing how he used to train with Billy Bland, even when he was just nineteen years old.

'There was no step up from Junior to Senior. I was built like a 12-year-old, even when I was sixteen. I was just skin and bone. In 1990 I would have been doing quite a lot of running with Billy.' He gave an example from his diary. '24 Feb 1990 – 10 mile with Billy up Borrowdale: Mt View, Stonethwaite, Rosthwaite, Grange, Watendlath, Mt View.' That was just a Saturday training run, at a time when Billy was still winning plenty of races.

Gavin Bland added that if you asked Billy Bland, he would say that he (Gavin) wasn't training hard, but Gavin refutes that. 'Following that session [*noted above*], soon afterwards I did 15 miles, 5 miles on road, 10 miles, 10 miles, 10 miles, 10 miles, then I did 5 in the morning and then I played rugby and twisted my ankle.' At this point he notes that his diary goes blank. He claims he wasn't doing big mileage. 'If you go out that gate and up

Steel Fell, your heart is doing 160 and you are just pitter-pattering, so I was getting fit without destroying myself. If I had tried to do what Billy did consistently then I'd have broken down. I wasn't injury prone. My brother played rugby for Keswick for 15 years and for two or three years in the early 1990s I would play for the third team. Just socially really.'

Gavin explains that he actually recced courses quite a lot, more than others may have realised at the time. A fortnight after his Three Shires/Mountain Trial weekend double of September 1993 he looked over the Black Mountains course on a Friday afternoon. 'We went down there in a minibus. There was a Welsh lad that Ken Ledward knew. He was called Benjy – why do I remember that! It was ground that I had no idea on. Rolling sort of stuff. We did the last half of it, walking. That was Billy's idea to go and recce. He once had us go half-way round the Peris course the day before because not knowing it was not good enough for him. Most folk would say you don't want to be doing that the day before a long race. But we were all used to strong walking and that is how we would do it.'

Gavin knows he was suited to the longer races. He accepts that he never really mastered Wasdale though. 'It was just at the wrong time of the year and it was just too far. I won it, but not confidently. I used to think at Borrowdale if I got to Honister and I was leading then I'd got it.'

Looking back, Gavin points out that he won loads of races by a few yards. In his own analysis he was a carthorse but at the end of a fell race he was the fastest of the carthorses. 'Does that make sense? Ian Holmes was a better runner than me but over the last field I would beat him. But I am not a sprinter though and would get beat by the bigger guys in a sprint as a pro. If I wasn't going to win or do myself justice, I would never screw myself into the ground to finish eighth or something. I would run in and that would be fine. One or two races you come second, and you think what I could have done differently.'

Gavin was starting as Billy was finishing, which Gavin thinks was a good thing. Was he as good as Billy Bland, though? Without seeming boastful, he replies quietly. 'On rough stuff I would say, yes I was as good as Billy. I was just the same on that stuff.' At that point Gavin's son Alex pops in to say hello. 'He doesn't believe I was a good runner!', chortles Gavin.

No one else ran such distances on the fells as Billy Bland did at the time of his peak performances. People like Dave Bedford and Ron Hill were doing even bigger mileages in traditional athletics. Billy's miles were nearly all on the fells where he ran with a kind of madness, rarely setting any specific target beyond running until he was ready to drop. It was not scientific. Looking at it, many would say there should have been more quality and not so much quantity.

Writing on his blog, coach/runner Rene Borg listed what the ideal athlete for the fells needed. 'The raw talent of Bill Teasdale, the technique of Kenny Stuart, the physical fortitude of Billy Bland, and the relentless mental strength of Iron Joss would make for a perfect athlete.' Although no such animal exists, Billy Bland was certainly the best there was at his peak, and arguably the best there has ever been. Justification for such a big assertion will be outlined in a later chapter.

I tried to question Billy on his own mental strength, but he insisted on playing that aspect of his makeup down.

'I never considered myself particularly hard anyway. My approach was to get as fit as I could and do the best I could on the day. Then I just tried my hardest. If someone was with yer and ran away from us, then that was it. I couldn't go as far as making myself sick over it or anything like that. Common sense kicks in. You have done what you can, and you are either out of petrol or you have learnt from earlier days to know when you are buggered. I got to know to get a bit of food down me. It did happen like. If I went wrong and had petrol left, then I would chase hard. If beaten the attitude I had was to come back another day.' Despite that response there are enough examples in the race accounts to show that he was certainly very strong mentally.

Billy sums his training up, and his success, thus:

'My secret was simple. I had the will to train where other more talented runners who had the ability to knock spots off anything I ever did lacked that will. I wasn't the best by any means. But I was a tryer. Because I was not the best, I had to train harder than everybody else, that is how I saw it. The harder you train, the better you get. Then you start beating people you didn't think you could beat.'

He adds, 'I prepared properly. Because I meant it. I can honestly say that I became as good as I could be.' With that attitude Billy Bland epitomises the maxim: *it's not the will to win – everyone has that – it's the will to prepare to win.*

Billy Bland was now prepared to win, and he consistently did. His finest performances came in the next couple of years, with his best championship season, and several course records being the result.

MAN AT THE TOP

As Billy Bland gradually increased his training, so his performances improved. In 1980 he had a real shot for the British Fell Championships title, even though he had developed into a runner who was suited to the medium and long distance races, and less so to the shorter ones, mainly due to his relatively poor basic speed.

Billy Bland had managed eighth, sixth, third and second in the British Fell Championships in the four years 1976–79. The winners in those years were Martin Weeks, Alan McGee, Mike Short and Andy Styan respectively. Looking back on the 1979 season, The *Fellrunner* Editor

(Andy Styan) commented in shorthand on Billy's season: 'Placed third last year, began campaign late – injury. Won Borrowdale, well placed in other long ones. Over shorter ones usually third to B. Robinson. With a selected race programme could aspire to top of the class', coincidentally where Styan currently sat.

At the time the championship races were chosen from a nominated fifteen race 'A' category calendar (made up of five 'Longs', five 'Mediums' and five 'Shorts'). Individuals were able to pick their best ten performances in those races, but they must pick three 'Long', three 'Medium' and three 'Short', with the tenth being any length they fancied.

Looking back on that 1980 season, Billy says, 'the year before I was second, so I knew I had a chance that year. The selection of races in place then gives you more scope than you have got now. I don't agree with the system they have now because you can get injured at one time of year and you miss one race how the hell are you going to compete. In 1980, say you won three long 'uns then you were a long way into it. Maybe someone else could win three short 'uns but couldn't win a long 'un, so it was interesting. I wasn't rubbish at short 'uns, but I did have difficulty ever winning a short race because it didn't suit me.'

On 23 Feb 1980 Billy Bland went up to Scotland to run in the Carnethy Hill Race. Just half an hour before the start the police decided that the fog that was down over the A702 Edinburgh–Biggar road was so dense as to warrant calling off the race. They felt that the accident risk of stopping traffic in foggy conditions on a normally fast main road was unacceptable. The organisers substituted a cross country race which did not cross the road. So, 120 runners lined up for the start; 17 ran the official cross-country course, while the rest took a chance, crossed the road and ran up the hill course anyway. Billy took the latter option, and was nominally second back, after Colin Donnelly.

Colin recently commented on why he ran the unofficial race. 'That is down to my rebellious streak. I think I probably would do it again. Nobody had come for a cross country race. We had come to have a go at the hills.' Having spoken at length to both of them, I see some similarities in character in Colin Donnelly and Billy Bland, with a tendency to go against the establishment strongly present in their makeup.

Billy Bland properly started his 1980 fell season with the category 'AM' Kentmere Horseshoe race on 30 March. He came up against an in-form Colin Donnelly (running for Aberdeen University), who beat him by just eight seconds on this tough 12-miler. There had been snow on the higher tops, sometimes knee-deep, but no problems with navigation for either of these two, as the clouds were blowing high. Billy remembers it well, as he does most of the races that year. 'There was nothing in the race until we were coming down the [Garburn] lane, because it went anti-clockwise then. While I was on that rough lane I was a match for Colin, and I think there is a bit of tarmac just before where it finishes and that was me done.' Billy carries on his analysis with what might be seem a surprising comment on walking in fell races. 'Kentmere is not really my sort of race, not enough rough stuff on the tops. Not much walking either. I liked a good walk. If it is steep a good walker can walk as fast as anyone can run, and you are not wasting energy doing it. You lean forward, pressing on your knees, rather than trying to run on your toes.' Having not raced in April, but trained hard, Billy came back at the 20-mile Duddon 'AL' race on 10 May. Being his own fiercest critic, he later described this as his worst performance of the year. He came a mere fourteenth place, some 22 minutes off the pace. This was despite being very fit and knowing he had trained extremely well recently. He says he just died completely, 'I think I was short of salts, or something.' Untypically, he had completely run out of steam, and was reduced to a walk, but recovered enough to get going again.

The next weekend (18 May) didn't go that much better for Billy. Running the 'AM' category Fairfield Horseshoe race against a good quality field he came eighth, and to rub it in, didn't even warrant a mention in the race report, which pointed out in passing that the athlete one place in front of him was the leading V40 runner. Billy freely admits to it not being his sort of race, claiming it to be too runnable. He did win it one time, but he wasn't in contention that day in 1980.

Looking back after the season, Billy commented that he had addressed the salt shortage that may have been behind these two poor performances by (as he put it), 'banging a lot of Accolade down and doing the diet'. Accolade was a popular isotonic drink of the time, and by 'the diet' Billy is referring to the carbo-loading diet that he sometimes used before very long races.

A carbohydrate-loading diet is a strategy to increase the amount of fuel stored in your muscles to improve your athletic performance. Carbohydrate loading generally involves greatly increasing the amount of carbohydrates you eat several days before a high-intensity endurance athletic event. You also typically scale back your activity level during carbohydrate loading – although Billy Bland didn't really take that option on board. He would deplete for three days, eating just protein, and then carbo-load for the next three days before a race.

Bland first tried carbo-loading in the lead up to his next race, which was another week later (24 May). After his early season results he was becoming desperate, but it was so successful for him that he would soon swear by it. 'All this stuff about it coming into effect after two hours is rubbish – for me it is there right away', is how he described it at the end of the season. 'Maybe it just works better for me than for others, but it certainly works.'

The race was the 'AL' category NCAA race from Honister, over 14 miles of rough terrain. He felt great again and knew that he was back on track. On a beautiful spring afternoon he romped home first, beating his only real challenger on the day, Mike Short, by just over a minute. By the end Billy had taken 11 minutes and more out of all the runners who were predicted to be leading contenders for the Championship that year. Billy thinks that he probably beat Short coming off Dale Head. 'He might have been in front on all the tops and I would catch him coming down. I do remember coming between Hindscarth and Dale Head with Mike in front of us. I knew a little way that everyone will know now that saved you twenty yards or so. That might have been the year I won a portable TV.'

This was a real show of form, and he went off to do three hard weeks training before attempting a double 'A' race challenge over the middle weekend of June. It started on the Saturday with the Ennerdale Horseshoe. This is acknowledged to be one of the toughest of fell races in the Lakes, with its course record time only exceeded by the Wasdale race.

Prizes for Ennerdale were donated by British Nuclear Fuels Limited (BNFL), for whom Joss Naylor worked at the time. It was a wet day and misty on the tops, resulting in only 110 of the 148 starters finishing. The weather didn't seem to affect Billy, who stormed home in 3:21:04, reducing the previous course record by over two and a half minutes, and leaving the next three athletes (Styan, Short and Whitfield) over 16 minutes in his wake. He had once again carbo-loaded prior to the race.

The race report in *The Fellrunner* concluded with the following comments, on a rogue runner's behaviour: 'A member of the promoting club was timed out but refused to retire, causing much anxiety before he arrived back, completely unrepentant, having been out for over nine hours.' It was also reported that it was, 'conceivable that Billy Bland could set a new kind of record that would surely merit recognition. That is to win every fell race promoted by CFRA in a year, Northern Counties, Ennerdale, and Muncaster.' He did do just that, all within three weeks.

It was fascinating to sit there 38 years later with Billy, looking at a photocopy of the race results, with splits for each check point, as he tries to reconstruct the race as it must have developed. 'I must have been clear fairly early on. It was typical Ennerdale weather, degenerating into a very wet afternoon. There was mist on the tops, which led to a record number of retirements. I must have somehow got away from him [Styan] so he couldn't see us, as six minutes is a lot to take out of him between two check-points. I was ten minutes ahead by Kirk Fell, so going away from him all the time. Sixteen minutes is a big win, but I had a few of them. I won Borrowdale by 16 mins, and 21 mins at different times. I had some fair time gaps at Wasdale and all. [*From Billy this doesn't come across*

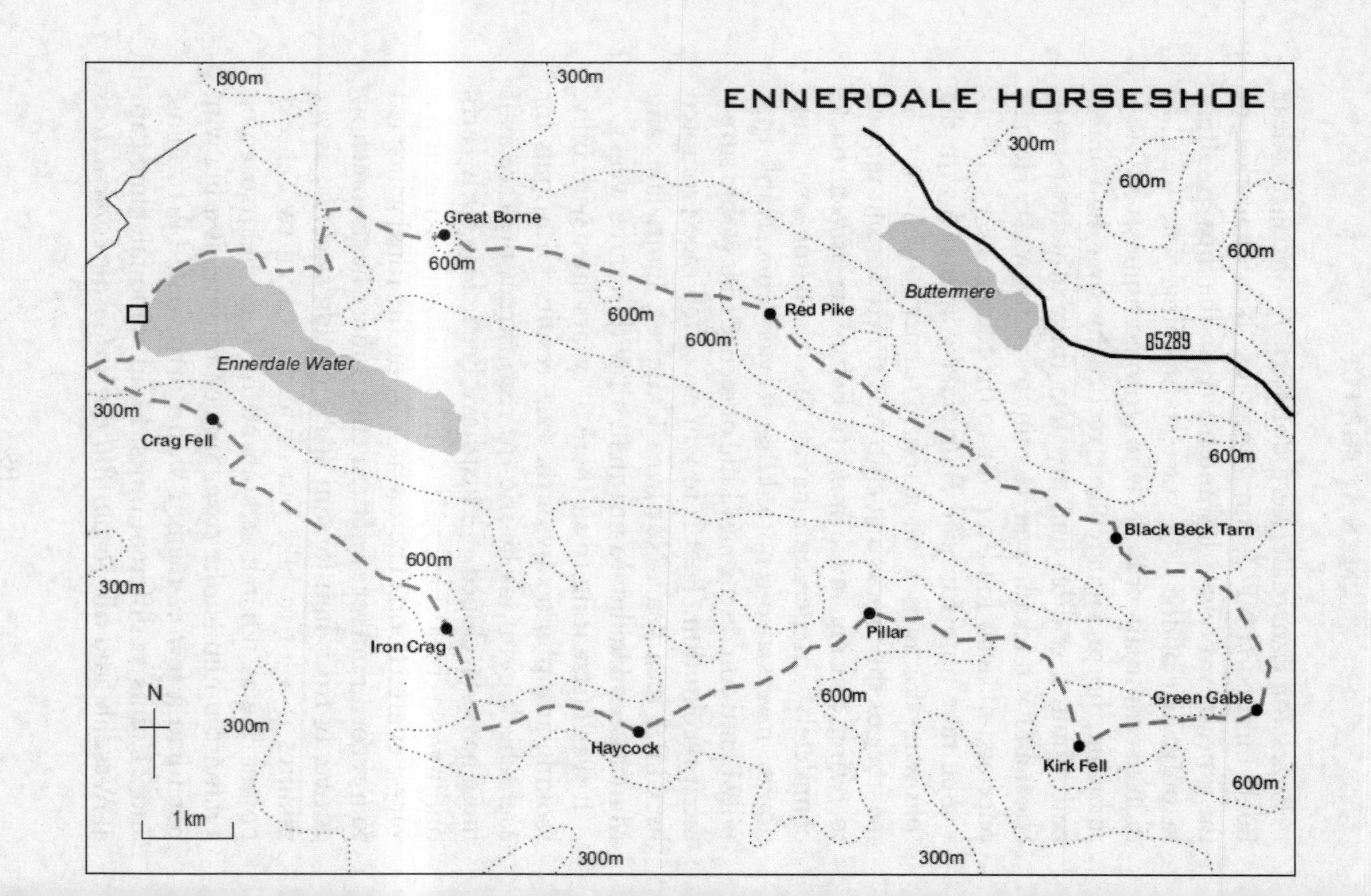
ENNERDALE HORSESHOE
300m
300m
300m
600m
600m
Great Borne
600m
600m
600m
Red Pike
Buttermere
B5289
Ennerdale Water
300m
Crag Fell
600m
Black Beck Tarn
600m
300m
Iron Crag
Pillar
N
600m
Green Gable
300m
Haycock
Kirk Fell
600m
1 km
300m
300m

as boasting, just a statement of fact] It was nice to get away and be on my own. I liked that. I just liked running on my own. Maybe at some point they had lost me in the mist', he concluded.

That Saturday evening Billy pursued one of his other interests, horse racing. He spent some time at Carlisle Races, and had some luck with his picks. The next afternoon he was on the starting line for the 'AM' category Muncaster Luck fell race. The ten miles caused him no real trouble and he easily came home first. This time it was Harry Jarrett chasing him, but Billy held him off by 48 seconds. He had achieved an amazing two-win 'A' race weekend. [*As a measure of this achievement, Billy tried the same double again the next year. He won Ennerdale, but Harry Jarrett turned the tables on him, to win Muncaster by 21 seconds.*] Reviewing the year, he noted that he had felt good at Ennerdale, and even better at Muncaster, reckoning that weekend's double his best performance of that championship year.

Talking about this race triggered a Muncaster memory from Billy. 'Another time at Muncaster I got tripped when someone caught my heels. I went down on the gravel. Trying to get up someone hit me from behind and I fell and knocked my forehead. Ann said I came past her with blood everywhere, but I carried on and finished second to Harry Jarrett.' He thinks it was the next year, referred to above, but is not sure now. That looks correct from the results.

Just one week later, Billy was up in Scotland to race the Eildon Two Hills race (on 21 June), looking for championship points in his first 'AS' category race of the season. After 27 minutes of running he had met his match in Harry Jarrett though, who took him out by eight seconds over the 4½-mile course. Billy says that he felt it was a horrible little race that just did not suit him. 'I won it once, but not that year. Third, second and first I think I went [*yes, in 1979, 1980 and 1981*]. It sets off from Melrose rugby club. That was where I first saw the message up in that clubhouse, *it is not the will to win, it is the will to prepare to win.* I have always remembered that. It registered in my head and I thought that is exactly what I am doing, preparing to win, and race days are a bonus day.'

By the end of June then, Billy had won two Longs and one Medium, and had seconds in a Medium and a Short (in seven races entered), setting him up nicely for a challenge for the title. Through the months of July and August though he upped the ante and produced even more consistent results.

First came the Skiddaw race (an 'AM') on 9 July. The ground was slippery from recent rains, and it was windy and overcast on the day. Jeff Norman coped with the conditions the best, being second at the summit to Andy Darby, and holding off Billy Bland on the descent to win by over a minute. Billy did 65:02, which was the fastest time he ever did there.

Just three days later and it was the Wasdale race (a 21 mile 'AL' race). Mist on the tops caused many a navigational issue, but not for Billy over some of his favourite (and best-known) terrain. He and Andy Styan got away over Whin Rigg. By Seatallan Billy was two minutes up, extending it to eight minutes by Pillar (by superior navigation), before Styan started cutting back his lead, which was less than three minutes by Esk Hause. Billy Bland was reckoned to be one of the best descenders, but was outshone here by Styan, who pulled nearly two minutes back from him on the descent from Scafell Pike

1. The Blands at Borrowdale School, 1954. [Billy 2nd row, 4th left; Stuart 3rd row, 2nd right; David 2nd row, 7th left; Ann 1st row, 2nd right]

2. Billy Bland, aged about 8

3. Lairthwaite school football team, 1959 [Standing, 2nd right: Howard Pattinson; Seated, 2nd right: Billy Bland]

4. Billy winning his first pro race at Patterdale in 1967

5. Braithwaite football team, 1970 [Billy: back row, 2nd left]

6. Billy heads Mike Short at the Blea Tarn road in the Langdale race, 1976

7. Goat Fell fell race, Arran, 1979 [Duncan Overton 2nd; Andy Styan 1st; Billy Bland 3rd]

8. Keswick AC's winning team at the Northern Counties fell champs, 1979 [Anthony Bland, Billy Bland, Bob Barnby]

9. Fellrunners of the year, 1980 [Billy Bland and Pauline Haworth/Stuart]

10. Billy's trophy haul from the 1980 season when he was Fellrunner of the Year

11. Saunders Lakeland Mountain Marathon, at the end of Day 1, 1981 [Race partner Stuart Bland is out of shot]

12. Training at the top end of Borrowdale, 1981

13. Posed photograph for an article on the BGR record that was published in the Daily Express

14. With John Wild after the 1982 Wasdale fell race

15. Two of Billy's training partners, Dave Hall and Jon Broxap – racing at the Blisco Dash, 1983

16. Leading Hugh Symonds in the 1983 Blisco Dash

17. Chris Bland and Billy taking a break from work

18. Descending at Ben Nevis, 1984

19. Survival of the Fittest on TV, 1984

20. Stuart Bland and Billy Bland supporting a BGR, 1984

21. Running for Britain, Causey Pike, 1985

22. Checking the rain gauge, up above Seathwaite

23. Winning at Wasdale, 1986

24. Buttermere Sailbeck, 1987

via Lingmell Nose. But Bland led him home by 1:17 for another 'Long' victory. Billy reflects, 'Yep, Styan quite possibly came down quicker than me. I might have been coming to the end of my tether then, but I think I bossed him farther back. I have the split times for that race somewhere.' Ann Bland recalls that she had a Mars bar and a can of Mackeson for him at the ambulance box at Styhead that day. With a laugh she adds, 'I think I got told off for standing in the wrong spot!' He hadn't carbo-loaded for this race, thinking that you can't do it too many times, and thus was suffering towards the end of the race.

The race splits tally with Billy's analysis. His lead over Styan was up to six minutes by Great Gable. Billy came down from Scafell Pike in 15:51, whilst Styan took 14:08. Billy adds a further thought. 'The way you come down summat in a long race having run three hours already or whatever is down to how much petrol you have left. You can be really good coming down hill but if your legs have gone then you gotta go with your legs. I didn't see anything in him that day to be frightened of, however good he was downhill.'

The very next day I got a message from Ann Bland, who I consider to be Billy's greatest supporter. Ann says she wouldn't go that far! 'We discussed times off Scafell Pike in the Wasdale race. In the year Billy set the Wasdale record (1982), he came off in 14 minutes flat, which may not have been bettered. Styan may have come off faster in the race you were talking about last night, but he is not the fastest.' That has resolved that then.

In the search for points in 'AM' races Billy then picked the Kinniside race on 19 July. It was run in a downpour with very poor visibility above 1,000 feet or so. Billy Bland and Harry Jarrett were away at the front of the field by the Blakeley Raise checkpoint, but went badly wrong after that, and sadly came in seventh and ninth respectively, giving a rare race victory to Donald Lee. When the leading four runners went wrong, Joe Ritson was running in a second group of three, with Donald Lee and Duncan Overton. They split up on descending Latterbarrow, and Ritson came homing thinking he was seventh, only to be told he was third. Joe Ritson is still running today in his early sixties. Like Billy Bland, he has a farming and stonemason thread in his family. When I chatted to him in the café at the Keswick Museum he also told me, 'I suspect I am related to Will Ritson, the one-time World's Greatest Liar, who ran the Wasdale Head Inn.' Joe Ritson recalls that Billy came in that day at Kinniside swearing away at having foolishly followed Harry Jarrett.

Billy tells the story behind that result. 'As I remember, again if it is that year, Jon Broxap and Harry Jarrett were going across Caw Fell Road, up to Flat Fell and I was with them going across to Latterbarrow in mist, as I describe it as three daft dogs. I shouted at them and instead of stopping to see why, they carried on. I was shouting, "you can't get to the top of Latterbarrow running downhill". We lost a bit of time before we corrected ourselves and tried to get back into the race.' Jon Broxap remembers it slightly differently. His recollection is that they were in Harry's 'backyard' on top of a hill and Billy was making disparaging remarks about Harry's ability with a compass. Broxap also acknowledges that Billy Bland was a better navigator than he let on. He adds, 'Billy often didn't need to navigate as he knew the terrain so well. He knew it intimately, but he could navigate if he needed to.' John McGee, the fourth of the errant group, came home in tenth, with Broxap eleventh.

Now Billy Bland really hit top form. On the next two weekends he chose to run two races on both occasions (all four being 'A' category ones), and in the process showed his remarkable ability to recover and re-focus.

On 26 to 28 July the Lochaber Three race series was held from Fort William. This consists of three races held from Saturday to Monday and gives a stiff challenge to anyone competing in all three. Billy Bland chose to run two of the races, and really staked his claim as man of the moment by winning them both.

On the Saturday it was the Melantee race ('AS' category). The 3.5 miles are certainly hard ones, with 1,500 feet of ascent, and on a hot day Billy went into an early lead, to win in 31:17, almost a minute ahead of Harry Jarrett. Billy liked this race, it being the middle one of a hat trick of wins there from 1979 to 81.

On the Sunday many were back for the Half Nevis race (an 'AM' category event), run over 6 miles of out and back on the lower part of Scotland's highest mountain, that is to the Red Burn and back. There was cloud as they set off and Billy won easily in 51:21, again from Harry Jarrett (53:23). He might have beaten his own course record of 50:23 (from the year before) had the halfway turn point been in the right place. Unfortunately, the marshal, not knowing himself where the exact location of the turn was, had decided to wait and see where the leader turned off, and then stand there. Bland, a basically honest person, didn't want to turn until he'd found the marshal. It was Catch 22. The result was that the whole field ran an extra 50 to 100 yards. Billy's win was the second in a run of four consecutive ones he had at the Half Nevis between 1979 and 82. Billy recalls, 'I thought you turned around right where you swing across Red Burn. Whether the marshal was farther on or what, I don't know. Melantee was very steep, which I liked, but you had to get to the hill across fields and stuff. If I could get to the bottom of the steep bit in touch, then the race was most probably mine. A good strong walk up and bomb down with enough to see you to a win. I never stopped for Cow Hill race on the Monday though, as I wanted to get to work and I had an eye on Borrowdale a week later.'

Back in the Lakes, the next weekend Billy started his next two-race challenge with his local Borrowdale race, a 17-mile category 'A' race which starts just a short jog from his house. On a boiling hot day Billy set off with a vengeance, having a two-minute lead by Esk Hause. He extended this throughout the tough course, to come home in 2:41:34, a massive 11:48 ahead of second placed Mike Short. [*Billy's consistently excellent results in this race are covered elsewhere in this book.*] However, he had carbo-loaded before this one, further proving its value to him.

Running his fourth race in just eight days, he then moved down to the other end of the Borrowdale valley to tackle the Latrigg race on the Sunday. Being just three miles, with 950 feet of ascent, it is not really a Billy Bland sort of course. Slippery underfoot on the day, Billy ran exceptionally well to come second to Alan McGee, being just 34 seconds behind at the finish (in 17:57). This scored him good points in his 'S' category efforts for the champs. [*Running slightly faster the next year he succeeded in doing the Borrowdale-Latrigg double, a remarkable achievement for someone reckoned to only be a long race specialist.*] Billy explains his appetite for racing doubles. 'If there was race locally, I would go to it. When I won the double the next year I presume Alan McGee hadn't been there [*he wasn't*]. I don't know how I ever won Latrigg, with that long lead out up Spooney Green Lane, which is runnable all the way.'

On 17 August Billy ran in the second Sedbergh race. The conditions were appalling, including thick mist, with many runners having difficulty navigating the upper fells. This included Billy Bland and Harry Jarrett, who were unable to locate The Calf checkpoint and ran in a little after the winner, only to both be disqualified for missing a checkpoint. John McGee had romped home to win in a new course record.

Despite this setback, Billy was on a roll now. He continued training hard and planned an excursion to the Yorkshire Dales to pick up another 'Short' race to give him a good spread of the required distances. On the 23 August he ran the fortieth edition of the Burnsall fell race. At just 1½ miles it is about as short as a fell race can be, and an interesting challenge for Billy. On a beautiful day he was no match for Mike Short on the ascent, but gave everyone a demonstration of running downhill to come from behind to pass all but Short, by just four seconds (in 13:39). Billy laughs, and just says, 'well it would look brilliant against Mike! If I could have got to the top with him I could have beaten him by a minute I would say, even on such a short race.'

Two weeks later Billy travelled up to Fort William again to run in the Ben Nevis race ('A' category, 12 miles, 4,400 feet), which he had won in 1978. Unfortunately, the weather wasn't playing ball, as it was wet and very windy, increasingly so the higher you went. The summit marshal claimed he could not reach his station, and the mountain rescue team rather dramatically advised that, 'anyone getting into difficulties would be dead within 25 minutes'. The race was cancelled by the organisers, knowing how many inexperienced hill runners can be on that particular start line. Many runners ran halfway as a kind of protest, and nine actually carried through to the summit, reporting conditions there no worse that it had been at halfway. Billy Bland (who had 'done the diet' for the event) was quoted at the time as saying, 'I reckon I could have got up OK, and other top runners would have been OK. They should have advised us of the situation and left it to us. I just can't see why the mountain rescue couldn't get up'.

Billy adds, 'I couldn't see anything wrong with it to be quite honest. But that is just the point of view of a selfish runner. I just went off home in a bad temper. I had gone there thinking I could win the race, but of course it could have been another disappointment, as I got beat there several times.'

The next event in Billy's personal race calendar was actually one that didn't count towards the championship, but one he really liked competing in. It was the Mountain Trial, sponsored by the Vaux Brewery at this time, and essentially a long orienteering event, held this year on 14 September from Longthwaite Youth Hostel – again just down from his home in Borrowdale for Billy.

Bill Smith thought that the Mountain Trial was, 'without doubt one of the toughest events in the fell runners' calendar, calling not only for a high standard of athletic stamina but also for a considerable degree of mountain craft, including the ability to navigate with map and compass'. That is why Billy liked it. In terms of pure racing, he thought that the Mountain Trial was the most demanding because, in normal races, he found that he could (as he noted in the history of the event), 'ease-off at times whereas in the Trial, he had to race all the way, not knowing how he fared against other competitors until all potential winners had finished' [*as start times are staggered, as per orienteering events*]. He acknowledges that he learned, quite early, of the locations of Trials via the farming community, but never the positions of controls. He spent hours studying maps beforehand, guessing at possible routes and considering map-marking on the day to be a waste of time. He 'sussed-out' controls during periods of forced walking.

It had rained buckets in the lead-up, with streams running fast, but on the day it was fine, though wet underfoot. Billy soon found that he had caught one of his main contenders, Peter Haines, who had a start time eight minutes ahead of him and was noted for his navigational abilities. But the two of them took very different routes mid-race, and Billy's time at the end was eventually just 55 seconds faster than Haines' was, with both taking nearly 5 hours. The LDMTA race report graphically explains how Billy suffered in the last mile or so: 'Descending from Blea Tarn he became aware of a walker with a heavy rucksack going just as fast as he was! He had almost reached his limit but managed to recover enough by sitting down [*for 6 minutes or so*] and taking in as many blaeberries as he could.'

Close your eyes and try to imagine Billy sitting down amongst the blaeberries in a race and picking them. Got the image? Billy elaborates on the story.

'In my own backyard it was. It set off from Longthwaite YHA but finished at the campsite at Stonethwaite, which is unusual to have a different start and finish. It went out to Littledale Reservoir, Haystacks, Glaramara, Codale Tarn and Blea Tarn. I must have been minutes clear earlier. I got to Blea Tarn and all that was left was getting back to

Borrowdale via John House bridge (up Langstrath). I came away from Blea Tarn and had run myself legless. Stupid really, but when you set off and you don't know where the opposition is, because of the staggered start times, you have to push yourself. I was far too aggressive on this occasion and I nearly blew it with Peter Haines, who never beat me normally. It was difficult. You didn't know for sure you had gone the best way, because clever planners give you alternatives. This feller was walking up there and watching the event. I really wanted to ask him for something to eat but I knew I shouldn't as you are not allowed to. Anyway, he was walking alongside us. I sat down looking over Langstrath and I saw what I thought was Peter Haines coming. I knew there were blaeberries about and I also knew the shortest way down. I was that out of petrol that I sat eating blaeberries for quite a bit. Bracken was waist high, but I saw Peter and thought it was go or bust. I staggered down to the bottom and maybe them blaeberries gave us a little bit more energy. I flopped over the line and saw John Richardson, who had been one of the planners, so I said to him, "you laal bugger, you should be made to run around this", as it was one of the longest ever Trials. I remember saying that and of course it was never my fault!'

Once again, failing to carbo-load prior to this race came back to bite him. This might seem a simplistic analysis, but Billy Bland is convinced that there was a direct correlation between his dietary preparations and results in the longer races of this season, where he was pushing himself to the limit so many times. He would use the diet a maximum of three or four times in any one season.

One week later and it was back to Championship duties at the Langdale race ('AL' category, 16 miles, 4,000 feet) on 20 September. Billy knew he had won the

Championship already. Mike Short needed to win the race simply to keep his chances alive, but he did not run, so Billy started the race knowing the title was his. The race organiser, Dave Meek, had moved the event from a Saturday to the Sunday but the move backfired, with a big drop in numbers racing. On a misty day several top athletes went awry, but Billy Bland came home first, followed in by Bob Whitfield.

Even having won the Championship Billy kept racing. On 5 October he ran the Moffat Chase ('AL' category, 20 miles, 5,000 feet) in mist, rain and high winds. Billy and Colin Donnelly were pushing each other hard and by the fifth (of seven) checkpoint were twenty minutes clear, but then got severely lost. With nothing to run for, except pride, Billy retired and Donnelly trailed home in thirtieth place.

On 15 November Billy Bland ran the Blisco Dash ('AS' category, 5 miles, 2,000 feet) to prove yet again that he COULD perform well in the shorter races. He won in damp conditions with mist on the tops, from Bob Whitfield again. To emphasise his ability even more pointedly, the next year he set a new course record for this short up and down race. Billy adds, 'I think I won four or five times there. The only downside for me was running to it and running back again. Running against Kenny Stuart he could get a lead on me there, I'd catch him on the downhill and he'd still do me down the road, and there were several who could do that.'

Billy's season ended with a bit of a whimper, when he could only finish twentieth the next day in the Copeland Chase, another orienteering style event ('O' category, 12 miles, 4,000 feet). He won that event once or twice but was obviously not going well that day.

But he had put himself about throughout the year, and finally became Fell Running Champion in that 1980 season. His race positions through the season for the three categories (in season order) had been Long: 14, 1, 1, 1, 1; Medium 2, 8, 1, 2, 7, 1; and Short 2, 1, 2, 2, 1. Taking the best of these to make up his 10 events gives eight firsts, and two seconds – not perfect, but pretty damned good. Second placer Mike Short had four firsts, five seconds, and a third.

In an Interview with Andy Styan in *The Fellrunner* issue of January 1981 (given after the Blisco Dash in November 1980) Billy was asked how it felt to have won at last? He replied that he was, 'very pleased about it obviously. It's something I always wanted. It's a bit of an anti-climax, though, particularly as I start to think of what I am going to do next year. I have said to a few people that I'm going to defend the title next year, which to me no-one has really set their stall out to do, but next year is another year and we'll just have to see what comes.'

Knowing how nervous he had been before races, and how he had sometimes not run through nerves, it was good to see him saying in this interview that after winning the British Fell Running Championships that year that he, 'always enjoyed the running in training, and loved racing'. It had only been in his pro race days, in his teens, that he hated racing. It had all changed now.

Who did he think was going to be challenging him the next year? 'The same five or six lads who've been pushing for the top this year. I can't see anyone new breaking in, but then you never know. There's you [Styan] and me and Mike Short. I think such as you and me and Bob Whitfield really have to work at it, whereas Mike's more of a natural. If he were to really try, he could dominate it – that's my opinion.'

As it happened, there was a brilliant newcomer on the scene in 1981. The challenge was to come from John Wild. Billy Bland was destined never to win the Championships again.

Recently I took the opportunity to ask Billy Bland why he only won the British Fell Running title just the once. He disingenuously replied that he just wasn't good enough. He expanded: 'It was the best ten races from fifteen races at that time and so you could pick races that suited yourself. Over the years it has got reduced, is it down to four now? If I had picked the championship races, I could have won three or four British titles, because I could have picked them to suit myself.'

He concluded, 'I really enjoyed my time climbing the ladder. When you start to be a winner then a certain part of the enjoyment goes out of it, because you are just there to be shot at. Once you have been a winner all you want to do is win, after that.' An interesting take on success.

Throughout his running career Billy Bland often had members of his own family as some of his most serious rivals. His brothers, cousins and nephews were fine runners, with varying degrees of longevity in the sport. A detour to look at their training, attitude and positions in the sport may also shine some light on Billy's achievements.

THE TIES THAT BIND

The remarkable thing about the other members of the Blands of Billy's generation is that apart from Billy they all came to fell running quite late in life. One can only wonder what levels some of them might have achieved if they had started earlier and had dedicated themselves so selflessly to training for the fells as Billy did. Local races were invariably the catalyst to the family members becoming involved in fell running.

In August 1974 the first Borrowdale race was held, organised by Chris Bland (Billy's cousin), and with its start on the land Billy's brother David Bland farmed. None of the Blands ran that day. Joss Naylor was top man at the time, but he wasn't running in that inaugural Borrowdale race either and it was won by Dave Halstead in 3:05:07.

David Bland (25 at the time and living at Nook Farm) decided to enter the second Borrowdale race in 1975, although he had no previous running experience. He finished twenty-ninth out of the 81 competitors, being greeted with a rousing ovation from the locals as he hobbled into the sports field. Sometime afterwards, in an interview, he commented on the event. 'I had not done much training and thought it would be a piece of cake. If anyone ever got their eyes opened that day, I did.' He was in the leading pack of ten athletes early on, but after Honister Pass his legs went, and he felt sick and dizzy. 'Coming off Dale Head I had to sit down and slide on my backside rather than fall on my head, being passed by loads of runners on this section. I've never been as happy to see a finish even to this day.'

Billy Bland (27 at the time) also decided to run that day. Borrowdale (at 17 miles) was a much longer race than Billy normally ran in as a pro, and he enjoyed it 'up to a point', but he thought that with a bit of training he might be able do well over the longer distances. He was quoted at the time as saying, 'before I started amateur racing, I used to read articles about Joss Naylor's performances and wondered what was the standard of amateur fell racing when a 36- or 38-year-old man was winning these races. I soon found out. What a marvellous fella he is!'

Billy Bland and his brother David began to train with the longer races in mind, although both acknowledging the need for speed work for shorter races such as Latrigg, which had been revived as an amateur race in 1973 by Keswick AC, the athletic club they joined shortly. David and Billy, having had indifferent starts to their amateur careers, both began to build a reputation as good runners locally. Later that year David competed at Langdale and then came a creditable fifth in the Wansfell Race at Christmas (1974), which turns out to be the first mention of any of the Bland family in *The Fellrunner* magazine. The race report also noted that that there was 'a very enjoyable pack run round the Troutbeck Horseshoe the next day, supported by about 20 runners'.

David Bland was one of those runners, describing it as a race rather than a run. 'Mike Nicholson was half a mile ahead of me and Billy after we had done 18 miles. I said, "are we going to catch him?" to which Billy replies, "well you can if you want". We got to Garburn Pass and just had to drop into the caravan site at Troutbeck, and I caught Mike and beat him. I still have the trophy. It was only ever run once. The trophy is a ram's head and it is an ugly thing. [*His son, Gavin, points out that it is on the front door of their farm at Thirlmere.*] Just then they were getting races on the skyline of every valley.'

Other highlights in David's reasonably short career were coming fourth at the Blisco Dash in 1975, beating Billy by two places in the process; and in 1976 being eleventh at Borrowdale, sixth at the Mountain Trial, and sixth at Langdale. In 1977 he started losing interest in fell racing, but still had a best result that year of fifth at Ennerdale.

David once joked that he didn't need a whistle in his race kit as he whistled sheep all day on his farm, and could 'do perfectly well without carrying one, thank you very much'. After he had finished competing, David Bland admitted that he wasn't the best trainer out there. 'I'd probably not go out training for a fortnight or so, and then a week before a race I'd go mad and train every night.' He also admitted that he would, 'set off to do eight miles on the road and end up doing four.' On Sundays he would go out with Billy and Stuart for a long run on the fells and, 'hate every stride because they were going too fast. But I enjoyed races, but it was always hard work because I was never as fit as I should have been. Farming took my time.'

Billy Bland's cousin Chris was a good all-rounder, playing cricket, rugby and football before trying fell running in 1975, aged 34. Legend has it that he was shocked one evening to find he was unable to run the mile from his home to the Scafell Hotel. He was over 14 stone at the time, way too much for someone 5ft 8ins tall. On New Year's Day 1975 he 'started trotting out at night for 2 to 3 miles with stacks of clothes on. The first 1½ stones came off fast.' Getting down to 12 stone, he started doing some races, but initially finished towards the back of race fields. Chris joined Keswick AC around the same time as David and Billy, going on to become Secretary and Chairman of the club.

Chris Bland was never really up at the front end of races, but become an excellent endurance runner, and later he completed the Bob Graham Round on a family attempt, which is described elsewhere in this book. He led a very full life, being very involved in his local church. He once said that, 'life is wasted if not used to the full. I have been on Scafell Pike before seven in the morning. What better than running past Angle Tarn at 6a.m.'

Chris completed his BGR in 1977 along with Jean Dawes, the first female to complete. In 1977 he was also seventh in the Keswick AC club champs, and four of the six people in front of him were the other Blands. Chris

Bland also liked orienteering and completed in events such as the Elite Class at the Karrimor Mountain Marathon, and the High Peak Marathon.

One of Chris's innovations was to attempt the 214 summits in the seven Wainwright guidebooks in seven days, one volume per day. Although he had to miss out 22 of the summits on two long days, he was not bothered, being pleased to raise considerable sums of money for a fund to repair the Borrowdale Church roof. He commented, 'that I failed to complete the entire programme no longer worries me, as before the event I was terrified of failing miserably. That things went so well was the greatest mental and physical boost that I could have hoped for.'

Sadly, Chris Bland committed suicide in 2003 in difficult circumstances. One of the extended Bland family said to me that, 'only Chris knows why he took his own life'.

Anthony Bland (Chris' brother) began fell running at the age of 28 because his brother and cousins were doing it. In his racing career he jumped straight in at the deep end, entering the 1976 Ennerdale race, and coming forty-fourth, followed by finishing seventeenth at Borrowdale later that year. His highest placings when he got more established were to be fourth at both Borrowdale and Ennerdale in 1977, and third at Duddon in 1978. He used to take his whippet on his runs up to 10 miles, until its age precluded it. Anthony and Chris Bland were both stonemasons. They did a lot of work at St Benedicts Church in Whitehaven, using Elterwater Slate.

Anthony Bland continuing running into the early 1980s without any major successes, and then tailed off, before coming back as he approached fifty. In 1996 he had eight V50 victories and won his age category at both the British and English championships. He continued running through the 90s and into the new millennium, before dropping off in 2003 and 2004. He came back well as a V60 winning six races in his new category in 2005.

The member of the family who perhaps had the greatest early impact on the fells was Billy's other brother, Stuart Bland. He had been employed up at Honister Quarry for seven years and had worked in manual jobs like road-working for a while but got back into farming again when he put in for the tenancy at Thorneythwaite Farm in 1975.

He started in 1976 at the local Borrowdale race, aged 30 and running unattached, after playing football for years. On taking up running Stuart Bland immediately showed superb descending ability, for which he justifiably became famous. When asked about that first Borrowdale race he replied, 'I remember running between the Esk Hause and Scafell Pike checkpoints in about twelfth position and thinking I would do well to hold that place. Anyway, once I got on the downhill between Scafell Pike and Sty Head, I was amazed at how I improved my position to third.' Going up Gable he held that position, to finish behind Billy Bland and Joss Naylor.

This debut by Stuart did not come without some prior training. The year before he had gone on a training run with Billy, following the Borrowdale course to Scafell and back. He had been reduced to a walk at times, but he persevered. About a week later he went solo from Rosthwaite round the full Borrowdale race route in 3:27. That encouraged him to do some regular training, which was eventually about an hour on the fells almost every night, despite his arduous farming life at Thorneythwaite Farm. 'I'm a one-man band', he commented. 'I suppose like all the other lads I do my training when the day's work is done.'

Immediately prior to his race debut he ran hard up Dale Head every night for a fortnight, showing for a while the singular attitude to training that Billy had. But Stuart had no illusions about his short distance speed, which was not brilliant, like Billy. His endurance became mighty impressive though. To keep his racing weight down to 11 stone he would run with extra clothes on to get up a good sweat.

One of his other race highlights was another third, at Ennerdale in 1978. Andy Styan beat Mike Short after a tough race that day with a winning time of 3:27:00, which beat Joss Naylor's previous record from 1972. Billy Bland had been in contention for much of the race, but was passed coming off Crag Fell by Stuart, who had charged through the field. After being 6 minutes adrift of Billy at Kirk Fell, Stuart had the satisfaction of beating his brother by nearly 2 minutes, with his 3:35:47 for third place.

At the Langdale race in 1976 the Bland family showed their amazing strength in depth. They easily won the first team prize for Keswick AC, with Billy third, Stuart fourth, and David sixth (and with Anthony spare in eleventh). David Bland mentioned what he called his 'claim to fame' from a Langdale race. 'It was when I got to Thunacar Knott in a Langdale race on a misty day and I knew exactly what I was doing from there. We were going down into Stake Pass and I was in the lead having been about thirtieth going up Thunacar Knott. Local knowledge gave me the best line. Everybody passed me again mind. I think the three brothers (Billy, Stuart and me) should have won the team but I think someone like Jon Broxap spoilt it.'

Hearing that story, Gavin chips in with a parallel one from his generation. 'I have a younger brother who ran as well, Peter. Peter, Jonny and I won a team prize at both Buttermere and Langdale. Two brothers and a cousin, nearly as good as them boys. Peter beat Billy at the Peris Horseshoe one year.'

There was a lovely picture of the Blands in an article that Ross Brewster wrote for the Evening News and Star in April 1977. It shows Stuart, David, Chris and Billy Bland running uphill in a line alongside each other. If you look closely you can see that it was a posed picture. It was shot in the field over the road from Billy's house. The photographer said, 'just jog back up and down the field'. 'And up again and down again,' Billy adds. Ann chips in that Anthony wouldn't come and do it, thinking it stupid.

Another tragedy overcame the Bland family, when Stuart Bland was diagnosed with cancer and sadly he passed away in May 2017. In the eulogy at his funeral it was said that that Stuart was very proud of Billy – something that Ann and Billy hadn't really known.

Ann Bland ran her first fell race in 1977 at Dale Head (aged 28), finishing third out of eight starters, behind Joan Lancaster and Anne Bland (Pete's wife). Ann modestly claims that she was rubbish. But, she adds, 'I think I ran Dale Head two or three times. Then I did half marathons a couple of times. The second one I was sponsored to get football kit for the kids at school. I didn't really like running against anybody, but I always ran for myself. I often went out for long runs with a dog. I also used to run up to higher ground to watch Billy when he was racing.'

Her running had started one Christmas time. Billy had been running earlier and he had gone down to Rosthwaite with the two kids to some friends. Ann continues, 'I thought I would just go and have a run. It was a really wet day and I had a pair of plimsolls. It started from that. The only thing I could do well was come downhill though. I did Dale Head because it was the ladies' race when Borrowdale was on at the time. I finished third but I came down well, got to the field at the bottom and was knackered. I also did the Blisco race.' She says that nobody forced her to do it, and adds a brilliant self put-down, saying, 'maybe I thought I was better than I was'. Billy's cousin Anthony told her, 'you will never make a fellrunner because you are the wrong shape and size'. Just the encouragement you need.

Two of Billy Bland's nephews also had quite an impact on the fell running scene. Jonny Bland (Stuart's son) and Gavin Bland (David's son) both started running fell races immediately on leaving school, following uncle Billy's path rather than their fathers' late-starting way into the sport.

Jonny Bland was born in September 1972 and grew up living at Thorneythwaite Farm, Seatoller, where his father Stuart Bland was the tenant farmer at the time. Jonny ran a few professional/guides races as a junior, for example finishing third in the Grasmere under-17 race in 1988 and going on to win the event in 1989. Both Jonny and Gavin joined Keswick AC in 1989, having changed code to the amateur one, in order to expand their range.

Jonny showed great promise in his first season, winning the Coniston junior race, and also finishing in the top ten in five senior races. He then took a year and half off from racing and came back with a vengeance, performing particularly well in long races. He came back in September 1991 with a third at Dale Head, and a second at Scafell Pike.

Like many others leading a farming life Jonny felt there were pluses and minuses about it as far as his running was concerned. In an interview in 1993 he said that on the one hand, 'it keeps me fit, what with gathering and clipping, and is bound to be better than sitting in an office.' However, 'at lambing time my training drops off to just an odd evening a week, and sometimes I don't feel like training at all if I've been shepherding all day.' In that same interview Jonny commented that he didn't do any special training for races he hoped to do well in. He said he just tried to get fit before the running season. He added that in longer races he found that, 'I'm getting stronger while others are slowing up a bit. I wouldn't say I'm a good navigator with map and compass, but I can manage if I take a bit of time.' He reckoned that cross country style races were good for getting him fit, but that he didn't enjoy them so much. 'However, such courses do improve my speed and fitness and make me try harder.'

In the early days, his father Stuart and uncle Billy gave him advice on how to run races and how to pace himself. They often used to show him around a course before a race, usually a fortnight beforehand. Jonny was a far better descender than climber, having a great technique for running downhill over rough ground, claiming that shepherding on that sort of ground on Glaramara helped in that aspect. He was not one for travelling miles to races as he didn't feel right for racing after sitting in a car for too long. He was lucky to experience no serious injuries, 'just the odd blistered foot when the ground is dry and hard, and the occasional twisted ankle when out training.'

Jonny Bland had a good year in 1992, running for the all-conquering (and newly founded) Borrowdale Fellrunners, when he won the Buttermere Horseshoe race, came second at Borrowdale, Wasdale and Dale Head, significantly all races local to him. Early in that season he also came eighth at the Grisedale Grind, where he had the satisfaction of a rare beating of both uncle Billy and nephew Gavin. Despite running a good number of races, he was only twenty-third in the British Championships that year.

Running many races again in 1993, but with inconsistent performances, Jonny won only at Wasdale that year, to finish fifteenth in the British Champs. This pattern was repeated for several years. Of 25 races competed at in 1994, Jonny won at only two, Tebay and Gatesgarth. The next season saw Jonny win at Ennerdale, Tebay, Langstrath, Wasdale and Scafell Pike, beginning to show his mettle at some of the classics. In 1996 there were wins at Skiddaw, Gunson Knott, Gategill, the Grisedale Horseshoe and at Dale Head. In 1997 Jonny had a quiet year, with his first win at Borrowdale being his only victory that year, beating Gavin Bland into second place by well over 3 minutes.

Still racing frequently, Jonny had a good finish to 1998, winning the Scafell Pike and Langdale races, finishing ninth at the British championships. In 1999 he finished in his highest British championships position of fifth, winning five races, including Langdale again. He was fifth in the championships again in 2000, despite winning only two races, although he equalled his highest ever English championships position of sixth as well.

The 2001 fell race season was virtually wiped out due to restrictions in place because of the foot and mouth outbreak. Cumbria was the worst affected area of the country, with almost 900 cases reported. This closed the fells for months as restrictions on moving farm animals was in place to try to stem the spread of the disease. After a near year-long race washout, Jonny came back in 2002 winning six races to take the very first Lakeland Classics Trophy (the trophy is scored on your best three results from: Duddon Valley, Ennerdale, Buttermere, Wasdale, Three Shires and Langdale). He had a quiet season in 2003, and then only raced twice in 2004, before racing more in 2005 but still with no victories. In 2006 Jonny raced five times, winning at Grisedale and Dodd Fell. He continued running intermittently in 2007, and then drifted out of competition in 2008–2009.

In summary, Jonny was a fine runner, but chose the wrong races to do really well in the championships, often concentrating on Lake District races which wouldn't have helped. He won well over 30 races in his career in 24 different events. As to the big ones, he won Wasdale three times, Ennerdale and Langdale twice, and Borrowdale once.

Gavin Bland says that Jonny Bland ran well for many years but that, 'once Jonny wasn't competitive, he wouldn't do it. Whereas I kept doing Borrowdales just for the sake of doing them really.'

This, and much more, was revealed recently when I had the chance to have a long chat with Gavin Bland at his farm near Thirlmere. He started by explaining his own background, before commenting on some of his running highlights and a little about his life as a farmer.

Gavin was born in the hospital in Penrith in November 1971 and lived at Nook Farm for the first ten years of his life. His father, David, had taken over the farm even though he was the youngest of the Bland brothers. Gavin was the oldest of three children. His brother Peter is 15 months younger than him and his sister Lisa was born in 1980.

Gavin went to Borrowdale School and then on to Keswick School, as it was by then. He went through school thinking all along that he was going into farming.

He was good at school but then he realised that he didn't really need all the things they were trying to teach him. He left school at 16 and saw a lot of classmates go to agricultural college. However, he had to come home and start working right away as he was needed on the farm. He still works with his father, as they farm as one business.

Gavin ran at school and by the second year at senior school he had just started getting good when he was diagnosed with Osgood-Schlatter's (severe knee pain experienced by some growing adolescents) and stopped doing any sport. He didn't really start again until he was aged 15–16. Gavin Bland spent a year on the professional scene before changing to the amateur code. Gavin's best pro race results in his one year of competition were coming second at Grasmere and also at Kilnsey.

Gavin explained the difficulties in the pro/am split at that time. 'We would be spending the summer going to see sheep shows and there were still (pro) races at the shows. At the time the sport was split into the two codes.'

Changing codes and joining Keswick AC in 1989, Gavin immediately finished third in the under-18s amateur race at Chew Valley. He reads from his diary. '3 Mar 1989. Chew Valley fell race u18s. First race in English championships. 3 miles, 900 feet. Time 22:44. Finished third. Prize a t-shirt.' At this last statement he laughs, presumably thinking about equally poor rewards in the recently departed pro races.

That year everywhere Billy and Stuart went they took Gavin and Jonny with them. That was what got Gavin into it.

Gavin explained why they changed codes. 'Jonny and I changed to amateur to do real fell races. Billy was just coming to the end of his reign and the pro scene was also just fizzling out. It wasn't what it used to be.'

Although often competing in junior races Gavin also showed his massive talent by competing in Senior events when he could. A week after Chew Valley he was already stepping up. He commented in an early profile, 'I ran my first senior race at Loughrigg a week later finishing tenth. It was a 9-mile course, further than I had ever run before, but I found it much easier than the flat-out pace of a short race and enjoyed the increased competition of running in a larger field.' In June 1989 Gavin and Jonny Bland are shown in the results in *The Fellrunner* as finishing first and second juniors, with Gavin an impressive sixth overall in the Coledale Horseshoe race.

Gavin explained the range of land he had to cover when shepherding, and how it affected his running. 'In winter we would start gathering above Ashness, and come right through High Seat, High Tove, Ullscarf and back to West Head. The other side we would go Hellvellyn, Nethermost, Dollywagon, and then help all our neighbours over Grasmere, Steel Fell way. All of this several times in each year.' If they had a good day gathering the fells there was no need to go for a run, and often he couldn't possibly face it anyway. 'We would fit the running round the gathering. I could never run well at lambing time, for a start, from the middle of April till the end of May. I was on my feet too much. They were long days. My body couldn't cope with it. I could go to a race and run but unlikely to be winning.'

Gavin Bland is obviously fiercely proud of his achievements. His first World Cup race was on 16 September 1989. Starting with a quote from his diary, he recalls the occasion. 'Seventh in Junior race. Second Englishman, being only the fourth best runner on the team. Red hot day. I still remember that one of the lads collapsed. I could cope with heat when I was young, as pasty skinned as I am!'

In 1990 his performances were being recognised, and he was again selected for the junior team for the World Cup race at Telfes, in Austria, where he finished in a brilliant second place. Gavin admits that the Junior World Cup was a nice incentive. 'We had been nowhere, never been abroad. There was no two weeks (holiday) in Spain when you worked on a farm. For a boy from the fells I got abroad for a couple of years courtesy of the FRA.'

His 1991 season really picked up and he managed to win some of the Lakeland classic races, including the Blisco Dash, and the longer Three Shires and Borrowdale races. He began to realise he was in with a chance of the British Champs title, and ended up finishing second to Keith Anderson, but having the consolation of winning the English Champs title, which had been competed for alongside the British Champs since 1986. He hadn't planned to target the English Champs, preferring to focus on World Cup races, saying that, 'running for England in the last four World Cups has been more satisfying'.

Talking with me, he recalled the finale that year, as he scanned his Wainwright-branded training diaries. 'I just went and did the races and ran against whoever was there. Keith Anderson was top of the tree at the time. I beat him at Borrowdale, and I knew then that I could win big races. I have never come as fast off Scafell Pike as I did then. I ran with Keith down the Corridor and going up Gable I knew I was better uphill than him and I left him. Strangely, I can read these diaries now and think, "did I really get to such and such a place?" Other races I can picture them still. Some people can remember them all, but I can't.'

In 1992, aged just 21, Gavin proved he could run long and short courses equally well. With victories at Borrowdale and Ben Nevis, he also won the short Butter Crag race in 12:43. He was adjudged the winner despite being given the same time as John Atkinson, after they had a helter-skelter descent together. This was just one example of where his proficiency at descending would serve him well, and garner him comparisons with the best descenders.

After the reigns of Joss and Billy, there was a changing of the guard in 1992 when Gavin Bland beat his uncle Billy into second by 3 minutes at Borrowdale. Gavin had first beaten Billy in a race at Borrowdale on 4 August 1990 (but did not win the race that time, coming second to Mark Rigby), and was really establishing himself. The 1993 Three Shires race was run in unsettled weather but still resulted in a new course record for Gavin Bland in 1:47:59.

Gavin fully admits to having been a lazy trainer, and even a lazy racer, liking to do just enough (a slightly different trait to that which Billy admitted to at his peak, as he raced everything full on). He hardly did any speed work but sharpened up by racing regularly. In the early days, he explained, 'I get fit fairly quickly. Billy's advice on racing is: a steady start always pays.'

Gavin also admitted to never training over courses, although he used to look around Long 'A' races. In 1993 he says he, 'looked around Duddon the week before the race with Billy, but we didn't look around Borrowdale or Ennerdale in one go but did them in stages. I can navigate if needs be but prefer to know where I'm going in a race. I won the Mountain Trial without ever using my compass.' I had thought that Gavin was not the best of navigators and casually mentioned that, only to be strongly reprimanded. He came back immediately. 'I dispute that completely. That was printed by someone once and it is absolutely not the case. I am a really good navigator. When we were doing the FRA relays, we had some good navigators in our teams. If there was a decision to be made, I wouldn't let them make it because 99 times out of 100 I would be right.' Suitably chastened, we moved on.

In 1993 Gavin Bland became the youngest ever winner of the Three Peaks race in appalling conditions. Gavin says it was his luckiest win ever. 'We had gone around the course a fortnight before, three of us – me, Scoffer and Bob Whitfield. I was absolutely knackered and hanging on. I thought, "what am I doing this for?" Meanwhile, Scoff fell off a sink and he couldn't run in the race. Paul Sheard was up there but went wrong halfway round, so myself and Mark Roberts ran around with Paul Mitchell, racing as we thought for second, third and fourth places. We got to the last field and Mark Croasdale, who had been in the lead, lost out as he had ran out of petrol coming off Ingleborough. Mark and I left Paul, who had showed us the way round, and sprint finished that last field and I won it.' Being reminded of the event, Scoffer said to me, without any apparent irony, 'I would have won the Three Peaks that day. I came second three times and third three times, but never won it.'

Gavin Bland is 5 feet 11 inches tall and weighed 10 stone at his racing peak. He admits to not being a brilliant climber. His stated preference is for steep, rough courses and he does better in longer races, giving Borrowdale and Ben Nevis as his favourite races. In the early days he claimed he wanted to run on the roads later, and wanted to beat Billy's Bob Graham Round record. But his career took a different path.

In 1997 he set the present course record of 1:45:8 for the Three Shires race. Although he couldn't find his diary for that year Gavin explained about having a difficult lead-up to that record. 'I had my appendix out in April. Billy took us to the Grand National race meeting on the Thursday. I got back and that night I had the appendix op. I was in real bad fettle till the middle of July. They stitched us up wrong. But I got right again and Borrowdale [in August] would be one of my first races back, and I ran well to come second behind our Jonny. If Borrowdale had been a week later I would have won it. Until the end of that October I was unbeatable. That was one of my mini peaks. Because I had been unable to eat I lost weight. That would be the second time I won the Ben as well.' He ends the story with a triumphant statement. 'I won the Ben race one more time than Billy.'

Gavin also commented at this point on the vagaries of memory. 'I once went to the Ben and finished second and I can't remember a thing about it. The two times I won I can remember them clear as day. I was coming to the road the second time with a good lead and was told my time wrong, so I didn't put it all in. If I had been told right I would have been a lot closer to Kenny's time than I got.' This is remarkably similar to Billy Bland when he was close to the record in 1978.

Then in 1999 it all came really good. Setting records that still stand at the Carnethy and the Edale Skyline races he finally achieved his ambition of being crowned as the best fell runner in Britain. He revealed that he was not happy with the way he had won it, having desperately wanted to win the vital last counter to seal the title in style.

'I have never been so disappointed as I was the day I ran Borrowdale, as I was only third in the race. I had to beat Ian Holmes and then I wouldn't have to go to the last race in Wales. I said to him, "I am not right". We were killing each other up the top of Langstrath. He was puffing as well and so we all regrouped. Going into Honister there were five of us. I was still thinking I am going to win as I have been the best runner all season. Then Simon Booth ran away and left us up Dale Head to take the win. I had beaten Holmsey by then, so I knew I had the championship won. I had thought I was going to win Borrowdale again. I was a seriously disappointed British Champion.'

The enforced break from running the fells that Foot and Mouth caused in 2001 also signalled the end of a period of good running for Gavin. 'But I never really stopped running until I was over 40. I made a big effort at 40, going for the Vet Champs. For me, I have to go running every day. It is psychological. Sometimes it is too hard, but as long as I have been, it is good.'

Gavin Bland began featuring less prominently in races but had occasional returns to good form, including winning a counter in the English Championships series at Langdale in 2003. Gavin remembers that win vividly. 'I was not very fit and it was a misty day. I said to Scoffer I was going to win, and he said no chance. We popped out of the mist and there it was. I was against Jebby and he can't run downhill!'

In 2004 Gavin raced sparingly but had a good win at the Mountain Trial, which was based locally to him at Thirlmere. In the event Scoffer took a bad fall. 'I slipped, landed on some rocks and had to retire, and then I had to have about 50 stitches', said Scoffer when he and Gavin were recounting it. 'They had to patch up his head', said Gavin, adding that, 'it would have killed a normal person. It was over between Helvellyn and Nethermost. We went over there this morning [*through work*] and I said, "be careful this is where Scoff nearly killed himself". Weirdly, I had been concerned about him all the way round that race, not knowing he had fallen. It was knowing I hadn't caught him up like I would expect to have.'

In 2005 Gavin raced a few times, with only a couple of wins. The 2006 season was a virtual washout due to a foot injury. Gavin had to have a toe operation that year because of it, but not without doing the Borrowdale race a day or two before the operation. 'I had a top joint in the big toe that was suffering from wear and tear. I went private and they said they will clean it out and it should give you 4 or 5 years more of running. If I was to start running seriously again, they would have to do the other big toe.' That Borrowdale race was an example of Gavin seriously under-performing, probably because of the injury. He came eighty-seventh in 4:10:53.

Despite some up and down form, Gavin reckoned that he had won a race every year since he started running. 'I don't know when that sequence ended, but it possibly lasted for 15 years.' A check of the stats shows that he seems to have won a race every year from 1991 to 2005 (excepting 2001 Foot and Mouth), an impressive run of 10 years. By comparison Billy Bland also won at least one race for 11 years in a row. That was from 1978 to 1988, and worth noting that his sequence would have been 15 years if it hadn't been for an anomalous barren year in 1989, as he won one each year up until 1993.

Gavin rarely competed in 2007–2011, and then tried

to come back as a Vet in 2012 but got injured again that year. He tried again in 2013 and did really well for a while, coming in the top ten at Black Combe and winning at the Silent Valley (Northern Ireland) Championships race. 'I was the fittest man in the country for about six weeks. I never missed a day's training all winter, and there was loads of snow that year. I lost a lot of weight. Silent Valley was a pig of a day, a man's race. I hadn't had a drink for two years and had a load of Guinness afterwards. Then I had a bursitis and couldn't run downhill. I went to the next Champs race in the Borders (at Yetholm) and I couldn't run.'

Gavin Bland just lost interest in being competitive from then on. He explains himself with regard to commitment, saying that to win a British Championship you have got to be really dedicated. 'When I did win it, I was dedicated. If I didn't give the time to it there was always a runner who was better. I was only super fit for short spells. When I was fit I was as good as anybody. I had to do a proper winter's training if I wanted to do well. Sometimes I played rugby in winter and arsed about like that. When training hard we used to do mile reps on the back road at Thirlmere. I don't miss training when I am not doing it, that is my problem. When I was injured, then I didn't miss racing. When I was fit, I would rather race than do three weeks training. I'd race to fitness. Uncle Billy wouldn't do a comeback race for the craic, but I would.'

Gavin even admitted that he had run the 2018 Borrowdale fell race when very unfit. He finished two hundred and twenty-eighth out of 239 finishers, in a time of 5:46:10. He got a huge cheer as he came in as the prizes were being given out. 'I thought halfway round I should have finished by now!', he laughs.

Looking back on the records that he set, and still holds, Gavin reckons the hardest to beat would be Carnethy. 'It was the first race of the season. There was an orienteer from Norway there called Bernt Bjornsgaard. He set off like a rocket. I raced for 44 minutes before I caught him and then beat him off the last top. I had to really race. That was a good record.'

I asked Gavin to analyse why it might have been that he couldn't beat Billy's times for any of the Lakes Classics, except the Three Shires. 'Because I very rarely had to really push it. If I had been in a race with Billy Bland and we had both been in our prime I would have run faster than I ran against others. Does that make sense? In my time we were all fairly evenly matched and it was rare that anyone thought they were going run the legs off everyone. Because if you did you would get beaten, wouldn't you? I would rather mooch round and win, than race round and finish fifth because I'd misjudged it.'

Billy Bland agrees with that assessment by Gavin. 'He was better than me, but he didn't achieve what he should have done. He was a different sort of racer to myself. I would set off to do the best I could. If that meant leaving somebody behind in the first half mile then that meant leaving them behind. Whereas Gavin was more of a racer. Not always going round as fast as he could. That was his character really.'

Gavin concludes that he did make the most of what he had, but that it was all in fits and starts. 'When I was at my peak I was as good as I could be. But I sometimes would go into a trough and finish 20th in a race and think, "well that is all right". When I wasn't fit, I still enjoyed going to races. That was slightly different to Billy. If he wasn't fit, he wouldn't go. Looking back, I shouldn't have played any rugby when I was 19 and 20, and if I could do it all again you would do it completely differently.' Notwithstanding that, as I walked across the farmyard to leave, he yelled after me, 'I might go on a massive diet and make a big comeback when I am 50!'

Billy and Stuart Bland helped Gavin and Jonny in the early days, as Billy explains. 'Rather than us preaching to them they used to listen to us two talking. My best advice to any young 'un is to run your own race. Don't go off like a bloody idiot, just learn how to race properly, and you will get your best results. Do what is good for you not what is good for somebody else. That is how those boys got into the scene, because we were still running then.'

Billy ends with a devastating put-down of Gavin, and a surprising admission about his own achievements. 'Gavin could have trained harder. Whatever his Three Shires record time is it could have been much faster, by training proper. Just like if I had trained like Kilian Jornet trains then I'd have been better.'

Having said that, Billy Bland isn't afraid to admit to his own shortcomings. I once asked him if he ever had any thoughts about coming of the fells to do marathon running for real, like Kenny Stuart and Dave Cannon had. If not, what was his reasoning. Back came a typically blunt reply, which highlighted a family characteristic. 'Well, I was too slow! No basic speed, me. Nowhere near what Kenny could do. There isn't a Bland that had any speed. Gavin used to think he could sprint at the end of a race. He looked as though he was sprinting because he had such an easy time earlier in the race. He could beat someone who was already buggered, basically. We Blands are no sprinters, we are distance men.'

That, then, is the Bland family. In their individual ways

all the family are driven. Unfortunately, some of them Billy Bland has had a massive domestic split from. One person neatly summed the family up. 'The Lakeland Grit of farming, plus the challenge of the fell running.'

The challenge for Billy Bland was to repeat his success of being top man on the fells in 1980. Everyone, of course, was now out to beat him in races, and it wasn't going to be easy.

GLORY DAYS

Having won the Fell Runner of the Year award in the championships in 1980, Billy Bland went on to have a long period of hugely successful running at the highest level in the sport. In his local 'Long' fell races he managed several enviable runs of consecutive victories, and set a good number of course records, two of which have not yet been beaten, many years on. He became an iconic figure, who was, and still is, revered across the sport.

His 1981 season started with a runout at the Chew Valley Skyline, a race that Billy Bland later used as a form marker as each season commenced. Billy fully acknowledges that outside the Lakes he sometimes was not exactly lost in races but had to be canny with his rivals. On this occasion he admits he followed somebody. 'I remember going down there and I was very fit and I went up the first hill and down into a ghyll and Bob Ashworth had broken clear and there were four or five other pretty good runners and I said, "does he know where he is going?", and they said "yeh, think he does". So, I set off after him. In the mist Bob could have run me to Manchester, I didn't have a clue where I was going.'

The report in *The Fellrunner* saw it slightly differently, recording that Billy caught up with Ashworth going up Ravenstone Edge, and goes on humorously, 'it was here that Bob made what was perhaps his only mistake of the day. When asked by Billy if he knew the way, instead of looking gormless and pretending he was on a fun run for national slimmers week, he admitted that he did and so acquired a shadow for the rest of the race. By Alphin Summit they had increased their lead to over 5 minutes. From here it was possible for Bland to leave a tiring Ashworth, but in recognition of his pathfinding, he sportingly held back and let the Rossendale man take the honours.' Billy adds, 'normally I didn't really like running with somebody and liked to know what I was doing.'

After another early season tester (coming third at the Edale Skyline, rather than running the Pendle race in the champs the day before), Billy's championship season started at Kentmere. It didn't go well though, as Billy was in a group that included Bob Whitfield, Jeff Norman, Mike Short and Colin Donnelly which went off course after Kentmere Pike, going off down Harter Fell. Billy retired. Although not wanting to sweep failures aside Billy says he can't really remember not finishing that day. 'I think we were headed for Branstree instead of turning into Nan Bield Pass. That was probably a case of forget about it till another day', he reasoned.

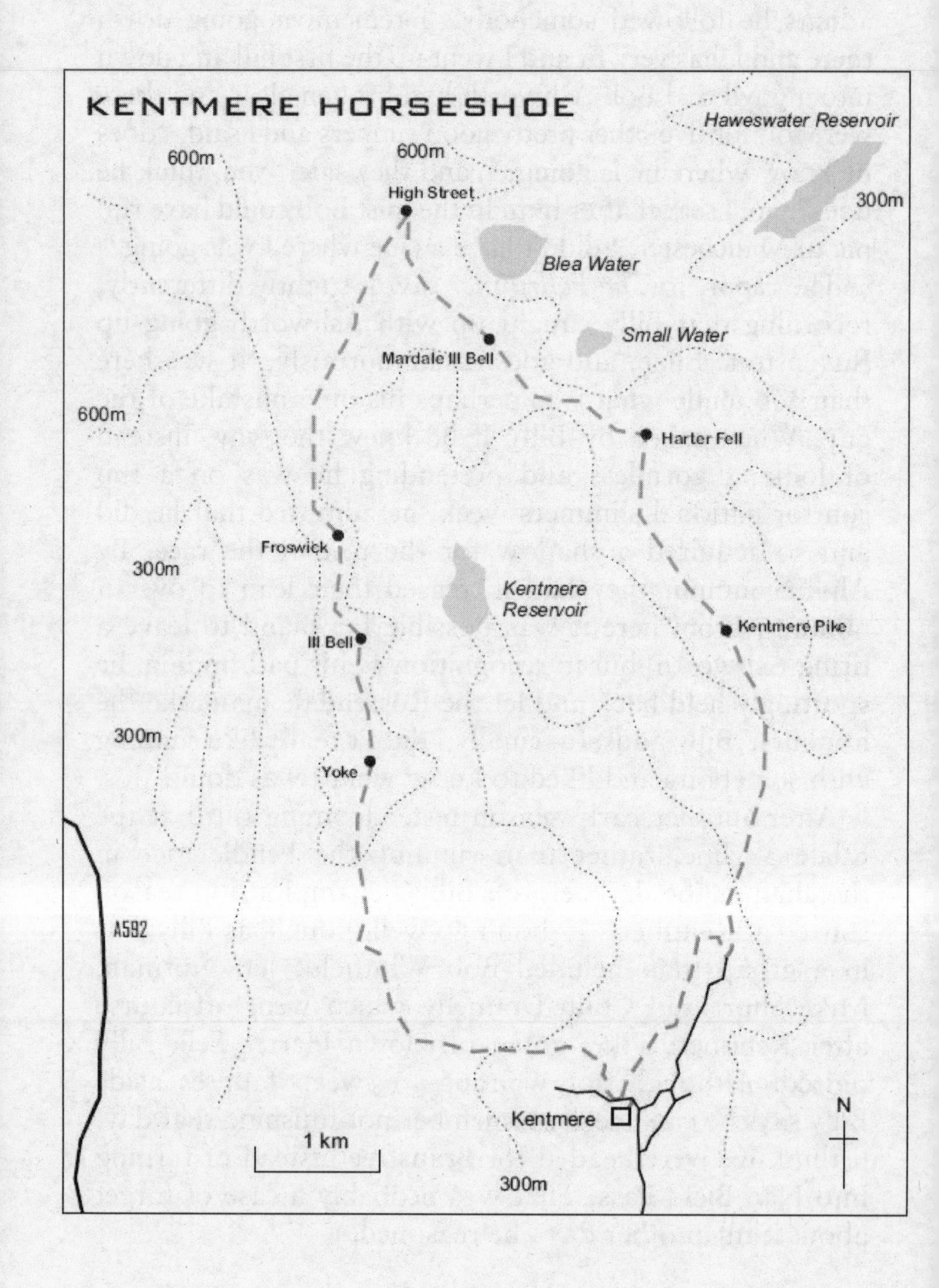
KENTMERE HORSESHOE
Haweswater Reservoir
600m
600m
High Street
300m
Blea Water
Small Water
Mardale Ill Bell
600m
Harter Fell
Froswick
300m
Kentmere
Reservoir
Ill Bell
Kentmere Pike
300m
Yoke
A592
N
Kentmere
1 km
300m

John Wild won that day, setting a new course record, even though the weather was so bad. He adds, 'I had recced the course, as I often did, and I wasn't a bad map reader. That is how I went the right way when the others didn't. I did go wrong incidentally. It was after the turning when you start to come back on yourself. I think a lot of people were surprised at that victory. You were in clouds soon after the start. I was in the lead after the first mile. I found it easy. I probably didn't know how to run fell races easy', John concludes with a wide smile on his face.

In May Billy again chose to miss a championships race at Ben Lomond (a 'Medium') and ran the 20-mile Duddon race the same day instead. He won in style with a new course record and a ten-minute gap over Andy Styan. After he had also won the NCAA race, and missed the 'Medium' champs race at Fairfield and the 'Long' Welsh 1000m Peaks Race, he came to the second 'Long' champs race at Ennerdale. Conditions were bad, with gale force winds, rain and mist. Billy left his rivals mid-race and came in with a three-minute advantage. Unfortunately, experienced fell runner Bob English strayed off course whilst on his way to the last checkpoint, took a fall and was later found unconscious from serious head wounds, and died on the way to hospital. Billy recalls the tragedy. 'Me and Stuart would go to Carlisle races sometimes. It happened at the Ennerdale race when Bob English died. I won the race, and we were wanting to bomb off to the horse races. We had stopped for the prize-giving, but didn't find out about Bob till after.'

Billy Bland came up against the old and the new at the next champs fixture, the 'Short' Butter Crag race. Coming fourth, he beat Harry Jarrett and Bob Whitfield, but was pipped by long-time rival Mike Short. Bland also lost out to young Shaun Livesey, and also saw that year's fell running sensation John Wild win with relative ease. Wild says he was trying to hang on to Mike Short at the top and doesn't think he did. But Wild passed him on the way down though, adding that he doesn't think Billy Bland had the speed for that race.

Interestingly, *Fellrunner* Editor Andy Styan had asked ten prominent fell runners who would win the champs that year and five had said Bland and three Wild. John Wild was charging towards the title, having won five out of the seven champs races at the time the predictions were revealed.

Hitting top form, Billy Bland then won the next seven races he entered, having been dealing with a nagging injury earlier in the season. He thinks that it was probably one of his shin splints episodes. He had to have a cortisone injection for it once. The non-champs Eildon Two Hills and Kinniside victories were split by another 'Long' champs win at Wasdale, by over 17 minutes. Then came two double race weekends, coming out on top each time. At the Melantee champs race Bland led all the way, and at the Half Nevis he clawed back a 100-metre deficit at the turn point, to beat Mike Short.

Then it was back to Borrowdale for Billy's third 'Long' champs win. He was never headed, after establishing a five-minute lead by Esk Hause. He came home in 2:34:38, a new course record, and nine minutes clear of Bob Whitfield, with John Wild coming in fifth. Billy took just 15 minutes to descend from Dale Head summit via the Tarn to the finish at Rosthwaite. Afterwards he was asked if he could go any faster on the Borrowdale course, and he reckoned not. 'Everything was perfect: ideal weather and conditions, including pressure from fellow competitors.

Someone else may go faster.' Billy didn't run any faster, and nor has anyone else. His outstanding record still stands from that 1981 race (not 1982 as per the FRA website). At Latrigg the next day Billy also set a record, this time because new forestry fences had necessitated a minor course change. He looked imperious, taking just 17:46 for this three miles up and back course.

A third in a non-champs Sedbergh Hills race was followed by a fourth for Billy Bland at Burnsall in a championships 'Short' race. John Wild won, on what he calls his kind of course, short and sharp. Wild enjoyed winning there three times altogether, whilst Bland would have been going there for championship points.

All the top runners then headed off for Ben Nevis two weeks later, which was a 'Medium' counting race. Bob Whitfield reached the summit in fifth place and takes up the story of the race. 'I caught Mike [Short] at the Red Burn to go second and I got a glimpse of Billy [Bland] coming out of the steps. I saw him again at the aluminium bridges and I knew I could have a go. I passed him halfway along the road, and, as I passed, he held out his hand to shake mine and said, "It's yours". It was a marvellous feeling going round the ring, but if only they'd tell you when you are so near the record.' In 1978 Billy Bland had crossed the line here only to find that he had missed the record by one second, and Bob had just had the same experience, finishing two seconds outside Dave Cannon's 1976 time. John Wild showed a little naivety that day, admitting that he had run up the Ben the day before. 'It was a bit daft really. I didn't race it but ran with my dog, who was called Ben.' Wild came ninth.

Langdale was not in the champs and was suffering from poor organisation at the time, with Andy Styan listing the problems in *Fellrunner* and calling for the organiser to give it up or hand it over to someone else (which he did eventually). The official results were not available, but unofficially Billy Bland got his revenge for the Ben, as he held off Bob Whitfield by just one second.

Billy Bland finished his championship season with two more counters, a fourth in the 'Long' Moffat Chase and a win at the Blisco Dash, again beating Bob Whitfield, this time by seven seconds. At the end of the season it was a comprehensive win for John Wild, with Billy Bland coming second, mostly because he retired at Kentmere and thus was one 'Medium' race short of a full set of counters. He had run 23 races in the year and won 12 of them. Could he have challenged John Wild's dominance if he had run that extra 'Medium'? Well, of the six times they met at champs races that year John won four and Billy two (Borrowdale and the Ben), so probably not, though it would have been closer than the 37-point gap that there was at the season's end.

At the end of October Billy Bland had entered the two-day Karrimor Mountain Marathon for the first time. He was partnered in the Elite category with his brother Stuart, which was based on the Scafell and Langdale Fells. The Blands led overnight, with heavy rain showers turning to sleet and then snow above 1000 feet. First away on Day Two, into a snowstorm at Greendale Tarn, the Blands retired during that second day. The event was won by Joss Naylor and Mike Walford after over 12 hours of tough running, with Pete Barron and Jon Broxap fourth. Pete Barron remembers it well. 'We were camping in Wasdale, below Middle Fell. It was the end of October and Billy and Stuart were camping next to us after Day One. They bailed it as the weather was awful. They were brilliant runners, but the mountain marathons are a bit more than that. I think Jon [Broxap] and I were good at that feeding and overnighting stuff.'

Jon Broxap's take was that Billy and Stuart just got fed up with the discomfort. 'Billy was never a camper, and I don't think Stuart was either. Two six-foot blokes in a tiny tent when it is snowy was not good. The camp site was up by Greendale Tarn, above Wasdale and it snowed overnight. I remember waking up to Pete saying, "what is this on the ground?" They probably had an awful night because Billy was used to his comforts. I don't even think he did much of the cooking at home. I think they had a rough night and thought they weren't going to win it and the temptation to jack it in there was just too much.'

Howard Pattinson also thought 'home comforts' might be a factor, thinking Billy didn't much liked the idea of sleeping in a tent. 'He would have had no trouble finding his way at the event, although Billy is probably not the best orienteer, to be fair. He would recce an area and hope he could get away with it. A lot of us are like that who know the Lakes well and do not come from an orienteering background. We rarely get out a map and compass. We mistakenly think we don't need to. As regards picking good lines on the BG or any fell race, a map in itself is not a lot of use. The line from Rossett Pike to Bowfell, commonly referred to as the 'Billy Bland rake' is not a route you find by studying a map, you have to work it out on the ground. Finding Broad Stand when coming from Scafell to the Pike is not easy, it's a route you need to be shown. I don't know, but I doubt if Billy has done many orienteering events in unfamiliar areas.'

Jon Broxap went on to explain one of the secrets of getting two-day mountain marathons right – food. 'Pete

Barron and I never really had a bad second day on a mountain marathon. Billy and Stuart also probably didn't get the food right that time. Don't get me wrong as I have had some bad nights in tents.'

As you might expect Billy Bland was very keen to tell the story of this event from his and Stuart's perspective, so here goes.

Billy and Stuart had won the Saunders Mountain Marathon earlier that year, over the weekend of 4–5 July, based at Rosthwaite. Stuart then suggested they do the Karrimor Mountain Marathon. Billy notes that they had won the Saunders by over an hour, on a shortened course as it had been run in an absolutely fierce rainstorm on the second day. Stuart had been responsible for all the kit, all of which you had to carry for two days, including sleeping bags, a tent and food. The Karrimor event was based at Stool End Farm, in Langdale. Billy takes up the story of their dropout.

I think we had a nine-minute lead on the first day. So, there are two of us in a one-man tent. Joss Naylor and Mike Walford were our next-door neighbours and I could hear them snoring, and there were hailstones hitting the tent. I knew before I went that I would have trouble sleeping in a tent. We never slept and there was snow in the campsite in the morning. Stuart says, "are you wet". I says "aye I am". Stuart was in a puddle of water. I said "bugger this, I am garn yam. It is stupid this, I am off". "You are bloody not", he says. I was all for getting up and walking home, down into the valley and over Sty Head to our house. But we stuck it out, with me having trouble with my foot sticking out of one shoe, which was buggered basically. You went away with the lead you had from day before. We went across to the

Ennerdale valley and then up Scarth Gap. Then on to the mines above Seathwaite, the old lead mines. As we were coming through by Blackbeck Tarn on the way to the mines Naylor and Walford caught us up. Stuart was suffering by then. We'd argued, and I was there under protest and didn't want to be there. He went to punch in at the checkpoint and he was talking all slurred. The next checkpoint we had to go to was near the bottom of Stake Pass. We got to Mountain View and I said, "I don't know where you are going but I am garn yam". Stuart didn't argue. So, we both went home.

Billy reckons that if you can't sleep and you know you can't sleep, and you have got wet clothes it is a hopeless situation. The Saunders was in summer and he was able to get out of the tent and have a walk about in the middle of the night. In the Saunders they had a decent lead on the first day and on the second day they were crossing the Newlands Valley and the organisers said, 'that is it, make your way back to Borrowdale'. It had been shortened due to the atrocious weather on the second day.

Billy did another Saunders Mountain Marathon with Bob Whitfield after that, from Braithwaite on 7–8 July 1984, but again with a distinct lack of success. On this one they got the figures transposed for one checkpoint. So, when they realised this at the end of the first day they retired and went home. Bob was really disappointed. Billy adds, 'I was injured at the time and was limping beforehand. It was the strangest thing. I walked into the Braithwaite Institute to register, limping, and we set off and I never felt a bloody thing. We went out a bit and stopped on a milk churn stand to mark the map up. We never did establish who made the mistake over the co-ordinates. There was a checkpoint in the wrong fold we went to, but it was on a different course. We probably would have been leading if we had gone to the correct control.'

Moving on, Billy Bland went into the 1982 season at the peak of his fitness and fully intending to challenge for the Fell Championship title, planning his full complement of races as the season got underway. John Wild was favourite to repeat his victory from 1981, although a new challenger was to burst on the scene like a supernova later in the year. Eschewing his normal tester of Chew Valley or Edale as a starting race this year, Billy ran the inaugural 15-mile Black Combe race instead, coming tenth on a day of sunshine and snow on the tops.

The first championships race was Kentmere, which hadn't gone well the year before for Billy, and was won again in fine weather by John Wild, beating his own course record from the year before. Billy came eleventh, in a race that he freely admits not to liking as it is not rough enough underfoot. Billy returned to winning ways at the beginning of May, convincingly taking a victory in the first Coniston race.

A week later Billy came up against Kenny Stuart for the first time in a race, at Duddon. And what a competitor Kenny Stuart turned out to be. After 21 miles (and 6500 feet of climbing) Billy and Kenny came into the finish field together and had a sprint out for the win, finishing with less than a second between them, with Kenny just taking it. Confusingly, Kenny Stuart was still a professional (later in the year he applied for reinstatement as an amateur) and some high profile amateur athletes, like Joss Naylor and Billy Bland, faced a potential AAA ban for competing in this amateur race with Kenny Stuart, but it seemed to pass without notice. Ken Ledward organised that race and encouraged all runners to enter. It wasn't run under AAA rules as far as Kenny Stuart can remember.

Kenny Stuart had sat on Billy's shoulder that day, and Billy once said about that, 'good on him'. Yet in another race Billy waited for Bob Whitfield to take the win as he had followed him. I asked Billy if that is what we should do, is that good race etiquette, and what Kenny should have done? He replied, 'well, it would have been nice if he had done it, but I wouldn't have thanked him because if I wasn't good enough to win I wasn't good enough. I wasn't bothered. I was brought up on defeat. Kenny just wasn't a particularly good navigator, and he didn't spend the same amount of time out on the fells as I did, getting to know the terrain.' Hearing of this comment from Billy Bland, Kenny Stuart replied calmly, 'if I had won as many races and done what I eventually did and that happened I would probably have said why don't we run in together. But at that time I was hungry and I was lean and mean. In those days people didn't really worry about sitting on people. When the Lancashire lads came to the Lakes, they might never have recced the race, and Billy knew it like the back of his hand, and Joss did as well. Loads of people just followed the person in front.'

The champs moved on with races at Fairfield, won by John Wild with Billy fourth, and Ennerdale, where Billy won from Bob Whitfield (and John Wild didn't run). In between, Billy won the Northern Counties race again.

After another little diversion, which we will come to later, Billy dominated the next champs race at Wasdale. He comfortably set a new course record of 3:25:21, beating Bob Whitfield by almost 20 minutes. John Wild struggled in twentieth place, saying he had just run out of juice. At the time Danny Hughes reckoned, 'even this record will not last long'. A measure of this performance is that it is a record also has not been beaten, some 36 years on.

Billy then took a third place at Kinniside. Joe Ritson finished fifth that day, and recently recalled the event. 'Both BBC and ITV Border had cameras there, probably expecting him to win, but this year he was beaten by Harry Jarrett and Jon Broxap. There were TV cameras at the start and finish and where the race crossed the Cold Fell road. But it was another day of low cloud and rain with poor visibility. I don't know if any archive footage of the race still exists, but I can remember them interviewing Billy and Harry Jarrett.'

Billy then attempted a familiar double-double weekend. There was a surprise in the first of the four races, in that Roger Boswell managed to beat Billy at Melantee, which was short and has a flat runout which never suited Billy. Normal service resumed at the Half Nevis the next day, with an easy win for Billy. A week later and it was the Borrowdale-Latrigg combo. At Borrowdale low cloud hampered navigation for some. The conditions presented Billy with no problems, and he led from John Wild at Esk Hause, five minutes up on the rest of the field. Wild made a brave effort to stay with Billy, but got dropped beyond Great Gable, lost his bearings and did not finish. Billy had extended his lead to 18 minutes at the finish.

Billy Bland expands on the situation. 'The year before I beat John [Wild] in the Borrowdale when he had to finish fifth or something to win the championship. He came along and he finished fifth. I was interviewed after I had won it and I said I was disappointed in John, as he hadn't come for a race, just to get a position. He heard about that and I think the next year he did come to nail me

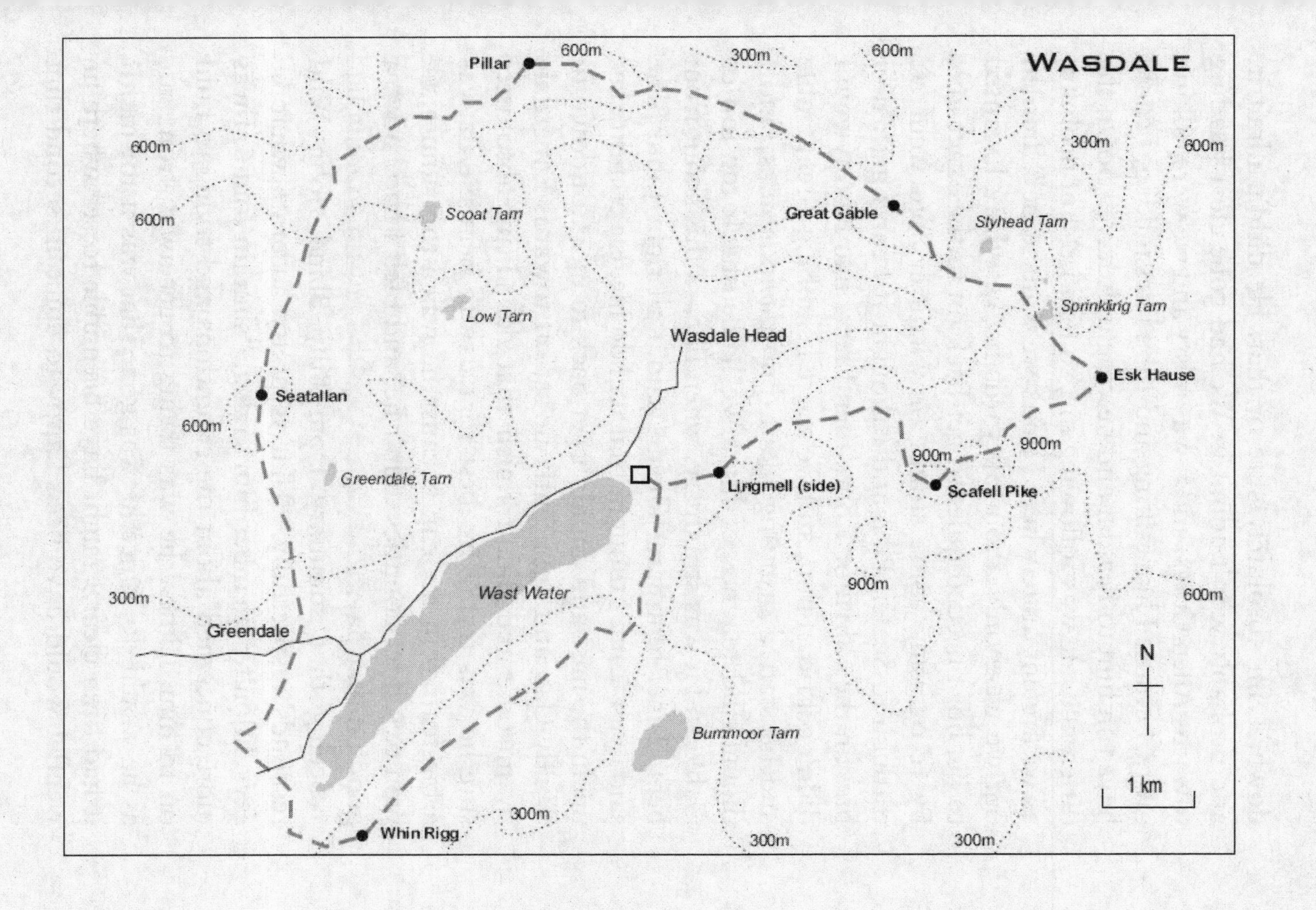
WASDALE
Pillar
Scoat Tarn
Low Tarn
Great Gable
Styhead Tarn
Sprinkling Tarn
Esk Hause
Wasdale Head
Seatallan
Lingmell (side)
Scafell Pike
Greendale Tarn
Wast Water
Greendale
Burnmoor Tarn
Whin Rigg
N
1 km
300m
600m
900m

down, I am absolutely sure of that. He didn't admit it, and probably won't admit it. We had gone clear heading towards Allen Crags, and it was misty and we were talking away, because I like talking and John likes talking. I could have run him to Kendal and he wouldn't have known the difference. He was following me, so I said, "shut up John, as we are not quite where I think we want to be". Turned out we were only about 30 yards below where I wanted to be, but I needed quiet to get back on to the exact line, by recognising some stones or whatever. We went on through to Scafell Pike and I thought if I can't get rid of him on the Corridor Route then I have had it. Anyway, I didn't get rid of him, and we started climbing Great Gable and he started grunting like a pig [*demonstrates*] and I thought I'd maybe got him. We had just left the top of Gable and it was still misty, when I heard this shout from behind me. John had fallen. I said, "all right John?", he said "yeh", and I thought that will do me. He couldn't see me in the mist and couldn't get back to me. Got down to Windy Gap and apparently he set off towards Ennerdale by mistake and didn't finish that day. I am absolutely sure he was trying his best that day to beat me. It was a big feather in my cap because he was a top runner, he won two inter-counties didn't he, and I felt I had nailed a good'un that day.'

Seeing that summary from Billy Bland, John Wild responds respectfully. 'That is pretty accurate what he says. I don't remember him saying, "shut up John". I was more concerned about the conditions and trying to hold on to him. I knew he was trying to get away from me, as he would do. Once he was gone that was it for me. If it had been clear I might have been able to see where he went! I would have been happy to come in second that day. It is no good having a map and compass if you don't know where you are. [*laughs*] It was his back garden, and you take every advantage that you have got. I have got no problems with that at all.'

John Wild was one of the few people who tried to take the race to Billy Bland at his peak. Although he admits that he was trying his best to beat Billy Bland that day, he adds a caveat. 'I have no qualms about it. I was hanging on to him. I hadn't a clue where I was that day. It was very bad conditions. I will say that hand on heart if I had been with him at the end that day I wouldn't have outsprinted him. I couldn't have lived with myself if I had done that. It wouldn't be worth the victory to me.'

The next day Billy won Latrigg from Malcolm Patterson, giving him three wins out of four races in the nine-day period. Joe Ritson reckons that this was his own best performance, because he almost won that day. 'It was Billy Bland that beat me, he was just too good. I ended up third behind Malcolm Patterson. They both passed me on the way down. They would have run Borrowdale the day before, mind.'

But now Kenny Stuart was to prove himself to be a new and very real rival for John Wild and Billy Bland, as was proved by the results through the rest of the season. On 22 August at Burnsall Kenny Stuart ran for the first time as an amateur, after his reinstatement from the pros had been approved by the authorities. Stuart had won the pro fell race at Burnsall in both 1980 and 1981. In overcast conditions John Wild took the race by the scruff of the neck and led Kenny Stuart by 80 metres at the summit and extended that on the descent to win by 33 seconds, with Billy Bland coming in fifth. John Wild's chance of winning the champs were not helped by him announcing that he was having an operation on his ankle in the following week. Wild's chance of winning the race were also threatened by an unusual event that shows something of his toughness and determination to beat his rivals, as he recently revealed. 'I lost my shoe leapfrogging the wall at the bottom and had to run in without it. I went back and dug it out of the mud afterwards.'

Two weeks later Billy Bland felt the full force of Kenny Stuart's commitment to racing. At the Ben Nevis race Kenny was leading at the summit, but Billy caught him on the descent, but lost out on the run-in. This was different to the earlier Duddon race they had, in that there is no real navigation involved and Kenny took the initiative to show his brilliant climbing skills, whilst Billy had the better descending technique. The outcome was the same though, this time Kenny winning by some 80 seconds in his first Ben Nevis race, something not many other runners have achieved.

Kenny may not have run the race before, but he had been up to Red Burn the day before, not having time to go any higher than that. Talking of the race recently, he recalls events as they unfolded. 'I did run it tactically in a roundabout sort of way. That day I knew Billy was going to come and catch me [*on the downhill*], it was inevitable. I played with him a bit, and I tried to get him to do a lot more than he was wanting to do. He was up for it as he was nearer me than he thought he might be. On the way down he caught me, and I stayed with him until the Red Burn and on the grass bank he belly-flopped. I thought he would get up from that as he had plenty left but I went right past and he didn't come back. Whether he was winded, or he realised that he had spent his lot, I have no idea.'

Then it was on to one of Billy's favourite events, the Mountain Trial, which this year was held in storm force winds and horizontal rain from Steel End, Thirlmere. Billy Bland was strangely out of sorts early on and was only forty-eighth on Glaramara, but then recovered his drive to take the lead by Easedale Tarn. The race report explains what happened, 'Billy's preference for working out check-point positions on the move nearly spelt disaster for him – on the fell he probably knows as well as anyone. He had wrongly identified the Glaramara control and, after spending ages searching for it, set off home, but on the descent saw a string of runners heading for it. The day had been saved!' In the end he came home for his third victory. Billy thinks that it was a case of repeating a transcription error of numbers for co-ordinates, a mistake he had made previously. 'I had got it into my head where I was going but there was nothing there. I worked the co-ordinates out as I went along. I ended up swearing a lot. So, I set off coming from the Red Beck area on the backside of Glaramara, whereas I should have been this side of Glaramara. I was on my way home and met runners so followed their line, checked in there and I decided to carry on, and did all right in the end.'

Billy then ran in the last three 'Short' champs races, which were all won by Kenny Stuart. At Thieveley Pike Billy slipped to twelth place, with John Wild sixth as he came back from his ankle operation. John Wild adds that he ran with the OK from his medical team. 'I was not being foolhardy, but I was chasing championship points', he says. At Butter Crag Billy just held off John Wild, with their fourth and fifth paces.

Billy could only watch the front of the race unfold and his course record be taken at the Blisco Dash. Bill Smith records that, 'John Wild led from Kenny Stuart at Blisco summit, both making their debut in this race, but they then strayed too far right (due east) coming away. When they presently realised and set about correcting their error, Stuart put one over Wild by jumping off a low crag. Meanwhile, Bob Whitfield, who did know the correct line off the summit, had plunged into the lead with a flying descent, only to be caught on the Blea Tarn road switchbacks by both Stuart and Wild. Kenny stormed home to a new record of 36:54.' John Wild recalls that he tried to be clever and instead of turning round and going back the same way as he came up, he tried to do a detour, and got a bit lost. 'It cost me the victory. I had done a recce two weeks before on a clear day and thought I could skirt round rather than bump into people coming up still. Kenny followed me, but only for a bit, and then doubled back to chase down Bob Whitfield, who had got into the lead.' Wild also adds, not really as an excuse, more stating the facts, that he had also twisted his ankle on the recce and couldn't train in between times.

In a loaded field Billy had finished sixth behind both Malcolm Patterson and Jon Broxap. Broxap recalls that the times were very good that day. 'The first eight that day were faster than it was won in 2018. It was not a high-profile race, but it got some amazing fields in those days.'

That second place sealed John Wild's winning the championships, by five points from Bob Whitfield. Wild had won seven out of his ten counting races. Billy Bland came third, another six points down, having won the three 'Long' races that he entered. In another long season Billy had run 22 races, winning 8 of them.

For two years Billy Bland had been beaten in the title race by John Wild. However, right in the middle that highly competitive 1982 season Billy decided to do the Bob Graham Round. He wanted to see what sort of time he could put up for that iconic challenge.

TOUGHER THAN THE REST

The Bob Graham Round is a 24-hour challenge in the Lake District that takes in 42 peaks, covers around 62 miles, and 27,000 feet of ascent. It was first completed by, and named after, the Keswick B&B owner Bob Graham in 1932, taking 23 hours 29 minutes. There it stood, until Alan Heaton repeated it in 1960, coming home in 22:18. By 1976 the fastest time had been reduced another four times and stood at 19:48 to John North.

In 1976 Billy Bland had put down a new fastest time of 18:50 [*discussed in more detail later*] and in 1977 Mike Nicholson reduced it again to 17:45.

Billy distinctly remembers that after he had done the 18:50 that he went home and went to bed without having a bath. He said never again, 'you won't bloody catch me going around there again'. But it wasn't long before Billy felt that his 18:50 round was not a true reflection of what he was capable of. He commented that his first effort:

'Kinda sowed the seeds for one day having another go. You heard people say that Mike Nicholson beat Billy Bland's record. Well yes he did, but it wasn't a record I was at all proud of, because I knew I was capable of better anyway. I was taking part in races and I was getting better. That was the best part of my running career if you like, the good part as you are getting better.'

In 1982 Bland was ready to really see what he could do about running a really fast time.

At the time I am not sure many people understood Billy's approach to doing it then, although he has explained it in detail more recently. When I was researching my book *The Round* he explained it to me, and that may have been the first time that bit of the story had been told by him.

His brother Stuart had started running, and he had recently come in third in the Borrowdale race. Billy expanded. 'Stuart thought he would do a Bob Graham, and he was going to have a go at doing it real serious, not just to go round in 24 hours. I began thinking that if my brother went and set a Bob Graham record then I wouldn't have wanted to take it off him. He was going in August, so I needed to be getting mine in. That is how I then went between winning at Ennerdale and Wasdale [*a four-week gap*]. What coach would have said that was a good idea? I just went out and I did it with some pacers.'

Billy didn't set out to do any time in particular, just to do it his way, which was to see how he felt on the day. He didn't do any recces on any legs, because he knew all the terrain well. He also didn't change his training. Even though it was to take place in between the Ennerdale and Wasdale races, which he says meant more to him than the Bob Graham Round, he kept up the training levels. 'I said to myself I will go and do the round, and of the three it would be third on my priorities. People have talked about it being the best thing I ever did. I pull folk up every time, and say it is not. The Bob Graham I did was just what I wanted to do on that day.'

The setup was quite simple then, and it was coordinated by Billy himself.

Kenny Stuart was the only pacer on the first section, from Keswick to Threlkeld, which is his backyard really, living as he did in Threlkeld. An interesting choice really, as Kenny never did a Bob Graham himself and didn't (as far as I am aware) support any other rounds. He was an absolutely top fell runner of course, who was just making his mark as a newly re-instated amateur that year. He also had the advantage of living in the shadow of Blencathra and trained on the fells that comprise that first leg, if going clockwise.

Although his memory of the occasion is somewhat blurred, Kenny Stuart recalls how fast it was run and the difference in circumstances surrounding it from say Kilian Jornet's attempt in 2018, which he witnessed. 'I used it as a long run as part of my training for that week. I was already bloody tired when we set out. I got to the end of my leg and Billy went on and I thought, "blooming heck, he is going at helluva pace, because I am knackered". Billy

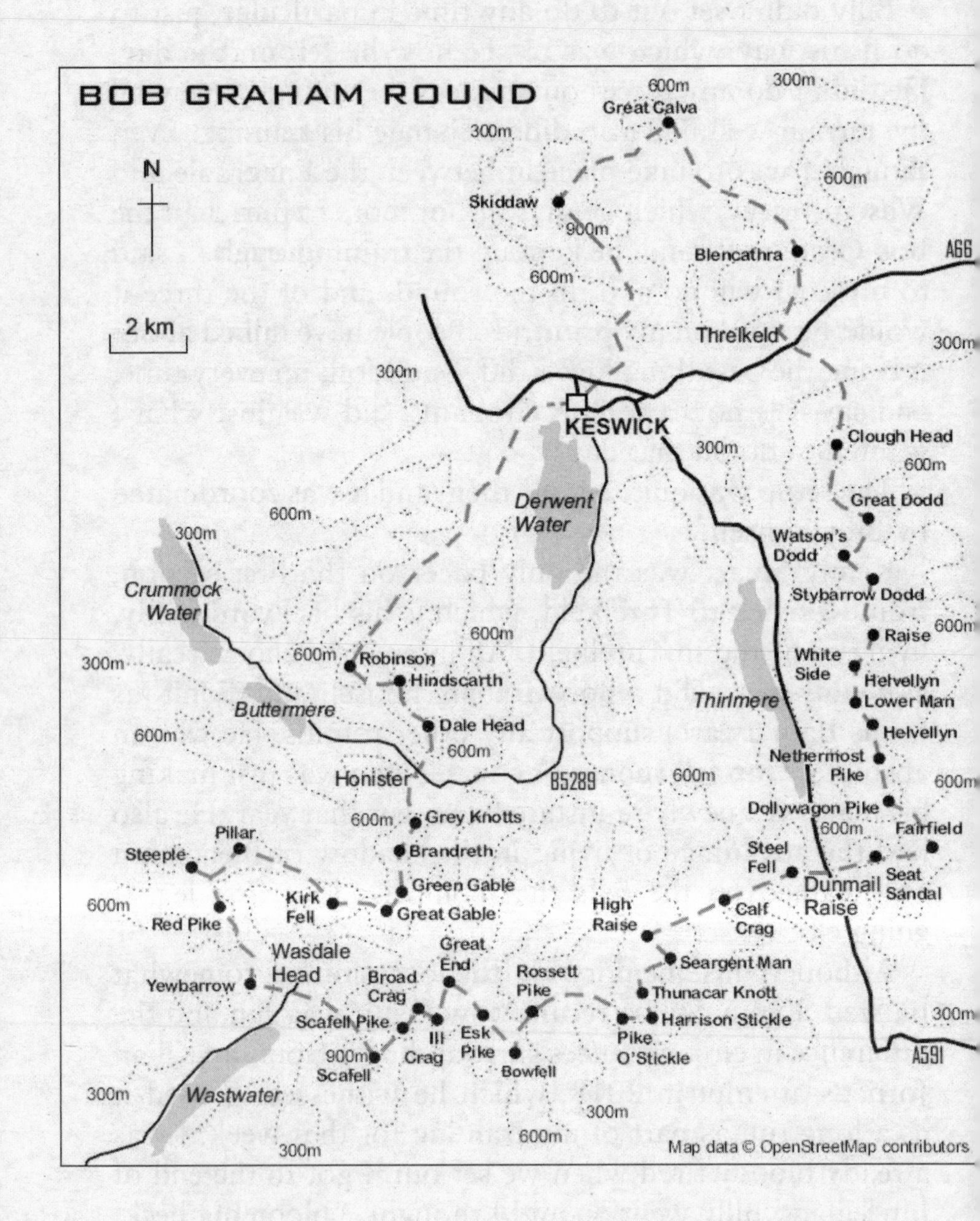
BOB GRAHAM ROUND
N
2 km
Great Calva
Skiddaw
Blencathra
Threlkeld
A66
KESWICK
Derwent Water
Clough Head
Great Dodd
Watson's Dodd
Stybarrow Dodd
Raise
White Side
Helvellyn Lower Man
Helvellyn
Nethermost Pike
Dollywagon Pike
Fairfield
Seat Sandal
Steel Fell
Dunmail Raise
Thirlmere
Calf Crag
High Raise
Seargent Man
Thunacar Knott
Harrison Stickle
Pike O'Stickle
Rossett Pike
Bowfell
Esk Pike
Great End
Ill Crag
Broad Crag
Scafell Pike
Scafell
Wastwater
Yewbarrow
Wasdale Head
Red Pike
Steeple
Pillar
Kirk Fell
Great Gable
Green Gable
Brandreth
Grey Knotts
Honister
B5289
Dale Head
Hindscarth
Robinson
Buttermere
Crummock Water
A591
300m
600m
900m
Map data © OpenStreetMap contributors

was the one pushing the pace, and I never felt comfortable even at that pace. We came down Halls Fell Ridge which I was reasonably familiar with. He took off from there and he finished the leg without me. I was tailing on behind by then. He knew where he was at.' There is a classic photo taken by someone near the end of the leg. It shows Billy just beginning to pull away from Kenny on the lane towards Threlkeld. Sadly, it is not of good enough quality to reproduce here.

Reflecting on the event, Kenny Stuart summed up how he saw it. 'He did his BGR so fast because no-one in that era had the capacity and speed to do that before. He was a racing athlete who went and took it on with his great stamina base. He was a lot classier runner than those attempting to do it up till then. To be honest he had everything going for him. He had all the best pacers. I could tell he would go very well, OR he would blow up. There were no mobile phones in those days, so you couldn't keep in contact with people, and I thought no more about it that day. I didn't know until the next day that he had run that time.'

In an earlier conversation Billy Bland had explained the setup. 'We were out of Keswick from the Moot Hall at 5a.m. I have still got a card with the times on. Kenny was on that leg – the little bugger could run, so we went well.' It had taken them 53 minutes to the top of Skiddaw, 1 hour 20 minutes to Great Calva, 1 hour 59 minutes to Blencathra, and 2 hours 13 minutes to Threlkeld, where he had a 3-minute pause. Billy left Threlkeld at 7:16a.m.

Kenny Stuart was always intending to do the BGR himself one day. 'I was always going to do the BGR at a later date, when slightly older, but unfortunately things didn't materialise that way.' It is fascinating to imagine what he might have achieved if he had done a round.

Pete Barron was a pacer on leg two. Pete is now in his sixties and has lived in Borrowdale for 40 years, during which time he has got to know Billy Bland really well, so has an interesting take on him and his achievements. Barron was a National Park Ranger in the Lakes for 23 years, working out of the Blencathra Centre. He worked for the YHA for a while before that, variously at Wasdale (where he started running), Honister, Grasmere and Keswick. He also ran Barrow House Youth Hostel for 10 years. Martin Mikkelsen-Barron [his son] was born at Barrow House and is an excellent fell runner. I interviewed Pete at his smart guest house in Keswick. He had to pause the interview twice while he welcomed new arrivals, making them cream teas to help them settle in.

Pete Barron gave me his memories of how the record round had gone from his point of view. 'I think Billy just asked us all to pace him, but it was quite informal. What I do remember on that day was that it was very fast, obviously. But it was race pace for some people. There was certainly more than me set off from Threlkeld, I think Ian Charlton and another two people [*there are only Pete Barron and Ian Charlton listed on Billy Bland's BGR ratification form*]. How far the others got I can't recall, but when we got to Dunmail there was only me and Billy still together. We were also the only two that did Fairfield and Seat Sandal. I was under a bit of pressure that day as I was navigating along the Helvellyn range in really bad weather. Places like Watson Dodd are not easy to find in bad weather. It was thick mist and for me to have got that wrong would have been a terrible thing. Billy might have been a bit upset!' As an aside: when Kilian Jornet did his round in 2018 he was blessed with fabulous weather, which he acknowledged.

Hearing that Pete Barron comment about navigating, Billy says that Pete, 'never let on to me that he was nervous on leg two. I think Ian Charlton may have gone down from Sticks Pass, as he was quite capable of being with us. He got under 3 hours at the Borrowdale race, so he was a good 'un. I also remember sending him off in front after Watson Dodd and him starting the climb up Stybarrow, where the actual summit is not very distinct. I wonder if sometimes people just follow the path up and call that it, but it isn't. It is out on a limb to the left. I could always see him and I didn't want to be zig-zagging about looking for it. He found it nicely.'

Pete Barron was very confident that his pace setting was good, but he does remember Billy making a point, and swearing, saying, 'we are not going fast enough'. 'But we had dropped people. So, we were not going too badly. You have to remember no-one had tried to run a round at that pace before', recalls Barron.

Pete Barron sets the scene for the support too. 'It wasn't like nav, drinks, food and clothes by nominated pacers, it was more relaxed than that. I had a bag on because I remember giving him a drink from it. But I was definitely navigating though on that leg.'

Fairfield was reached by going straight down the eroded part of Dollywagon Pike. Pete adds a note of caution here. 'I have had this conversation with Billy, in that the Bob Graham isn't doing the landscape a great deal of good in some places, and one classic is Grisedale Tarn up to Fairfield, where a new runners track has appeared. There isn't an easy balance between wanting people to come into the fells, but on the other hand achieving recognition in the fell running world that the impact is there for all to see. It is recces rather than races that might be the cause of much of these problems, as so many people do them, and directly use the accepted BGR lines between summits.'

Coming down to Dunmail Raise on Billy's round the support team that was taking over for leg three was Stuart Bland and Jon Broxap. Broxap knew Billy from having done some training with him and had already done his own Bob Graham Round. 'I did a BGR with Pete Barron. We did it in 1978, and we are numbers 89 and 90 on the list or something like that.' Jon Broxap's time was 20:16.

Jon Broxap says that it is that long ago that he can't specifically remember how he came to be a pacer for Billy on the BG record round. 'Billy put it together and I was there and free. At the time I think I had moved to Patterdale YHA, and I had intended to do the second leg over Helvellyn, because it was easier from work for me. Mere mortals usually do that at night, but Billy didn't need to as he was going so fast. But I could do it with him between shifts. I think it was a case of who was free to do what, and it worked for me to do that third section. It wasn't a natural one that I would have chosen because going with Stuart and Billy running over all those rocks was a tough ask. Billy had an amazing ability to run hard over rocks and make it look like a piece of tarmac. His foot plant was brilliant, no movement and the terrain didn't faze him at all.'

Billy Bland may have surprised a few people by doing his fast round in the middle of a successful race sequence, but Jon Broxap doesn't think doing it then was a spur of the moment thing. 'I think he thought about it, but don't think he planned his season around it. He thought, "let's go for it full on". That year he was very fit, and he just went for it. It was very understated in a way. But there was that brotherly rivalry too.'

Equally Broxap wasn't surprised he was going that fast. 'You know with Billy it is going to be full gas. I think he had indicated that he was looking at 16 hours or something, but you should take that with a pinch of salt. You knew you weren't in for an easy day, put it like that.'

Pacers' roles on Bob Graham Rounds differ. Quite often they are feeding the runner, and sometimes 'guiding' them too. With Billy it was very much a case of supporting rather than the usual pacing, as Jon Broxap recalls. 'I remember trying to get him to eat, but he never really did that. He was always off for the next summit. Tony Cresswell was doing his act of trying to find us and feed him, and he wouldn't take anything from him, unfortunately. It was full on, almost race pace. I remember it was overcast but not thick cloud. There was light cloud on the tops. Mostly dry, so weather-wise quite good conditions. I remember the photo from Wasdale, and it was greyish and definitely not sunny. It certainly never affected the navigation.'

Broxap makes the point that Billy Bland understates how good a navigator he was, and that his local knowledge was second to none. 'He was brought up there, it is his backyard, and he had trained over that ground and knew every little trod. That was his strength. He knew everything intimately.'

On the round they went up over Broad Stand. Broxap explained the set-up there. 'I remember being thrown up it by Stuart. There was no rope in place. Billy is not quite 6 feet and Stuart was 6 feet and they could get up it fine. Billy reached up and with a bit of a shimmy up and push from Stuart he was over it. I got shoved up the same. Then Tony (Cresswell) and Stuart got pulled up or shoved up.

The rock was dry and it was OK. If it had been wet it would have been a different matter, mind you.'

I asked Jon Broxap if the taking of a can of Mackeson by Billy at Wasdale was a myth or not, at which point he responded with a chuckle. 'I have got a photo of that. Martin Stone had it and he captioned it something like, "a real fell runner with a proper sports drink". He had one at Wasdale and also another one at Honister as well.' Broxap couldn't get a lift back to Borrowdale as no-one had a car over at Wasdale. Stuart Bland and Jon Broxap ran from Wasdale to Thorneythwaite [*Stuart's farm in Borrowdale*] and then they got a lift up to Honister with Billy's uncle Billy. Then Stuart and Jon ran the last leg to Keswick.

Tony Cresswell appears as a fairly minor actor in Billy's fast round but had a presence well beyond that. After several abortive attempts to arrange a meeting, I eventually managed to catch him at his house in the Northern Lakes just before he moved up to Scotland. More than one person had warned me that he was a good talker, and they were not wrong. He told some great stories about how things were in that era.

The brilliant thing about fell running in them days was 'the friendliness', Cresswell says. 'There was no hierarchy. It didn't matter which club you were from, we all got along together. There was a great competitive edge, but we all advised each other. I feel extraordinarily lucky that I had my time when I did. A lot of the big races and records were in my time. I just happened to be there, rather than had anything to do with them particularly.'

On being involved in Billy Bland's record round Cresswell recalls that, 'Jon Broxap rang me and told me that Billy was having a go at the BGR record. He says, "can you come out?" I said, "of course". It was just low key. He was just going to see what he could do. I was at Ambleside at the time, so I drove up Langdale and parked at the Old Dungeon Ghyll pub. I ran up from there, picking them up at the head of Langdale and went from there. Billy had literally told his brother, he told Broxap, Joss and maybe a few others. Billy knew it was a soft record, but he never predicted what he might do.'

Tony Cresswell was on the Broad Stand section and gives his take on it. 'That was a riot, but there was no danger going over it freestyle. These fell runners are all spindly things. I think Stuart got pushed up first and then pulled Billy up. Then he pulled Broxap up and I was last. Stuart got hold of my hand and said, "hell you are heavier than Brox". It can be a pretty hairy spot, but we were fine.'

Tony Cresswell described his attempts to feed Billy. 'I had a Joe Brown rucksack on my back with flasks of tea and chocolate oatcake, and sarnies, fruitcake and everything. It was bouncing around on my back. I said to him, "are you going to have any of this shit!" In his own quiet way he says, "no I don't wanna eat nowt". The perceived wisdom is that you have to get something on board before it clouts you. But some people can't manage to get food on board on the go.'

Cresswell wasn't able to support any more as he had to get back to work in Ambleside, which meant getting back to his car at Langdale. He went back over Sty Head, via Sprinkling Tarn and back to Rossett Pass and down from there. 'It was a helluva day out for me', he concludes.

Taking over as support from Wasdale Head were Joss Naylor and Martin Stone. Once again Billy Bland had the very best support possible. Joss Naylor lived in the

Wasdale valley and knew this terrain intimately, whilst Martin Stone was an excellent navigator, who five years later did a solo and unsupported Bob Graham Round. By Wasdale the support team were wondering if Billy had gone too fast and could possibly hang on without having a massive bad patch. I asked Martin Stone if there was any talk in the team about what time to expect Billy to do. All Martin could recall is that they were expecting it to be within a couple of hours of the time that Billy finally achieved.

This same question was put to Billy at one of his talks recently. As question-master I suggested that there was a feeling that he said he had set out to do 16 hours. 'Well, no', he replied, then added something that becomes relevant later on that day. 'I knew I was gonna break it. I had done my 18 hours 50 minutes round without trying, basically. I had become a lot better runner after that, so I did know I would break it. But I had no idea what time I was gonna do. All I wanted to do, which was a great way to do it, was just run as I felt. I wanted to do what I wanted to do, and not get dictated to by anybody. I wanted to be the boss on the day, and I didn't really need anybody to show the way, cos I knew the way.'

Martin Stone adds that he felt privileged to be part of the occasion. 'It is also quite possibly one of the very few Bob Graham Rounds where no vehicle has gone around to Wasdale. Billy insisted that was far too over the top, so Bob Whitfield and I had to walk over from Borrowdale with the Mackeson and some of his wife's fruit cake in our sacks. That was how it was.'

Martin added some of this detail at one of Billy's talks, where he was in the audience, and on that occasion Billy took the story up. 'Yep, Joss was there too and you

[Martin] went to Sail Pass. I got to the top of Yewbarrow and Joss says, "I'll just give your legs a shake out". This has become known as the Naylor Shake, which you may have heard about. It is supposed to shake the lactic acid out. There was nowt wrong with my legs, but he wanted to do it anyway!' You need to imagine Billy Bland lying on his back with his legs in the air for Joss to give them a good shakeout.

Billy takes the story forward. 'Martin was there on Kirk Fell and I heard him or Joss say, "he is gonna get under 14 hours". I don't know whether I was supposed to hear, but I did, and subconsciously we must have just picked up the pace a little. Then coming off Grey Knotts I just ran out of petrol and had to sit down. I was looking at Honister a few hundred yards away and I needed to be down there, but I had gone all dizzy. Changing the pace is definitely something you shouldn't do, because you will bring on a bad patch. We then spent 13 minutes at Honister sorting me out. I refuelled and off we went again.'

Those supporters that were stood down at Honister could see Billy sat down and were thinking, 'what you playing at, get up'. Billy didn't plan to stop but going back to his earlier comment about 'not being dictated to by anybody', he felt afterwards that someone else had set that faster pace against his natural inclination, and that it had backfired quite dramatically.

His refuelling at Honister rescued the day, and on a lighter note Billy recalls that he, 'also met various people on the route, Pete Parkins at Ore Gap, and I remember having sandwiches and coffee with him. Not for a long time, just a minute or so. That was the manner that it was done in. Not like now when people think they can't stop, I don't go for that at all.'

Chris Bland was nominated road access support for the round and he ran in on leg five with the team. Pete Barron came back in to support on this last leg from Honister back to Keswick, along with Chris, David, Stuart Bland, and Martin Stone. Barron adds, 'Billy seemed to be going well, although obviously quite tired by then. We were not slow going down that road. I have been so fortunate to mix it with people like Billy (on that event) and Jon Broxap on the Broxap Round.'

That last leg did go really well, and according to Tony Cresswell, he, 'speeded up if anything and from Newlands into Keswick it was a job for any, including the fresh, to live with him. So, at 6:54p.m. just 13:54 [*officially 13:53*] after setting out, Billy shaved a clear 3 hours 51 minutes off the record.'

Jon Broxap ran in on leg five with the others and recalls that, 'along the road he was on fire. Billy was not a big drinker and I can't remember us going to the pub after his round. We were just stunned with his time really.' Tony Cresswell adds that it was typical Billy, with no fuss afterwards, before giving his analysis of Billy and his pacers.

'Pete Barron and all those guys were the best runners you will ever come across, but they are very quiet conservative guys, like Billy. That was the best thing about them, being under-spoken if you will. My perception is that Billy knew he was good, but he didn't want to put over that kind of persona. That is what a lot of us really liked about the guy. He had tunnel vision on his objectives.'

The Westmorland Gazette of 25 June 1982 carried an article entitled '*Fell record annihilated*', which included an estimate of the speed he had been running at on the flatish last part of leg five, and a revised 'official' time:

> Billy Bland of Borrowdale crushed the previous record for the Bob Graham Round at the weekend. Starting out from Keswick at 5a.m. on Sunday morning, Billy was back before 7p.m. to complete the round in 13 hours 53 minutes – an amazing 3 hours 52 minutes faster than Mike Nicholson's previous all-time best.
>
> The 33-year-old stonewaller – was accompanied by a relay of fellow runners, but they struggled to stay with him on some of the rougher sections and he was still running seven-minute miles on the last three miles of road into Keswick.

It also made the National newspapers, with a long report by Ronald Faux entitled *'The multi-marathon man'* being printed in *The Times* on Wednesday 30 June 1982. As well as the formal details of the event it added some 'colour' for its readers, which these next paragraphs illustrate.

> Billy Bland, of Borrowdale, ranks unassumingly among the top British runners. He can move faster across mountain tops than most other mortals but because the fell running world neither courts nor receives loud publicity his achievement in knocking nearly four hours off the record of one of the toughest cross-country races slipped by almost unreported last week.
>
> The Bob Graham Round of 42 Lake District peaks is claimed by those who are stout of leg to be the most demanding test of physical fitness available to British athletes.
>
> He [Bland] has built up a formidable record as a fell runner. He is leanly built with a shock of sandy hair

> and comes from a family of long-distance runners. He has been beaten only once in a long distance fell race in the past three years and that was in a bad patch.

Leaving aside him calling it a cross-country race, and the thought that anything could be considered 'the most demanding test available', it was rather ironical that the sport not courting publicity should be getting three columns in the sports pages of one of the world's leading newspapers on such an insignificant mountain challenge. But it did provide some great quotes from Billy, which I couldn't help thinking were something of a wind-up from him, but Billy claims weren't:

On the time: 'I was a lot faster than I thought I would be. In fact, there are them as won't believe I've done it.'

On bad patches: 'I do have them, but I know when they are coming because my eyelids start to flutter. I just bang in another Mars bar and wait for it to hit the system.'

On the Ben Nevis race: 'I got to the top in decent time and set off down, and my legs just gave out. I went base over apex.'

On Joss Naylor's 72 peaks record: 'I'd like him to keep that record for the rest of his life. I'm not saying I could do it even, but unless someone else takes it off him I'll leave it at that.'

Expanding on that first quote recently, Billy explains. 'I did know that by knocking that much off [the record] people would think, "has he done it?". I think about that sometimes. It is a real good job that people like Jebby nearly got there, and then Kilian broke it, as that just kills that argument stone dead.' Continuing with this surprising sign of insecurity Billy adds, 'at that time people that didn't like us so much might have thought that.'

On the second quote he adds that for him, 'dizziness came on because he was out of petrol. You start to go dizzy. You know it is coming. You don't know a long time beforehand, otherwise you would do something about it.' This shows a lack of understanding of nutrition really though, as now most runners would know to deal with both hydration and the need to re-fuel on the go by taking something on board BEFORE the signs occur.

There was also an article in the *Daily Express* of Saturday 31 July 1982, which was an appalling example of journalese. Five short extracts will serve to illustrate how misguided was this reporting of the event, and of the man himself. The article was written after a visit to Billy and Ann to interview them and take a couple of photos, and was entitled: '*Lonely as a cloud – Billy Bland of Borrowdale is tackling his third marathon of the day*'.

> Bionic Billy Bland must be the fittest man in Britain. He has engines in his legs, a powerhouse in his chest, and the best cartilages in the business.
>
> Billy is tall, lean, wiry, blond and has the most amazing Paul Newman eyes, and lashes as long as his stride
>
> ...smart turquoise blue vest and shorts, and matching coloured running shoes.
>
> ...making mountain goats seem as they have balls and chains anchored to their legs
>
> ...away up on those fells, where the sheep have shorter legs on one side, to enable them to stand up and graze.

This was from a journalist who, to quote from their bio, was one of the youngest journalists to reach Fleet Street and while on the *Daily Express* won two national awards for her feature writing.

So, there it was, an amazing new record for the Bob Graham Round that few have even got near to and was to stand for 36 years. It was done on Billy's terms, with friends and family supporting him.

Over time Billy Bland has been asked many questions about the performance, to the point of being somewhat fed up of the continued attention. Typically, it might be, 'did you think after the 13:53 that maybe you could go faster?' To that his reply was, 'if someone had gone faster, when I was still able, I would have gone for it, I guess. But I am certainly in no condition to go back now!'

There was also a misconception that, fast though the round was, that it was all done at race pace. Someone asked once, 'were you going at race speed, like the Wasdale say?' Again, Billy gives a measured reply, which included advice for anyone who might choose to try to emulate him. 'I would be under that pace. I was just running by feel. You kind of know what you are capable of. I did very little running up the hills, as I was a good strong walker anyway. Anyone trying to break it, they need to be good at downhill, as that is where they might lose time. Probably need to be better at going up too. I was born a good downhill runner. I mean that, born a downhill runner, because if you are not a good 'un from day one you will never be a good 'un. You might get better, but you'll not be a good 'un.'

Before the record was broken, Billy Bland had a very clear view as to why the record lasted so long and was keen to see someone have a decent crack at beating it. 'It has been given too much respect. At the time I was setting records and winning most of the Lakes long races. So, I can see why maybe people at the time thought they couldn't beat it. It stood for too long. I am sick of hearing about it actually! Come on, get on with it. You need fuel, and you need fitness. It is nothing to do with speed, you just need to maintain pace. It is not easy. If you have not done enough training you will have bad patches.'

He has been asked if when looking back, there was anyone he thought, at the time, could have beaten his time. 'Back in the '80s, that was the most likely time actually. But maybe they didn't fancy it. Bob Whitfield, then later on Simon Booth, both could have had a chance. My nephew Gavin Bland – the lazy sod – he could have wiped the floor with any of them.'

There was an amusing moment at one of Billy's talks, when he was asked if a woman could take the outright record? This question raised a cheer from the audience. Billy just responded, 'erm, no', to much laughter. He continued, 'I have absolute admiration for Jasmin Paris, and it is her that has raised the game for other women. Good on her. But she couldn't do that time. A woman is basically 10% athletically below what a man is. I am not being sexist, but I have great admiration for women and the way they go about these events, and they are not as macho about it as us men.'

While researching *The Round* I visited Bob Graham's grave in Borrowdale churchyard, just half a mile from where Billy Bland lives. I couldn't make out the writing on the headstone. So, I decided to try to arrange for it to be lifted and cleaned up. I asked for Billy's help in finding a suitable firm to do the work, and we visited the grave together one day. Billy surprised me by saying, 'I was aware that it was there but had never been to look at it.' Believe it or not, the inscription said that the Bob Graham Round was 130 miles long. At that time they thought the distance was that far. Billy chuckled, 'they had either gone a long way between tops or got it wrong. It is only half as far really.'

FURTHER ON UP THE ROAD

Much of the action of the 1983 season has been covered in *Running Hard: The Story of a Rivalry*, but that was written from the point of view of the main championship rivals – Kenny Stuart and John Wild. Billy Bland was racing strongly that year, but it is not a season that particularly sticks in Billy's mind, as he noted recently. 'I used to watch Kenny Stuart and John Wild from behind mostly. I probably got an odd victory that year, Borrowdale maybe, and I did stop Kenny getting a full house [of wins] in the championship one year.' He did indeed, but that came later.

Billy's 1983 season started in April with a fifth place

at Blisco, which had changed its race date to earlier in the year. The report notes that, 'Billy Bland, overcoming a slipped disc, made a more cautious start but used the descent to move up to fifth'. Initially Billy couldn't recall having a slipped disc. He then remembers what it might have been about. 'I was on a roof at Miles Jessop's house at Grasmere when I felt that someone had stuck a bloody knife in me. It just did me in.' He went to a chiropractor in Penrith who he says had a walking stick. 'He put us up on a bench and pushed my leg over one way and my shoulder the other way. He said after, "does that feel any better?" And I said, "well I don't know". He had a stick and he was puffed out and well knackered after doing the treatment. He says, "see this stick. It is a stick not a bloody magic wand". [*Laughs*] It came all right in the end, but then everything comes all right in time.'

Billy then had a second place at Coniston, before winning the Duddon race at the beginning of May. The next week was the first 'Long' championships race. The NCAA event was won by Kenny Stuart, by over three minutes from Billy. Kenny had benefitted from Billy Bland's generosity, as he had taken Kenny around the course earlier in the week, as he was having to learn a lot of new courses as he established himself as an amateur. Running the champs Fairfield race a week later, Billy could only watch from eighth place as Wild and Stuart battled it out up front, finishing in that order. John Wild remembers it well. 'That was a tough sprint finish, over the last 300 yards or so on the track. I couldn't shake him off on the descent. I called Kenny all sorts of names afterwards! A good race and a pleasing victory.'

Billy saw no problem in showing a close rival around courses. 'We were in the same club and I was not interested in winning a race if I wasn't the best there. There is no point, and it means nowt. If you set off and you win because you are the best one there, then there is a satisfaction in it. But by keeping something a secret and then going a shorter way then that is not for me. Not just with Kenny, I showed any amount of people round courses.' Billy seems to have temporarily forgotten the occasions where he did employ such tactics when knowing good lines and short cuts, and using them.

Kenny Stuart remembers the recce with Billy well, saying they just did the finish bit really, the race finishing at Honister at that time. 'We did the bit coming off Whiteless Pike. I think it would be up to the Newlands Valley road and on to the side of Robinson and back to the mines at Honister. We ran from Billy's house the wrong way round, and then back again. There weren't many places on that race where you could get really lost, unless it was misty. It was very steep but very open in that you could see quite a way. There wasn't a lot of rough stuff, which was Billy's forte of course.'

Billy Bland concludes, 'It is about conducting yourself in the sport the way you should do. I am very happy with the way I did that. I don't think I ever cheated anybody. If you help somebody along the way and they can beat you, then so be it. It was the same with Mike Fanning and Gavin Bland. I knew they would topple me eventually, but I was quite happy to help them.'

Another two weeks on saw both Kenny Stuart and Billy Bland contesting the Welsh 1000m Peaks Race for the first time. Kenny Stuart's tactic was to follow whoever took the lead. Going up Snowdon, with eighteen or so miles under their belts, there were John Wild, Kenny Stuart and Billy Bland slogging it out up the PYG track. Kenny Stuart recalls, 'I wasn't sure what to do. I thought I'd try on the climb up Snowdon as there's a path all the way. The three of us climbed Snowdon together. Billy dropped off three quarters of the way up and I thought it was mine. In the end it was nothing to do with fitness – John was just harder.' John Wild remembers that he was starting to get cramp and hoping Billy would win to take the points off Kenny. In Wild's opinion the Welsh 1000m Peaks Race is not as hard as Wasdale, even with finishing at the Snowdon summit. 'You had to do a sprint finish. I don't know about it levelling off, you still have to get to the trig point. You just dig in, don't you?'

Billy Bland then had a big win at Ennerdale, before also dominating the Wasdale championship race, on what turned out to be a boiling hot day. Billy claimed afterwards that he was untroubled, keeping himself cool carrying a sponge to dip in every stream he found, coming home over 20 minutes ahead of second-placed Tony Richardson, who would have been still coming off the top of Scafell Pike as Billy crossed the line. Although he ducked this race to sort out a temporary blip in his form, Kenny Stuart said at the time that he was confident that he could, 'give Billy a race over this course but don't know if I'd have beaten him on a hot day like this'. Two confident athletes then, letting each other know how they were going, as part of their mental strategy, perhaps.

Billy had a sixth place at Kinniside, in a race won by Kenny Stuart. It was another red-hot day and John Wild admits he just couldn't hold Stuart on the hills. Bland followed this with a second place at Bootle Black Combe to Graham Huddlestone, before taking Kenny and John on again at his local Borrowdale race, his fourth champs 'Long' of the year.

John Wild was again hoping for Billy to do him a favour by beating Kenny, but Billy couldn't seem to climb as well as usual that day and was being left by Esk Hause. He caught John and Kenny going along the Corridor Route, but eventually lost third place to Shaun Livesey. Wild liked Borrowdale, as it was more runnable than Wasdale, and confirms that it was only on the last bit that Kenny got away.

Kenny adds that, 'Billy himself had shown me over the course. He has helped me a lot, as has John. Billy came back to us down the Corridor and out towards Sty Head we got him again. He turned around to us and said it was no good and he doesn't say that unless he means it.' With Billy getting beaten at the age of 37 a local said to him after this race, "well that is the last of your wins then". Billy said, "no, I don't think so. I just haven't had a very good day." Billy won the next five Borrowdale races, rather proving his point.

Billy came sixth the next day at Latrigg, and a month later fifth at Ben Nevis, when John Wild set a new record of 1:25:35. This was the occasion of the legendary post-Ben naked/underpants relay race through the streets of Fort William. Billy Bland declined to streak, so the Keswick team were disqualified from the relay. Billy Bland shows his sensible side by explaining that they used to stay with a Mr and Mrs Chisholm in Fort William, and that stuff was just not his scene. 'I can laugh about it, as it is just a bit of fun isn't it. That John Wild he was wild sometimes. I was there when there was similar behaviour at the Royal Victoria Hotel after the Snowdon race, but I wasn't taking part in it.'

Ten days after the Ben Nevis Race Billy only managed second in the Mountain Trial, a rare failure to win that event. It was the first time it had been sponsored by Ordnance Survey and crazily they had decided NOT to provide special race maps. Many runners obtained maps from an OS agent and cut them down to the grid size prescribed by the organiser. When the OS saw the maps being mutilated, they changed their mind. Billy's second place was actually impressive, because, as usual he didn't mark up his map, then later dropped his route card which blew away. He says he swept the fell to find the final control.

Having finished with championships races for the year, Billy then won two events that were being inaugurated that year – the Three Shires and the Buttermere races – before finishing his season with a third place at the Copeland Chase. Racing seventeen times throughout the season, Billy won five times, finishing sixth overall in the champs, despite not having a full set of ten counting events.

The 1984 season started late and not particularly well for Billy Bland. Coming eleventh in a championship race at Coniston on 5 May presaged a year when he only competed in four championship races, leading some to consider him to be semi-retired from the scene.

As has been noted earlier, Billy did his second Saunders Mountain Marathon this summer, and he was carrying an injury through the early part of the season, which he was eventually able to shake off.

A fourth place on the new Northern Counties course was followed by a win at Duddon, and a fifth at Ennerdale, where Billy just couldn't stick with the pace of Kenny Stuart and Hugh Symonds when they opened up a lead in the second half of the race. Hugh Symonds is always great value to interview, and I didn't hesitate when he invited me to drive up to Sedbergh to meet him when he was in the country for a while in between his long cycling trips. He had the coffee on and his training diaries out ready.

Hugh Symonds reckons that the Ennerdale was one of his favourite races. His race diary entry for that one just says, 'good run'. Hugh admits that he never beat Kenny Stuart. He came close at Coniston, and he beat him to the top of the Ben once, but says, 'that isn't the race, it is to the bottom'. Kenny Stuart reckons he just had a very good run that day. 'I stayed with them until the flat before Iron Crag where there was some good running. I think Hugh Symonds was still with me, and I left him and finished quite strongly.'

Kenny Stuart was having a fabulous season and was unbeaten in championship races so far. He won Skiddaw in a new course record on 1 July, with Billy off the pace in fourth place (but showcasing Keswick AC's strength at the time as he was their third scorer, with Rod Pilbeam being third). Proving that he had still got it, Billy scorched round the Wasdale course to beat Hugh Symonds, holding him off on the rough stuff and taking him out on the run-in. Hugh Symonds remembers being very frustrated at being second that day because he had led Billy on the way up Scafell, but he didn't know the course sufficiently well, 'to just ping off the top and get on to Lingmell and into the finish. He ran faster than me down the hill, fair and square. He deserved to win', he says now.

A week later Billy Bland came fourth at Kinniside, following three Cumberland Fellrunners home.

On 4 August there was a race that defined Billy Bland's season, and Kenny Stuart's too. It was the Borrowdale championships race on Billy's home patch, and Kenny had missed the previous championship race at Moel Siabod to prepare for it. For Billy though it was one of the few times that he felt he had run well that year. It was over Broad Crag that gaps started to appear in the leaders as Billy opened up a slight lead in the mist from Shaun Livesey, Kenny Stuart and Jon Broxap. At Scafell Pike these four were four minutes clear.

I assumed Jon Broxap would have had a good view of the race as it unfolded from his position in the lead group, but it seems not, as he explained. 'Billy's tactic at Borrowdale was to set off and challenge people to stay with him if they could. He did it in a lot of long races. Soon I would be so far behind I would see nothing of him. He knew that course so intimately that there would be a point where he could just change up and disappear. Kenny would either be able to keep with him, or not, depending on how he was feeling.'

Billy extended his lead to four minutes by the time the summit of Great Gable was reached. Along the Corridor Kenny overtook Shaun to open up a three-minute gap on him at the Gable checkpoint. Kenny was unable to close the gap on the good running to Honister as Billy piled on the pressure to secure a gap of seven minutes. Climbing up Dale Head Kenny managed to pull back a minute, but barring disasters there was no way he was going to catch Billy. The long descent to Rosthwaite saw Billy stretch his lead to nearly ten minutes. Billy's pride was restored. The outcome meant that Kenny Stuart was denied a fantastic achievement. At the end of the season he was that close to an unprecedented 'perfect' season, as he had won the necessary three Short races, three Medium races (+1 spare in each of those categories), and this was to be his third Long win (having already won the Northern Counties and Ennerdale). But Billy Bland had stopped him.

Although he had won two 'Longs' already that season

Kenny hadn't especially thought he could win Borrowdale. 'I would be running because it was a champs race', he says now. 'Anything can go wrong in Borrowdale of course, especially if it is misty.'

Later that month Billy Bland almost became a TV star. This was something that just dropped into a conversation we were having one day. It was a topic I certainly knew nothing about beforehand, so we explored it in detail. At the time, the 1980s, there was a programme called Survival of the Fittest, which had been going for three or four seasons and they were looking for more sports people to participate.

Billy takes up the story. 'Survival of the Fittest came to pass because someone had noticed that I had recently set the Bob Graham record, I think. I wasn't sure if I wanted to do it as they were various things you had to take part in that I hadn't done before. I had just beaten Kenny Stuart at the Borrowdale race. I wouldn't commit at first, but anyway I went – so we had a week down in Wales doing various things, in Betws y Coed [*at Plas y Brenin*].'

Billy has a DVD showing the event in grainy detail. It describes the nine events that made up the challenge, but mostly concentrates on the fell running event, in which the contestants raced up Snowdon, via Crib Goch. The others were: endurance run, abseil, assault course, log cutting, downhill run (running down Y Garn), aerial ropes course, canoeing, and log carry. Billy claims he wasn't much good at anything but the running, but still managed to come a very respectable second overall, three points off the leading competitor. The winner was Jim Wood, an Army PTI Sergeant and former Olympian at Biathlon. Wood had been ultra-consistent, his fourth place in the mountain race being his lowest place throughout the event.

Border TV messed up and Billy's episode never went out on the TV locally. His edition went out on Harlech TV (in Wales) but not on Border TV in Cumbria, as Billy explains. 'There was a tale about it which was probably true. It had come out on Border TV that it was gonna be on, but when it came on it was the next one after. They must have had it canned for quite a while. They missed ours out and put out t'other. Someone picked up wrong 'un and ours never went out up here.' It was shown in public once when Paul Cornforth took the video and extracted the running bits for a presentation at Kong Adventure in Keswick.

The DVD is a particularly useful historical record as there was so little video recording in those days, and it may be unique in showing Billy Bland running in his pomp. The mountain race was to the summit of Snowdon from Pen y Pass, via the knife edge of Crib Goch. Billy seems to be ascending with ease and to run surefootedly on even the roughest ground, inviting a comparison with a mountain goat. He easily won the mountain race, from Tony Cresswell. Cresswell had been a pacer on Billy's Bob Graham record round two years before, and was described in the commentary as having been, 'forceful, courageous and entertaining all week'. There is no mention of Billy being any of those three things. What he was though was efficient. Throughout the series of programmes they had used that route beforehand and the record to the Snowdon summit was 47 minutes. Billy beat it by over 2 minutes, so had ascended Snowdon by that long and tricky route in under 45 minutes.

The fuzzy helicopter photography shows all the competitors setting off by the road, crossing The Horns, and then tackling Crib Goch and Crib-y-Ddysgl, before the final steps up to the summit. Billy looks majestic, particularly as he scorns the organiser's proffered small glass of fruit juice about halfway up. Straight afterwards, sweating slightly, he gives an awkward post-event interview. 'It was not bad. Don't normally race over that stuff. You just make sure you don't fall off.' He then offered the suggestion that he was in control really, by saying, 'in a [*normal*] fell race you might have to go faster if you have company. But I haven't messed about, like.' And then delivered the *coup de grace*. 'I just kept it going steady. If they can't beat me in the first 20 minutes, they won't beat me at all.'

I had the chance to hear Tony Cresswell's version of events recently. He says that it was embarrassing, and he doesn't know why he was invited. He had heard of that event as it had run for some years. It was organised by outdoor enthusiasts from the armed services. There would invite top people from the army, navy, and air force and also top rock climbers and other sportsmen. Tony explains his involvement. 'I seem to remember Harlech TV speaking to Pete Bland and asking who they should approach from fell running. When they rang me, I said, "you got the wrong bloke if you want a top runner". But I did it.'

In the end Cresswell thoroughly enjoyed it. 'The only bit I was a bit miffed about was that we were made to look jessies. But that was what they wanted. They want TV, they don't want everyone being brilliant. They were hoping someone would catch their nadgers on Crib Goch, or something, as that would make good TV!'

'The guys were great, the camera crews were great, and Harlech TV were wonderful. There were two events each day for four days, and then the fell run up Snowdon on the last day. When we finished Billy and I got a helicopter off the top of Snowdon. The overall winner bloke, Jim Wood, couldn't bend his legs at the end. He was screwed. He couldn't make it to the helicopter and had to come down by train', chortles Cresswell.

Cresswell finished by describing why he enjoyed the running events. 'I was second behind Billy on the two runs. Billy was grateful to me because I took out the guy that won it. For the downhill (off Y Garn) I said, "I will be off here in 10 minutes". Billy says, "who are you kidding, if you break ten minutes then you'll win it". It was rough with no track like. I came down it and broke ten minutes. Billy did about seven and a half. We screamed down there. Jim Wood knew he had to track me, and I blew his legs away. I don't know which day in the sequence it was, but Wood was stuffed for the next day!'

Soon after that excitement Billy was back running Ben Nevis, on 1 September, it again being a championship event. He came a strong fifth, but the day was Kenny Stuart's. Kenny had again missed the championships race at Sedbergh to prepare specifically for this one, and delivered a new course record, beating John Wild's 1:25:35 from the year before by just one second, having chased Hugh Symonds to the summit turn. Hugh Symonds recalls that he felt very good going up. 'I think it was the fastest time I ever did at the Ben that day. It was 1:27:05 and I was third. It was quite meaningful because I was first to the top and Kenny went off fast and I think it was Jack Maitland that was second.'

A week later Billy had what was a routine win at the Mountain Trial in gale force conditions. Despite the best efforts of Jon Broxap, Jack Maitland and Joss Naylor, Billy won by almost 32 minutes on a course out by Ullswater. Billy finished his season with a third at the Three Shires, and then further wins at Langdale and the Copeland Chase, giving him 6 wins out of 13 races in a somewhat uneven year. He finished nineteenth in the championship, because of the lack of counting races.

Billy Bland set about the 1985 season with a much greater commitment than he had the previous year, completing enough championship races to have a real chance of going for the title again. He ran 19 races in all, of which 10 were in the championships.

He started the year with the first championship race at the Edale Skyline. The weather turned bad during the event, with snow swirling around the runners. There was a big group of the main contenders at Mam Tor, but by Lord's Seat it had thinned out. Last year's champion, Kenny Stuart, had a virus and dropped out here, leaving Bob Ashworth and Billy Bland heading a smaller group. Ashworth found the best line home to finish almost a minute up on Billy.

Running only championship races in April, Billy came third behind Kenny Stuart and Jack Maitland at the Kentmere Horseshoe, and second to Kenny Stuart at the Blisco Dash. May was a busy month with five races, three of which were the three in the middle week that constituted the Reebok International Mountain Challenge, which is discussed later. On the first weekend of the month there was a championship race at Coniston, in which Billy came third to in-form Kenny Stuart and Jack Maitland.

On the last weekend of the month Billy won the Welsh 1000m Peaks Race (a 'Long' champs one) in appalling conditions from Bob Whitfield and Kenny Stuart. There was a typical blunt explanation of the win from Billy. 'Yeh, we got shot of Kenny that day. I remember saying to Bob Whitfield before we got to Pen y Pass that we would get

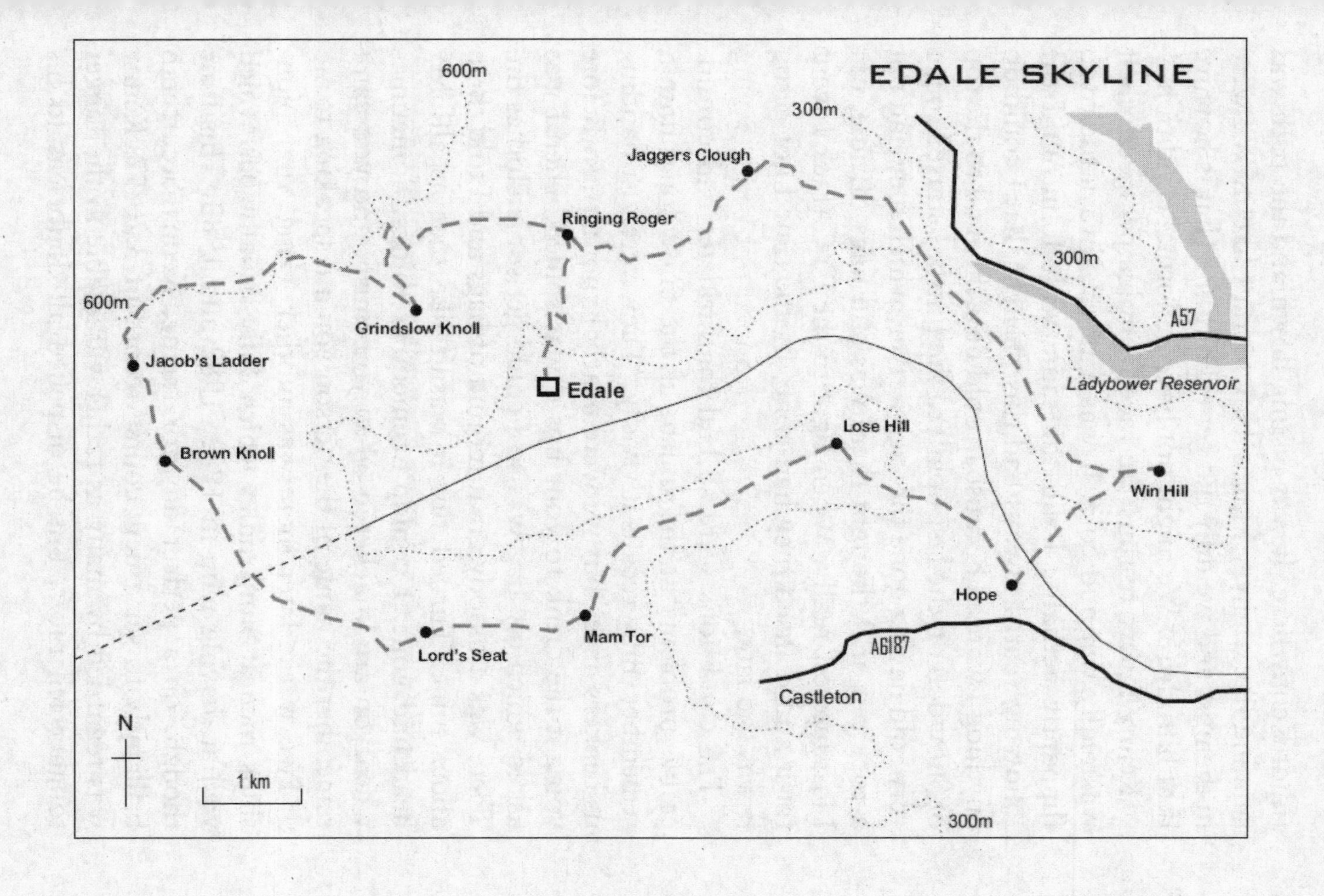
EDALE SKYLINE
600m
300m
Jaggers Clough
Ringing Roger
300m
A57
Grindslow Knoll
600m
Jacob's Ladder
Edale
Ladybower Reservoir
Lose Hill
Brown Knoll
Win Hill
Hope
Mam Tor
Lord's Seat
A6187
Castleton
N
1 km
300m

rid of Kenny here. It was pissing down and the path was running like a ghyll. I knew he wouldn't like it. We were in the mist and we duly did get rid of him. That is how we beat him there. We might not have in normal conditions.'

Kenny Stuart re-runs the race from his perspective. 'It was really wet and cold. It was a race I always took too flippantly actually. I did the same with John Wild the following year. I always had this thought that I could do anything I wanted because I could beat them all to the top of Snowdon on the last uphill to the finish. I started to get very cold having gone through a river, which they had put a rope out at. I thought there was still bags of time, but I lost interest really. When I got to the PYG track I went for it and realised they had gone. By the time I got going it was too late.'

The conditions were so bad that athletes had considerable problems at the finish, at the Snowdon summit, remember. Billy recalls it vividly. 'They were just handing us beakers of tea but we were nearly hypothermic. Before you got the drink to your lips it was spilled. Then I was asked which my bag was so I could get some clothes on. There was a bloody great mound of bags and I told them about mine. Turned out it wasn't like that at all! My head had gone. I couldn't remember things. Sometimes when you are knackered when you finish, and you can't remember the name of the person you are speaking to.'

Two weeks later there was another 'Long' championships race at Ennerdale, which Billy usually performed well at, having won in 1981, 1982 and 1983. This time though, on a perfect day for racing, Kenny Stuart ran brilliantly to set a new course record of 3:20:57. Kenny was regarded by many as rather vulnerable in the longer tougher fell races, but he dispelled all doubts as to his ability in this department as he sped round the formidable Ennerdale Horseshoe in a new record time and well clear of his regular shadow of Jack Maitland. Billy came in third, and recently he came out with a rather negative response to Kenny's achievement, casting doubt on its veracity, before claiming it doesn't bother him. Kenny broke the record by seven seconds, but Billy queries the distance run that particular year. 'It was dubious as the start and finish were in different places. It used to start away from the Scout camp and finish at the same place. That year I am sure it started at the same place but finished at the Scout camp, which wouldn't have been as far. I couldn't give a toss about it though, as Kenny was a better runner. He no doubt used me all the way round. There is no way he went out there on his own, as that wasn't his way.' For the record Kenny beat Jack Maitland by three minutes, and Billy by another 3 minutes that day.

Kenny Stuart takes umbrage at Billy disputing his record. 'I did those two Ennerdale races back to back and I didn't think the start and finish was any different. I didn't go out to break that record. It just happened on the day, which was a great day for racing. I didn't even run with a watch. That wasn't the only classic long race I broke the record for – I did it at the Three Peaks once. But I never set the record at Borrowdale, which is a really good one.'

Billy Bland then had a purple patch, winning five races in a row, at Royal Dockray, Melantee (in a 'Short' champs race), Half Nevis (the next day), Wasdale (in his slowest winning time) and his local race at Borrowdale.

Billy fought hard in the remaining three championship races. First, he came second to Kenny Stuart at Gategill, and then had a third behind Symonds and Maitland at the Ben Nevis race (Kenny didn't run). Symonds remembers it well, and with justification. 'The fact that Kenny didn't run meant that I thought that was possibly the only chance I'd get to win the Ben. Running off the top Jack [Maitland] was catching me. I said to myself I can't let this happen. I have got to run off this hill in front. And I did.' Hugh's diary just recorded it thus: '1st! Wow. A real surprise. 56 seconds slower than the year before.'

In the third champs race Billy was third at Langdale. In this race Billy was beaten by Jack Maitland and Shaun Livesey, with Kenny Stuart fourth, having been in the lead at Pike O'Blisco, but somehow going wrong on the final descent to let in Jack Maitland for his first ever British Championship win.

Kenny reiterated what happened at Langdale at day. 'I was going to win the championship and just needed to get in the first four or five, I think. I was leading coming off Blisco and took the wrong line. Then three or four people passed me, but I managed to still retain fourth position. Colin Donnelly was one of them. I should have won Langdale that day, but I never did win it.'

In between these counters Billy won the inaugural Gunson Knott race, on a course that he had devised to accompany the Shepherd's Meet. Looking for a traditional course Billy says, 'Gunson Knott, the first of the Crinkles, allowed a route unblemished by tarmac or even footpaths along Oxendale and up the steep grassy front to the 2,680 feet summit and back'. Billy devised the course with the help of Dave Wilkinson. The farmer had asked Billy about having a race there, connected to the Shepherd's Meet. Billy adds that it was ideal for him, but barely long enough.

Gary Devine tells a story which illustrates how well

Billy Bland knew that particular terrain, and also how he was prepared to use it to his advantage. 'I remember once overtaking Billy Bland who, as you know, did not take kindly to being overtaken. It was near the end of Gunson Knott [*in a different year*] and we were lying fourth or fifth and I thought "fantastic, I've overtaken Billy"; but he then re-appeared in front of me because he had just dropped back to let me pass and then take a shorter line. I learned from that and now do it myself.'

Billy also won the Mountain Trial, which was held in in water-logged Eskdale. I know that to my cost as I also ran it and got a ducking in the final river crossing as I lost my footing, right in view of my wife and my best mate, coming home some considerable time after the winner.

Billy rounded out his season with a fourth place at the 1.5-mile Butter Crag race, finishing just over a minute behind Kenny Stuart, who was making up for previous day's disappointment when he went off course (at Langdale). Kenny lowered his own course record from the year before, finishing in 12:22. In summary Billy Bland had won 7 out of his 19 races, and came second in the championship table, 16 points behind Kenny Stuart, but 24 ahead of third placer Shaun Livesey.

The scoring system for the 1986 season changed for the Fell Championships. The British Championships went down to just six races, with two each in England, Wales and Scotland. A nine race English Championships was also instigated, watering down the whole championship focus to my mind. That year neither John Wild nor Kenny Stuart were competing regularly on the fells. But the British championships were still very competitive.

Billy Bland was competing regularly, managing 17 races in the season in all, and had a good go at challenging for the (British) championship. He started with an early second place at Chew Valley in cold and snowy conditions, and also warmed up in March with a win at the Edale Skyline and a sixth at Black Combe. He then travelled to Wales for the first championship race, coming fifth at the Llanbedr to Blaenavon 'Long' race, which was won by Jack Maitland – showing he finally meant business this year. Billy seemed to remember more about the trip itself than the race. 'Three of us from the club went down, possibly Rod Pilbeam and Mike Fanning and I. We stopped in this pub somewhere in Llanbedr. I got up early as I like to get up and out. I went out to see if I could get a paper. I got a bollocking off the landlord because I hadn't locked the door. If you had put a pot of paint down in that street there would have been a riot.' Being unsure what he meant by that last remark I asked him to explain. What he meant was that it was a very run down area and needed a lick of paint. He also added that you wouldn't have seen him so far south if it hadn't been a counter in the champs.

Billy followed this with a ninth at Coniston and fourth at the Buttermere Sailbeck race, before returning to Wales for the 'Medium' Moel Eilio championship race. Here he was surprisingly off kilter, coming in ninth, almost three minutes behind Maitland. Billy had a reasonably successful non-championship month of May, winning the Welsh 1000m Peaks Race, and coming second at Blencathra (to Rod Pilbeam) and Ennerdale (to Hugh Symonds).

At that Ennerdale race Billy reportedly sat down for five minutes at the start of the race. It was certainly unusual behaviour, which he explains was a reaction to being followed by others in races. 'I didn't sit down I stood, but anyway. I didn't think I was fit enough to win it and I think I had been injured or something. I travelled over and said to my cousin, "I am going to stand on the line for 5 minutes today". I didn't want people just sitting on me all the way round, giving me a hard time. If I was up there in the lead I would be trying my best, whereas further back I could pick my own race. Anyway, I ended up second, with a faster time than the winner, which I think was Hugh Symonds. It was just because I didn't think I could win that I ran like that.'

I mentioned this to Hugh in an interview for this book and he said, 'did he say he ran a faster time than me that day? We need the results for that! My diary shows: I did a slower time than the year when Kenny was first. I did 3 hours 38 minutes 59 seconds. Some fast bits, otherwise easy. The following day the entry says that I was not too stiff.' Billy seems to be correct, as he recorded a time of 3:42:50 according to *The Fellrunner*, so if the five-minute wait is accurate then his running time was 3:37:50, which is 1 minute 9 seconds faster than Hugh had run. Billy says Danny Hughes timed his wait and it is accurate.

Proving that he was still 'the Man' at one of his most local races, Billy won Wasdale in July by over four minutes from Hugh Symonds, in what would appear from the results had been in a routine manner. But *The Fellrunner* carried no report of the race. I knew that Ann Bland always supported Billy at his races and on this occasion she says that, on a horrible wet day she ran to Beck Head (between Kirk Fell and Great Gable), and he never appeared, after Jack Maitland had come through at the front of the race. Billy Bland recounts what had happened.

'I'll tell you the story. I had written the bearings on the back of my hand and I was clear on top of Seatallan. Prior to setting off, old Joss comes over and says to me,

"26 double paces from cairn and dive off down screes". I had the correct bearing on my hand and had won before, so I didn't bother with the compass. I counted the steps like and went down the side and got to the bottom and it was like a grassy dish. You are supposed to head for Pots of Ashness as it is called. I am thinking this isn't great. I thought there is a bit of a groove between Haycock and Scoat and I thought I was going up that groove. I knew by then I was lost, and I thought I was on the left-hand side of Haycock. I knew if I kept going for it I would hit the wall that comes down from the top of Scoat. When I got to the wall it was Little Gowder Crag and that was completely the wrong side of Haycock. I had to go up Haycock, down the dip and up on to Scoat. When I got to Pillar I asked how many had gone through, and I think it was maybe 8 [*Ann says 15. After some quite aggressive toing and froing they agreed to disagree*]. I had done the diet and was thinking I could beat that record, and I still think I might have done. I thought I would just go as far as Ann and bail out there. But she says, "they are just there". Well they were halfway up Gable and I was at Beck Head. I knew that some of them were surely having a good day as they were all together. So, if I catch them some will have more petrol than me, as I had been chasing hard to make up ground. By the bottom of Gable I still hadn't caught them, but from there I picked them off one at a time. Then there was just Hugh Symonds in front. There is a bit of a main path up past Sprinkling Tarn and there are two paths on from there after Great End. Hugh set off up the higher path. He kept turning his head, so I thought I'll make out I am going the same way. Then I switched back down on to the bottom path. As soon as he saw me on the bottom path he ran out of confidence and came back across to my path. So, I was playing him like a violin like. I think he beat me on to the Pike and then he went wrong going towards Lingmell and I got him and won.'

Hugh Symonds says that is fair comment from Billy, but that he didn't know he had got so lost earlier in the race, which surprised him. Symonds adds, 'the reason I went wrong on Lingmell is that it is like a nose and I went around the edge of it. It had been a clear of clouds earlier, but some mist appeared from nowhere when I was in the lead from Scafell by a few minutes. I got lost in that mist. I came out of the mist on Lingmell and I looked down on to the pub and I had just gone around the hill when I should have gone down the hill. My heart just dropped. It was a race I really wanted to win, was Wasdale, and I should have won it.'

Billy fashioned another Borrowdale win the next month, seemingly by a stunning 37 minutes according to *The Fellrunner*, which gave his time as 2:32:38. I should have realised this was wrong as it is faster than the course record, which Billy set in 1981. When I discussed it with him, Billy was adamant that he did not win it by 37 minutes. 'I won there by 16 minutes a couple of times. I won Langdale by 20 minutes and Mountain Trial by half an hour, but I didn't win Borrowdale by 37 minutes. I remember that year. I did 2:52 on a real windy day. It was so wild that the wind was picking up little stones from the footpath. I was the only one under three hours and I think I was 16 minutes ahead.' This suggests it was a misprint. A look at Ann Bland's results file proved this to be the case. *Fellrunner* had reported it as 2:32:38, instead of the correct 2:52:38.

His last two championship races were a third at Gategill,

and a sixth at the Ben, where Colin Donnelly won and missed the course record by just 14 seconds. Billy closed out his season with another win at the Mountain Trial (from Braithwaite), and two sixth places at Langdale and Wansfell. He had five wins during the season, was fourth in the British Championships and equal fourth in the inaugural English Championships.

During this 1986 season Billy Bland supported a couple of friends on their Bob Graham Rounds. He also supported others on their major endurance efforts. We take a step back to have a look at them, and also his own first Bob Graham Round effort, in 1976.

WHEN YOU NEED ME

It was Chris Bland that talked with Billy Bland about the Bob Graham Round (BGR) and what it was. He was the catalyst behind Billy doing his first BGR. 'I was probably aware of it at the time, but I was more into racing, as I was when the record was set in 1982', says Billy now. There were only just over 50 completions before Billy did his round. 'Both the BGR and fell running were just taking off in 1976 really. It has grown and grown since. Various books have come out and it has increased in visibility.' Billy adds that Rob Jebb made a comment when he did his 14:30 round (in 2016), to the effect that he was amazed that he got more recognition for that than any of his many race wins.

On a beautiful moonlit night in August 1976 Billy Bland set off from Keswick Moot Hall on a Bob Graham Round, having suggested he was on a 23-hour schedule. At this point in his career he had only ever won one race since turning to the amateur branch of the sport – that was the Borrowdale race the weekend beforehand. Chris, Anthony and David Bland set out with him that day, more as contenders themselves than as supporters for Billy.

Uncharacteristically Billy wrote an account of this round. This extract is edited down from the one published in Fred Rogerson's *History and Records of Notable Fell Walks, 1864–1972, Within the Lake District*.

> After having three or four hours sleep in the afternoon, seven of us set off for a nice, steady, uneventful section, arriving at Threlkeld on schedule, hoping that daylight wouldn't come – the conditions for running being ideal.
>
> We reached Clough Head together, apart from Neil [Shuttleworth] who was now beginning to lag behind. Howard [Pattinson] insisted that Calfhow Pike was one of the tops included so, being a little ahead of schedule the two of us added this. Having a job to hold Howard back as we were all tending to split up slightly, but we managed to stay together until we met Fred Rogerson at Grisedale Tarn with a welcome flask of tea, then on to Fairfield and Seat Sandal. Neil was now a long way behind, and we were starting to leave Chris. We arrived at Dunmail 30 minutes ahead of schedule.
>
> After breakfasting on tinned fruit in a 25-minute rest, four of us set off up Steel Fell with Mike Nicholson and Mike Walford as pacers, leaving Chris who said he was

going to hang on for Neil (eventually he set off on his own). We stayed together until High White Stones then we began to leave Howard and Mike Walford, the three of us pressing on with Mike Nicholson. We arrived at Rossett Pike at 10a.m., where Joss Naylor had kindly left an orange drink.

It was beginning to get very hot, but we were still going well. We reached Bowfell at 10.28 I was going rather better than David and Anthony, so Mike decided that we should press on by ourselves. At 11.29 we arrived at Scafell Pike and decided that Broad Stand would be a much better way to get up as everything was dry and should cause no problems. [*Billy adds now that they had split up by then so there was just him and one other and that he used to go up Broad Stand on his own in training sometimes.*] We made a fast descent to arrive at Wasdale Head at 12.15, for a 26-minute stay and more tinned fruit.

As we set off up Yewbarrow I turned around and saw David and Anthony arriving at Wasdale Head. After having a struggle to climb Yewbarrow we arrived at the top at 13.21 and went on to Red Pike and Steeple, both of us both suffering from the intense heat. Then on to Pillar, now going well again but getting very thirsty as there was little water because of the dry time we had been having. On reaching Black Sail, Mike decided to go for water – leaving me to do Kirk Fell and meet him at Beck Head. I reached Kirk Fell at 15.11, had a chat with a climber, being glad to see him to prove I'd been there. I dropped into Beck Head feeling shattered and cramming Mars bars in, one after the other, together with all the water Mike had brought. After five minutes rest I set off up Gable, Mike deciding to go for more

> water. After struggling up Gable I arrived at 15.45, the water/Mars bars getting through my system and I began to go well again. I met Mike on Green Gable and we then did Brandreth and Grey Knotts where we again met up with that man, Fred Rogerson with his cine camera, then down on to Honister Pass arriving at 16:20.
>
> After thanking Mike for the excellent job he'd done, and now feeling really good, I set off up Dale Head with Mike Walford after five minutes rest. We arrived at Dale Head at 16:49, Hindscarth 17:03, Robinson 17:24, then down on to the Newlands road – the hardest part of the course for me, Mike having to really urge me on. We arrived at Keswick at 18:50, downed two bottles of cider – and I said, 'never again'.

Billy Bland was delighted that David and Anthony made it in together, with Howard later finishing on his own but still within 24 hours. Chris didn't make it though, probably due to the fact that the team had split up. Chris Bland did go back to it and did the BGR in 22:50 on June 25–26 1977.

Discussing this 18:50 round with Billy, I wanted to get more detail about that fantastic effort. He offered some interesting reflections on the event, admittedly with hindsight 40 years on. As he remembered it, the team was himself, Anthony Bland (his cousin), David Bland (brother), Chris Bland (cousin) and Howard Pattinson (who Billy went to school with). He seemed to want to deflect criticism he had received for the group breaking up as it went around.

'The idea of doing the round came from my cousin Chris Bland. By doing it I became the fifty-second person to complete the round. I can't remember what time we started, but we were all supposed to go round together, just to do it. We went over the Skiddaw range together, and then up on to the Dodds. Chris was first to start struggling because he was always going to be the weakest of us. Anyway, Howard started going 'come on Chris' and that sort of thing. A little bit of ... [*a pause, and then the thought was not articulated*]. Somebody was nipping away and wanting us to go faster. I am not even sure that Chris answered back at the time (as to it being too fast for him).'

'That is water under the bridge now. [*Although both Billy and Howard still mention it!*] Let's face it we were only a few hours into the job anyway. It started to split up. Once we split up – which wasn't instigated by me, although plenty think it would be, but it wasn't. Then we started to splinter, and because we had plenty of pacers everyone had someone to go with. Or maybe Anthony and David went together for a long time, and they may have finished together, I can't remember. Anyway, even before Dunmail, I can't remember if Anthony and David were still with me or Howard was with us, I sort of pressed on from there and ended up doing much of the round without them. I was on my own before Scafell or thereabouts, and ended up with 18:50, was it. I think it was a new record [*it was*]. I was just left with the memory that it was a useless effort; I could knock spots off it. After 1976 I became a lot better runner.'

Howard Pattinson offered a slightly different perspective on the event. 'I bumped into Billy and he said, "we are going at the weekend, why don't you come along". I agreed. I hadn't done a round before and I set off with them. I don't particularly remember Neil Shuttleworth being involved, but he did turn up, I think. But Neil was never really in it. I was pretty fit at the time.' Howard comments 'in latter day reports of this round, as the only non-Bland to complete, I am often not mentioned.' In Billy's report, which I have quoted verbatim in a previous book, it reads as though Billy blames Howard for the group splitting up and for Chris Bland not completing. Really getting into his stride, Pattinson adds 'on the first two sections I was relaxed and fairly easy, but was already thinking "Chris is not going to do this, he is not fit enough", and Billy is quoted as saying he was "having a job to hold Howard back".'

Pattinson further comments, 'According to that report, Billy suggested that I thought that Calfhow Pike was one of the 42. What I had said to him, and we might have been 50 yards apart at the time, was, "did Joss count Calfhow Pike, as one of his 72?". That was the issue, but it was made to look as though I didn't know what the 42 were. It may not mean anything much to anyone else, but it did to me. We did Calfhow Pike anyway as we were waiting for Chris to catch up. My memory is that Billy, David, Anthony and I got to Dunmail and decided to go on. Chris was some way behind with Neil. After Steel Fell, I had a bad patch and got dropped. Subsequently, David and Anthony were also dropped, and Billy went on. What you can say is, that four people attempting a round together is asking for trouble, because at some time you are going to have people going at different paces. You either have a strict regime where you all stick together, or you have pacers to cover all eventualities. For quite a while afterwards Chris blamed me. The blame was short-lived. In 1977 Chris was a pacer on my anti-clockwise round with Chris Dodd and Frank Thomas. Chris also formed a team of four, Chris

Dodd, Frank and I, in the High Peak Marathon.'

Billy and Howard are going to have to agree to differ on the details, as Billy came back with, 'Howard was the one that was nipping away at the pace, especially at Chris. We didn't need to agree to stick together. Chris was arranging it and it wouldn't seem fair to piss off and leave him. We were all trying to do it so there were no pacers as such.'

Sometime after the event Billy added that he really, 'had just been messing around, so that time was crap. Mike Nicholson came along in 1977 and took the record to 17:45, I think. I carried on racing, and started winning Ennerdale, Wasdale, and Borrowdale. I always had in my mind that someday I'll see what I can do. I had conversations with different people and that, to get a feel for it.'

Of course, Billy eventually did see what he could do, and it was the stunning 13:53 for the Bob Graham Round in 1982.

Mindful of the axiom that a slow marathon is harder than a fast one, I asked Billy at one of his talks which round he felt the worst after, the 18:50 or the 13:53. He immediately replied that it was the 18:50 one, mostly because he was a whole lot fitter when he did the 13:53. He then expanded on his reasoning. 'A lot of people talk about pain and going through the pain barrier. I have never felt pain in my life when running, and I mean that. I used to train with young Mike Fanning when he was coming through. He would say, "my legs are screaming". I'd say, "what the hell are you on about Fanning", as I never experienced that. I faded away and had to lie down, but have never been in pain. Maybe I have been lucky.' An audience member interjected at this point, 'maybe you were not pushing yourself enough!' Not taking the bait, Billy continued, 'I consider I trained hard, but I may have given up too easy sometimes. John Wild would run till he was sick. You wouldn't catch me doing that, I'd just slow down. My strong point was preparing myself for what I was going to do.'

In talking with Pete Barron, it emerged that he and Billy Bland had instigated another round a few years later, which hasn't received the same level of interest as the Bob Graham Round. Pete recalls the set-up. 'When I was at Honister [*YHA hostel*] we did quite a few runs together. One run that stands out in my mind which we did together was the Borrowdale Watershed. To my knowledge it has still never been done since. We started at Cat Bells and ran round to Walla Crag, via all the tops that drain into Borrowdale, including Great End, and the Langdale Pikes. Ann Bland was supporting at Sty Head. I think it was 28 miles. We didn't make a big deal of it, kind of did it and went home again. It was a good day out. Of course, when we got to Walla Crag Billy had gone on ahead and was sat there waiting for me!'

Pete couldn't remember exactly when it was, but Billy recalls that, 'it was in the 1980s for sure. We just decided to do it. I had to wait for him on Walla Crag that day. It is a wonder I waited so long actually. It wasn't about setting records. Was it six hours or summat? It was just something to do really.'

What is also not that well known is that after his 1982 record round Billy Bland decided to have another attempt at the BGR, vowing that he would walk every step of the way, and not run any of it – not even on the downhills. This he did in 1989, accompanied all the way by witnesses to verify the feat. He walked round in an astonishing 20 hours 48 minutes, going so fast that he nearly missed his supporters at Wasdale. For this walk he was accompanied by seventeen-year-old Gavin Bland. Billy wore road shoes and got blistered feet. In the report in the *42 Peaks* booklet, Billy Bland says:

> I started getting fed up as I couldn't get it over as fast as I wanted – after running fell races for 15 years with virtually no injuries, two days after the walk I had a problem with my knee – torn ligaments, most likely caused by holding back downhill, which was the hardest part of the round.

The two Blands had separated by 10 minutes during the walk-in to Keswick (they went anti-clockwise), both getting under 21 hours without running a step. The difference was that this time some of the peaks had to be climbed through the night because of their slower pace.

It seemed to me that by walking the BGR Billy was trying to make a point. 'Perhaps', he says. 'I had a discussion with Ken Ledward and I said I could walk it. I said if I can't do it walking at three mile an hour I'll eat hay with a horse [*another fine Cumbrian expression*]. I said to Gavin, do you fancy it, and away we went. We were going to beat the pacers to Wasdale, so we sat down on Scoat Fell and had an orange to kill time. They weren't there so we went on and they intercepted us.'

Billy Bland would seem to be a candidate for the extended rounds where people try to get as many peaks as possible done in 24 hours, in effect an extended BGR. At the time Billy was at his peak that record was held by Joss Naylor, with his 72 peaks – which was achieved in 1975.

Howard Pattinson acknowledges that he made an attempt in 1981, with Chris Dodd, at 65 peaks. It was planned as a joint attempt with no additional support on the fells. Howard comments, 'Chris had dropped out and I was basically on my own. I got it wrong coming to Dunmail at night between High Raise and Calf Crag and lost some time there. Although Chris had organised some help for the night section over Helvellyn, I had had enough and called it a day. Somebody should have said, no, you must go on because you can do 63 or something. I regret that to this day.' However, in 1990 Howard completed a 58 peaks round, including the BG42. He adds 'I think, and I have discussed this with Billy, that he should have gone for the 72. At the time he thought no-one else could beat Joss's round, but he should have done it, he was capable.'

Pattinson adds a point that illustrates that he and Billy Bland were similar characters. 'Billy did say to me, "why didn't you ask me to support your 65 peaks effort?" I said, "there is no point as you are too quick". I needed to be in control of the pace.'

Until recently I had always assumed that Billy had not ever thought of trying for the maximum peaks record. But he did have a go in 1983, after having become British Champion, as Billy explains. 'Not many folk know this, but I did have a go although I never actually wanted to. I got talked into it by Fred Rogerson and my cousin Chris. I had no thought of wanting to take it off Joss. I went to bed that night to get up for 5a.m. in the morning to go and start at Braithwaite, and I never slept a wink. I didn't want to go. Call it what you like, I didn't want to do it. I had got talked into doing something that I didn't want to do, which didn't happen often. It was real hot day the day before, and I know this sounds like excuses, but me and Chris laid nine cubic metres of concrete in the afternoon in that heat. That didn't do us any good. I was just not firing on that day, physically or mentally. I was in reach of doing it at Broad Crag or Ill Crag, but I didn't want to be there, so I just sat down and said, "that is it, I am not going any further". It was about as near as I was to home then too. I do think that I could have done it if I had wanted to, but I didn't want to. That is silly thinking, actually, and I should have gone for it on another day. That is how I see it. I couldn't give a toss what anyone else thinks. Similarly, if anyone wanted me to go out to Spain to race, well no I didn't want to go.'

Howard Pattinson was not the only person that thought Billy should have gone for the extended round. Joss Naylor thought so too. In an interview with Andy Hyslop in *Climber and Rambler* Magazine in March 1983, Joss had this to say about the possibility of it happening. 'Well, given the right day I think Billy could go well – adding a few onto the 72 peaks record. He knows where his weaknesses are, he's got to have plenty of food, and I hope he does it. *You wouldn't feel any remorse if he took the record from you?* Not at all, because he'll have to work hard to do it and on the day he'll suffer. I paced him from Wasdale when he did the Bob Graham Round in 13 hours and he was going well that day.'

With all that in mind I asked Billy what he felt about people trying to do a double Bob Graham. He expressed a pretty clear view on the matter, and perhaps not the view you might expect from such an accomplished athlete. 'Personally, I think they have a screw loose [*laughs*]. There are a few people who have absolutely bottomed themselves, Steve Birkinshaw is one, nice lad that he is, but he suffered after his Wainwrights effort. We have talked about this, and I think he went too far with himself. Then there was Roger Baumeister who was first to do a double BG, but he had problems in his head after that. I'll say this about winter Bob Graham's as well, I think that is stupid. Bravado, call it what you will. It is not common sense as far as I am concerned.'

Another fact that may not be so well known is how many times Billy has helped others out on their Bob Graham Rounds. The first significant support role that Billy played was on his brother Stuart's round. This was a month later than Billy's 13:53 record round, in August 1982.

Billy recalls Stuart's round and how he too had a Naylor shake done to him. 'Joss had done the shake to me [*on my round*], and I don't know whether it is so much the shake as someone showing concern over you. Because you do, when you are buggered you withdraw into yourself. I never considered myself buggered on my round, but I think Joss was quite anxious about me at the time. So, we did a shake on Stuart, but really what he wanted was a pep talk. He did the same as I did at Honister, he ran out of petrol coming down off Scafell. But in the end he was just an hour and 3 minutes slower than me.'

Kenny Stuart repeated his pacing of the first leg of Stuart's round, and agreed he was going really well early on. 'He was a very strong lad was Stuart Bland', says Kenny Stuart, 'but not in the same class as Billy. Racing class I mean. The most talent Bland (as a runner) was Gavin. I think he could have broken the Bob Graham Round record.'

Gavin did think about doing a fast round at one point but explains why he didn't. 'It is a long way is the Bob Graham. When we were at our best it just wasn't popular. It was after Askwith's book that it really went up in popularity. Jonny Bland has never done the Bob Graham. The day that Billy and I walked it Jonny did the first leg with us (to Honister) and I bet he still wishes he had carried on with us that day just to do it.'

After coming third in the Borrowdale race earlier in that summer Stuart Bland had been heard to say about the BGR, 'I know I can do 16 hours...'. Tony Cresswell takes up the story of Stuart's round, in a piece in the *Fellrunner:*

> I got up to see Stuart off from Keswick. Kenny Stuart went along as he had done for Billy, but in August it was still dark [*at the start*]. Pete Barron and Ian Charlton went on from Threlkeld, again as for Billy. I couldn't make Dunmail again (jobs have uses!) and this time I dashed down Borrowdale and up Grains to Esk Hause, electing to wait on Esk Pike. This was a grand day and views were extensive and the approaching runners were spotted on Bowfell. Billy and David Bland, with John Gibbison, were with Stuart but the regularity of Stuart's drinks hinted towards a slowing. The pace was very swift, and Billy confirmed that at the time Stuart was well up with his own times. Stuart was reluctant to eat and sensed a fading, and after a drier and easier Broad Stand we dropped off Scafell. Part way down Stuart lay down and Billy saw his chance to try the 'Naylor shake' – a delightful little remedy performed by the said bod on Billy when he wavered on Yewbarrow. It was as much as I could do to obey instructions, but with Billy holding his arms and me his legs we picked him up and shook the living daylights out of him. Gripping a Mars bar between his teeth for anaesthetic, poor Stu was shaken like a rag doll between two guard dogs.
>
> It worked though; his eyes were all over his head, but on we all trooped to Wasdale! It was during this time that Stuart lost that bit of time that made the difference

> between his and Billy's rounds. Off went the pair of them up Yewbarrow with Billy giving, shall we say, words of encouragement. I had feared it might all end in a punch-up on Pillar, but Joss turned up and set off in pursuit as umpire. In true Bland style, Stuart got better as time went on and blazed into Keswick to record 14:56. While slightly overshadowed by Billy's effort, it ought to be remembered that this was a 'first time' effort and in as much was a voyage into the unknown.

Before detailing some other support roles on rounds Billy Bland reflected on the ethos of supporting others. 'Whoever you have helped, you seem to get sucked in,' is how Billy puts it. 'If you do Dunmail to Wasdale with someone you quite often go to Keswick to see them finish. It is usually an enjoyable thing to do. Ralph Stephenson was a joiner and he said he couldn't do it. I told him he could, it's not that difficult. But you can't just step off the street and do it, you have to prepare yourself. He did it too, in 1983.'

Billy also helped on Gillian Wilkinson's round in 1986. 'They [Dave and Gillian Wilkinson] helped us set up Borrowdale Fellrunners. I did hers and quite a few other BGR supports. Ann was often supporting as well.'

In 1986 Joss Naylor did his complete traverse of the Wainwrights (in 7 days). Billy Bland was one of his pacers on Day 7, which Joss described in the booklet, *Joss Naylor MBE was here*:

> I was to be accompanied on this next section by one of Britain's best ever fell runners, Billy Bland from Borrowdale. Here's a man who'll give you a straight answer, we've had some mighty tussles in fell races

> and this is the man who I believe may well go on to capture some fell endurance records; that is unless his new found success at golf doesn't get in the way of his training.
>
> Billy and I chatted almost non-stop, he pointed out places of interest, places he'd known since a lad, and me every now and again commenting that I'd been through this section during a fell race in the 60s or 70s.

Billy Bland also supported Joss Naylor on his 60 (peaks) at 60 (years old) challenge in 1996, as he recalls. 'I had been asked to go to the top of Glaramara and he said what time he would be coming along. I went about 50 minutes early to be sure. I am never late for owt. I waited a bit and could see the filming helicopter hovering above Esk Hause. I realised he had been and gone. He was going too bloody fast again. So, I legged it as fast as I could with a sack on my back. I caught him up down the Corridor Route. I went on to Gable with him and told him he was going too fast too early. Joss said, "d'you think so?". He was tired by the end after that pace he had set. Same old Joss.' He says it was just a case of turning up because he had been asked.

When we were talking about supporting others Billy launched into a story about a round where he didn't get on so well with the contender. 'A dentist was doing a round; our David was pacing early on and Stuart and I were going on from Dunmail to do leg 3. He came in there and he was on a 23-hour schedule and he had already lost three quarters of an hour. He was posing about at Dunmail with a camera and all that, and had also been doing so farther back, and David had just been letting him. I said to Stuart, "we are wasting our time here". I gave the dentist a lecture, saying, "put that camera away now, because if you want to do this Bob Graham Round you had better start hitting your times or we will be garn yam from t'Esk Hause, cos you are not going to waste our time as well as your own." He made a reference in his report to my parentage. He wouldn't speak to me for a bit, but he came around eventually.'

Billy also helped Scoffer [Schofield] on his round, in 2003. 'I can't remember which bit I had helped him on, but I went back to Newlands Church and on a bit to meet him. He did just over 17 hours by a minute or two. He says to me, "I could bawl [*cry*]". He had bottomed himself.'

In 2005 Boff Whalley decided to do the Bob Graham Round. Not because of the challenge, but mainly because of the history and culture of it. Boff relayed the story to me. 'I thought, OK I don't do that long distance stuff really, but it is really important that I did it. I did a bit more long training and reconnoitred it all, and had people helping me. On the last leg Gary [Devine] was going to do it but couldn't because he was ill. He said he would find someone, but I was worried. Anyway, for the last leg Billy and Gavin Bland turned up saying, "Scoffer told us we had to come here". Networking. Beautiful. I know Gavin a bit and towards the end he was saying "you could put a sprint on and get under 23 hours". I said, "look, I'm not interested I am just enjoying it, inside 24 hours is fine". I was happy with that.'

Gavin Bland calls it the nicest night there has ever been in the Lake District. Some claim! But he explains. 'You could see the Isle of Man, you could see North Wales. "Boff, it doesn't get any better than this", I said to him.'

On me mentioning him supporting Boff Whalley, Billy adds, 'it was nothing really. I just went from Honister back to Keswick with him and Gavin. Scoff was doing the arranging.'

Tony Cresswell mentioned that he did a support for Clare Regan in 2007. He talked her into going anti-clockwise. 'Everyone in the early days did it anticlockwise. I still advocate that. Clockwise is not the right way.' He also got Billy Bland involved. 'I said to Billy, "what you doing on Saturday night? Get your arse over Dunmail for us and have a wander round the Helvellyn range will you". He says, "have I got to?" Clare wasn't very confident, but she was not too knackered and was on schedule – aiming for 23:10 or something. I introduced her to her pacers at Dunmail, saying, "and this is Billy Bland". She suddenly got another mile an hour out of herself. It made a massive impact on her. She was well good enough to do it anyway, but thinking she had Billy Bland out there spurred her on and absolutely made her day.'

Billy remembers it but plays down his influence. 'I wouldn't know about that. I just turned up to help somebody. Actually, I think she was at Market Square when Kilian Jornet finished and asked me to sign summat. I might be wrong.'

Billy and Gavin turning up to support Boff Whalley, his pleasure in doing it just as he wanted, and the effect on Clare Regan of Billy coming out, both nicely illustrate the unique challenge that is the Bob Graham Round.

THIS HARD LAND

Billy Bland continued to compete through the latter part of the 1980s, extending his active career until the mid-1990s. In 1987 Billy Bland was still trying to compete in the championships but finding it harder to mount a real challenge. The British championship at this time consisted of six races, two each in the Long, Medium and Short categories, with the runner's best four counting, provided they included one from each of the three categories.

Billy started off 1987 with his traditional season-opener, at Chew Valley, on a very claggy day. It was so bad that the checkpoint marshals had trouble locating their stations. According to the race report, 'the spirit of the fells was well demonstrated by the runners on their way down from the marshal-less Featherbed. They sped down tight-lipped, with no intention of giving the game away to the poor souls slogging their way up.' The finish was exceptionally tight, with Malcolm Patterson beating Bob Ashworth by one second, with Billy Bland a further second down. Apparently, Billy had been heard to say on the start line that he really wanted to win that day.

Billy raced hard in the early season, but without any major successes. He came fifth in the Blisco Dash, won Coniston, came seventh at Ben Lomond, and then sixth at Buttermere Sailbeck.

He hit top form in late May and early June, winning his next four races. It was poor weather at Fairfield, but Billy won quite convincingly, giving notice of his abilities being undiminished as he approached 40 years old. He then won at Jura, and won Duddon, followed by a near five-minute win against a strong field at Ennerdale.

Colin Donnelly was now breaking course records for fun. At Y Garn he took the record by 2 minutes, with Billy coming in eighth, and then at the Moffat Chase Donnelly set another record, beating in-form Rod Pilbeam and Billy Bland. In chatting with Allan Greenwood he recalled something that Jack Maitland had once told him. He (Maitland) and Colin Donnelly were up with the leading runners on the climb that day. As Jack passed Colin – the runners being bent over on the steep ascent – Jack dropped his shorts and mooned at him! Apparently, Colin had done the same to Jack at some point before then.

Normal service was resumed at Wasdale, where Billy won for the eighth consecutive time; and Borrowdale (his ninth win there, this time by over 20 minutes, having just become a Vet to boot). Billy's next race was at Latrigg, where he came a close second behind Robin Bergstrand. Billy won his next two long events, at the Arrochar Alps and the Mountain Trial, held in clear weather from Grasmere.

On 26 September the Cumberland Fell Runners Association held an 'International race' up and down Scafell, with teams attending from all the home countries, plus Italy, France and Belgium. Although more used to uphill only mountain races, Italy's Battista Scanzi beat Colin Donnelly by over a minute. In a class field, Billy Bland came in twelth, and was easily first Vet.

A week later Billy was running for Keswick AC in the Ian Hodgson Relay, where rain and poor visibility made good navigation crucial. Billy was paired with Rod Pilbeam on the last leg, setting a new leg record as they brought the team home some six minutes clear of Rossendale Harriers, with Kendal third. Billy then finished off his season with his fifth win at Langdale. Bob Ashworth, Malcolm Patterson, Bob Whitfield and Billy were in contention throughout, with Whitfield and Bland pulling away across Crinkle Crags, before Billy topped Blisco first to eventually win by just over a minute.

At the season's end Billy Bland had won seven races, out of the 16 competed in, and he came fourth in the British Championships, well behind a rampant Colin Donnelly. His only championship race win though was Ennerdale, but he ran consistently across the board all season.

The scoring system for the British Championships changed yet again in 1988. Now there were nine nominated races, three in each category, with which you scored your six best, provided there were two from each category. This was moving back to the harder system at the beginning of the 1980s. Billy Bland ran a large number of races during the year, but with just one champs counter to spare, dropping his eleventh place at the Buckden Pike 'Short' race.

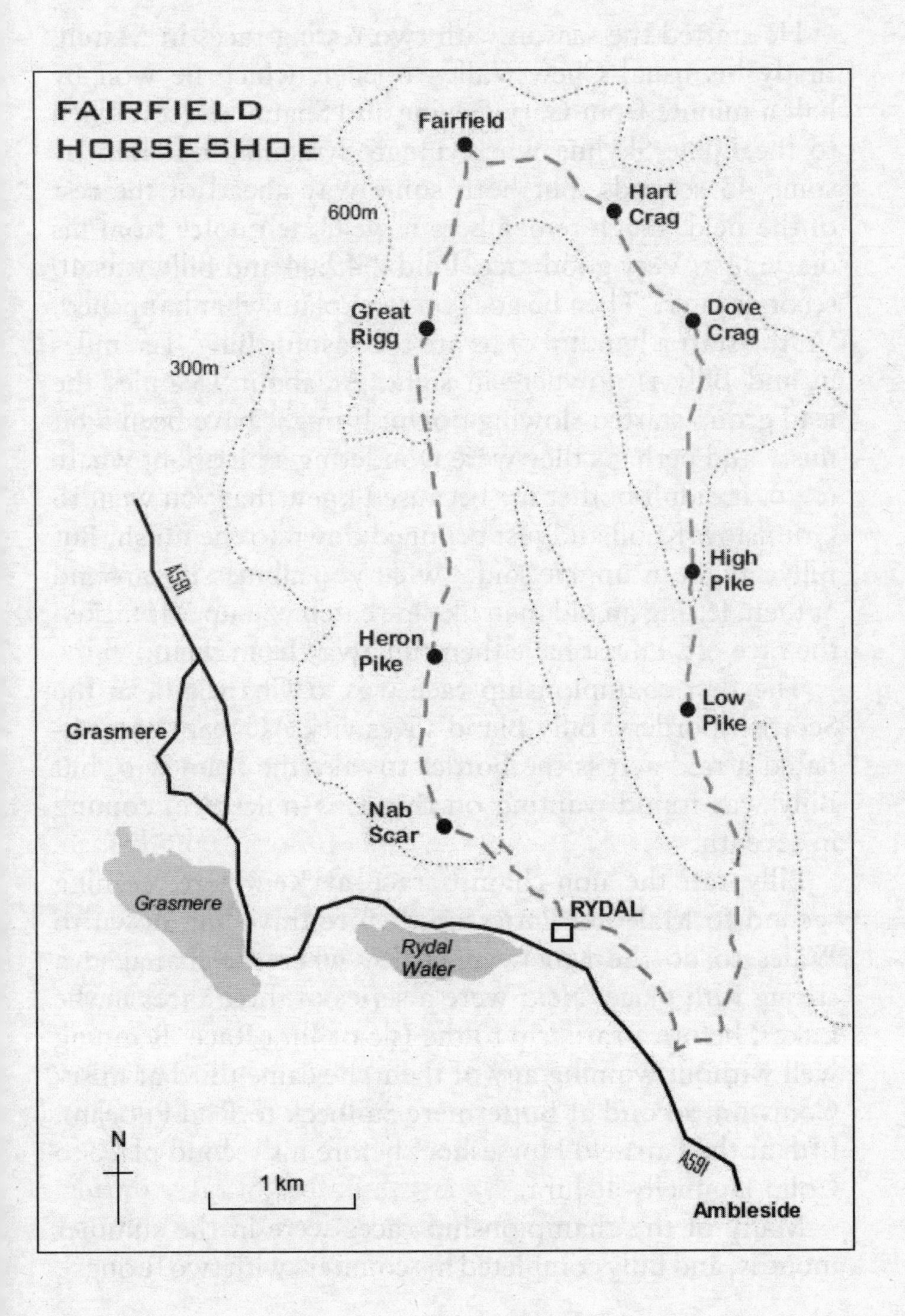
FAIRFIELD
HORSESHOE
Fairfield
Hart Crag
600m
Great Rigg
Dove Crag
300m
A591
High Pike
Heron Pike
Grasmere
Low Pike
Nab Scar
RYDAL
Grasmere
Rydal Water
A591
N
1 km
Ambleside

He started the season with two testing races in March, firstly his usual Chew Valley opener, which he won by half a minute from Gary Devine and Shaun Livesey. Then to the Edale Skyline where Hugh Symonds beat him by some 45 seconds, but both some way ahead of the rest of the field. Hugh remembers it well. He quotes from his diary: '1st. Very good race. I did 2:49:04 and Billy was 40 seconds later.' Then he goes on to explain what happened. 'At the start a handful of us are too fast for Billy. Ten miles in and Billy is nowhere in sight. At about 15 miles the lead group started slowing down. It might have been a bit misty and perhaps they were wondering a bit about where to go. It didn't bother me because I knew that you went to Grindslow Knoll and just dropped down to the finish. But Billy caught us up. He said, "what you all messing around at then, letting an old man like me catch you up." It kicked the race off. I must have then run away from them.'

The first championship race was at Chapelgill, in the Scottish Borders. Billy Bland's Keswick AC team co-ordinated a raid across the border to take the team win, but Billy was found wanting on this 1.75-mile race, coming in seventh.

Billy ran the non-champs race at Kentmere, coming second to Malcolm Patterson, before travelling down to Wales to do the Moelwyn Peaks, where he managed a strong fifth place. Next were a series of three races in the Lakes, before a rare trip to the Isle of Jura Race. Running well without winning any of them, he came third at misty Coniston, second at Buttermere Sailbeck to Rod Pilbeam, fifth at the Fairfield Horseshoe, before his second place to Colin Donnelly at Jura.

Many of the championship races were in the summer months, and Billy completed his counters with two 'Longs', two more 'Shorts', and another 'Medium'. Firstly, he ran the 20-mile Duddon race, which he always liked. He came second to Shaun Livesey, but ahead of a large and stellar field, which included many of the contenders for the title, including Colin Donnelly, who was third. A week later Billy was third to Hugh Symonds at Ennerdale. Buckden Pike was not going to be a good one for him, and so it proved, as he came in eleventh.

Things perked up on the familiar territory of the Wasdale race, which he won for the ninth successive time, and became the first Vet to win the event. The race report, by Danny Hughes, had an intriguing comment about these two facts. 'Sadly, it looks unlikely that he will surpass Joss' nine successive victories in the Ennerdale Horseshoe since he announced to me, in very convincing terms, that he would definitely retire at the end of the season.' Hughes added, 'However, have we another Keswick runner with potential to take over his mantle? Mike Fanning's position as runner-up in both the Ennerdale and Wasdale suggest big things for his future in long distance events.' On being shown this comment Billy confirms, 'that will be right as Joss never won it as a Vet. I certainly won it as a Vet. I had won it nine times in a row. I felt that nine was enough for anybody, and the fire was going out.'

With hindsight, I can report that Billy did not win Wasdale again, but also that he had another four very good seasons on the fells to come yet. Although Mike Fanning was a very good runner, he sadly didn't live up to the hype from Hughes either, as Billy explains.

'The hype was right for Mike Fanning. I have run with him and I knew he was good. He came here one night and wanted to train with us. We went to the Pike and back and as soon as we left here it was a bloody race. Nobody said anything but I knew what was going on. This was like ten days before the Borrowdale race. He had been telling folk he was going to win it. He had come to nail me down that night, and he didn't. I had to wait for him coming down Langstrath. I think we had done 1:47 from here to the top of Scafell Pike. In the Borrowdale race we both come up the lane together and I said, "you young bugger, but I know when I beat you. It was the other night when you came training". He was a good runner, but he went to college, where he struggled for a bit. He is a judge now! College life finished him as a runner though. Back then he was ready to knock me off my perch like I knocked Naylor off his. I remember saying to Fanning get it in sharpish as Gavin Bland will nail you soon enough.'

On 30 July Billy travelled up to run Melantee, but could only secure an eighth place this time, before competing in his last championship race of the year at Gunson Knott in mid-August. Here he had a race-long tussle with Colin Donnelly and Gary Devine, before having to give best to them both. Somewhat bizarrely, there was a tug-or-war contest after the race, in which two teams of fell runners made it to the semi-final to decide who met what *The Fellrunner* reported as the 'semi-professional Dungeon Ghyll bouncers, six blokes who would have fared well in the prize bull contest earlier in the day in the final.' The report concluded that, 'Pudsey and Bramley huffed and puffed, and all fell down into sticky mud; and the Assorted Fellrunners team tugged their way into the final. Both teams sat on the floor, eyes rolling and chests heaving.'

Not expecting a 'yes', I asked Billy if he was in that tug-of-war team, as I really couldn't imagine it. Quick as a flash, he was back with confirmation that he was. 'I can't remember who was in the team. It obviously wasn't so bad though. If you can hold that rope and hold them for a while, then fatigue will get fat 'uns before it gets fit 'uns wont it? We lost the final but whatever. I was determined, and I was a building worker. I wasn't heavy but I'd be stronger than a lot of fell racers because of the work I did. We had tugs-of-war at the Borrowdale Show sometimes.' This got me thinking about his power to weight ratio, and whether he would have made a good rock climber. He says it is not something he took a fancy to – claiming he wasn't strong enough in the arms. Ann adds that, 'Stuart and Billy used to regularly take sheep off crags when they got stuck. They had no fear of heights.'

In the middle of this run of races for points in the title race Billy ran into a third place at Ennerdale, behind Andy Styan and the aforementioned young Mike Fanning. Two days before Melantee Billy came second to Gary Devine in the Rydal Round. One week later Billy Bland got his revenge over Mike Fanning, beating him by over a minute at Borrowdale, his tenth win there. Fanning was now being called Billy's protege. Billy adds, 'he used to come here a lot for a chat when he was a teenager. I was happy to help him, or anybody for that matter.'

Bland had four more races that season, but no more victories. In September he came third in the Mountain Trial, and second at Dale Head. Having beaten Bland by one place at the Mountain Trial Mike Fanning was full of confidence, leading Billy off the Dale Head summit and just taking the win despite almost being caught by Billy with his lightning descent over his home ground. Bland finished with another weekend race double – second at Langdale to Bob Whitfield, followed the next day with a third place at the short and sharp Butter Crag race.

Despite only winning three races, Billy Bland had a

good year and took third place in the championships, behind Colin Donnelly and Shaun Livesey. At the awards he took home four individual trophies – second in the English Champs, third in British, and vet 40 winner in both – and two team trophies with Keswick in the British and English champs. Not a bad haul for a guy who had retired.

In 1989 Billy Bland competed in just one race on the fells. This was on 28 May at Saddleworth, where he finished outside the top twenty. This was because he had to have a hernia operation eleven weeks before the Mount Cameroon Race of Hope. This was held in January 1989 and is described elsewhere in this book.

For 1990 Billy Bland was back on the racing scene, although not challenging for the champs, entering no British Champs races, and only two in the English Champs. His first race was not until May when he came eighth in the Buttermere Sailbeck race. Danny Hughes ruefully remarked that, 'the once mighty Keswick were reduced to relying on their still strong but inevitably fading veterans [Dave] Spedding and Bland, who as well as being second and third counters for their club, were first two veterans home'. Billy comments that although that was not long before the start of Borrowdale Fellrunners it was not really the catalyst.

Billy still enjoyed trips to Scotland to race, coming third at the Isle of Jura Race, before winning Blencathra on 5 June. He bettered the Vets record by five minutes, and sportingly refused the Vets prize as he had won the race outright. Ann adds that, 'it is Billy's view that if you win something you deserve the prize. He must have been in a good mood that day!' I speculated that it must have been one of his best Vets performances. An irate 'no' came back, as he charged through some Vets records he had set. 'Compared to a 2:41 in Borrowdale, come on! How many can beat that nowadays. I set a Vets record at Wasdale in 3:30 something, and I'll have got the Ennerdale Vets record, without a doubt. What about Jura, even with not liking the long run in to the finish on the road, that is possibly a Vets record too.' A check in the book about the Jura race shows his best Vets time was 3:09:36 in 1988, and none faster by anyone else as a Vet according to the website results.

There were very strong winds for the 25th Skiddaw race in July, which was an English Champs race and a selection race for the World Cup team, so a top quality field. Billy could only manage fifteenth and second Vet in a race he hadn't run for 10 years. In August Billy was fourth at Borrowdale.

Gavin Bland reckons he should have won that race, as he explains. 'We start clipping sheep in July. In the lead up to Borrowdale, if it is a late Borrowdale (like the second week, which is as late as it can be), we would have finished, and I would be recovered from clipping. This time I went up Borrowdale beforehand looking at bits of the course with Billy and was goosed, and even more goosed when I got back. Billy said, "you need to start off steady, don't go off trying to win. Try to get round your first one". I think I was about twenty-second on Scafell Pike, but that might be completely made up. But I was with Bob Ashworth and we passed Billy going into Honister. Mark Rigby won the race and I came second. I still to this day think that if I had set off to win then I would have won. I did win it in 1991, 1992 and 1993. And should have every time for the next twenty years if you ask Billy!' Gavin certainly seriously mis-remembered how far down the field he was.

The lowest he was at any point was fifth, but he did pull through to take Billy Bland and Bob Ashworth later on.

Billy comments, 'I did say run within yourself because you will not win it. I may have said he wouldn't beat me, never mind everyone else.' They laughed about that one afterwards he says. Billy admits now that if Gavin had committed to it, he probably would have won it. Ann does point out that Gavin might not have lasted it out if he had gone for it.

Talking through Gavin's early races, we conclude that this was actually the first time he ever beat uncle Billy. 4 August 1990 then, a milestone date. Mark Rigby won the weekend for two at the Scafell Hotel, commenting that it was hard fought win. 'I just couldn't let up. I had to run the last climb up Dale Head, because I knew they [Gavin and Billy] were helping each other.'

Billy was then seventh at Gategill (in a race won by Gavin, who according to the report was 'beginning to show authority at the front of a fell running field'), and second at Gunson Knott (to Mike Fanning). Four races were packed into September, starting with second Vet, but outside the top ten at Hades Hill; and followed by a comprehensive win at the Mountain Trial, held in the Duddon Valley. Towards the end of the month Billy came fourth at his local Dale Head race, receiving no mercy in race organiser Ann Bland's report, being referred to as 'the old crock.'

A week later Billy was third at Scafell. Despite leading at the summit, he was beaten by Ian Holmes and Mike Fanning. Billy's only comment was, 'I was first at the top? Must have been misty and they all got lost.' The report in *Up and Down* magazine describes how the race unfolded. 'Steve Hicks led to Lingmell, but over the rocks

Billy Bland showed the way off, with Fanning and Holmes content to play the waiting game. Back across Lingmell the race was on with the comparative youngsters taking advantage of Billy's supposedly weak ankles.' Here were signs of the body weakening. Those ankles have become more problematic later in life.

On 7 October Keswick put out a strong team for the popular Ian Hodgson Relay, and they were led to victory on leg four by Billy Bland and young James Bulman, as they stretched out to win by just over three minutes. They ran the fastest leg four in the process. Billy thought that was the best event of the year. 'I used to love it, and I told the Hodgson family that. It is a great team event. James Bulman was going a bit wild, but was a good lad basically.'

Billy finished his season by taking first Vets place, for eleventh overall at Langdale. He also enjoyed seeing his young nephew Gavin take first place, a minute ahead of Ian Holmes. It was a strange season really. Despite only completing two races in the best four from six English Championships, Billy managed to finish eleventh Senior and third Vet. If you count the relay, he won three times out of fourteen starts.

At the beginning of the 1991 season a shockwave went through the Cumbrian fell running scene, which eventually rippled through the sport. At their committee meeting in February Keswick AC were surprised to receive two resignations, from club secretary Dave Wilkinson and committee member Billy Bland. Subsequently Mike Fanning, James Bulman, Ann Bland and Gavin Bland also joined the ranks of those leaving the club.

It was said to be about competition and the future direction of the club, as Billy notes: 'We had some good runners at Keswick, but they had started to look at the international scene rather than turning out for the club. I was for turning out for everything. Some club members were not playing their part in the club teams.'

Because of the resignations the club held a well-attended EGM, at which a vote of confidence was given to the remaining committee. After the vote, club chairman Pete Skelton commented, 'The feeling is that we were very sorry to lose all these members, especially Billy and Dave, who have given sterling service in their club posts and in fell running generally. They would all be welcome back at any time, no matter what the outcome of their resignations.' Gavin Bland bravely attended that meeting and was assured that when the new club folded, he would be welcome back at the Keswick club.

Soon the breakaways applied to the Northern Counties AAA and the FRA to affiliate a new club, named Borrowdale Fellrunners. There were stories that this new club would only be accepting members by invitation from Billy Bland.

Billy Bland strongly denies this, stating that he didn't leave Keswick to start another club. 'But a week later I thought, well I am coming to the end of my running days so why not start a club up here. I spoke to one or two, and Dave Wilkinson would be one of them, and we decided to start Borrowdale Fellrunners. We had no money at the start of the new club and we threw in £50 each. I happened to meet Miles Jessop when I was out on a run a week or so after I had left Keswick. Miles was a life member at Keswick and ran the Scafell Hotel. I happened to say to him what our situation was, and nowt was said. A few days later he knocked on the door and gave us £500. It did cause a bit of trouble, although it shouldn't have. There were some when the club started that put rumours about and causing a bit of mischief. It was said that we were just starting a club by invitation only, and it never was that. They [*the FRA*] banned us from competing as a club for 2 years, which was way outside what they could do I think.' It was actually only a one-year ban in the end.

This discussion leads Billy off on a tangent, and he disappears for a moment to come back with a Borrowdale Fellrunners t-shirt with a graphic on the front. Billy then dives into a story about cuckoos and spring, and a Borrowdale myth. If you are born in Borrowdale, you are a Borrowdale cuckoo. You haven't to be born in a hospital, it must be at home. Here is the myth. When the cuckoo is here it is spring, and back in the day the locals wanted to have an eternal spring. So, they built walls around the valley to keep it in. 'Because of a wall gap the cuckoo got out and there is no eternal spring. It is a load of rubbish but there you have it. It makes Borrowdale folk look like idiots!', chortles Billy. 'The first cuckoo is usually between 22 and 26 April. But it was early this year, it came on the 19th.' Ann adds that there aren't many 'cuckoos' left. The last time a person was actually born in the valley was 12 years ago. 'Our Andrea is 48 and she was the last one before that, because there wasn't time to get to hospital.' Ann herself was born in Carlisle hospital.

Billy then interprets the club t-shirt design of for my benefit. 'When Borrowdale Fellrunners started, they wanted a logo and I was the only person that came up with one. It has an egg, and a bird, and there's a wall gap that the cuckoo flew out of', he explains.

Billy finishes his analysis with a rather sad prediction for the future of the club as we move to the end of the second decade of the 2000s. 'There aren't enough young people in the club these days. If there comes a time when no-one is interested in Borrowdale Fellrunners then it will fall. So be it.' Borrowdale has always been a very informal club. Billy says that was fine by him as in his years in Keswick AC he just did his own thing but liked running in a team. Borrowdale has a committee and a constitution and that is it. The AGM lasts about 15 minutes. In the early days there was just a list of telephone numbers. If anyone fancied a run they'd ring you. Billy had no formal role, and one of the few formal ones was the President, who was Ken Ledward.

An indication of the ethos of the Borrowdale Fellrunners can be gleaned from another of Scoffer's stories. When challenged he admitted it was him that wrote a piece in *The Fellrunner* (in February 2001) entitled *Purple Peril Unmasked*. He profiled leading members of the club, with no holds barred, and put pictures of famous people to represent each of them. I asked him whether Billy Bland had minded being characterised as the Victor Meldrew of the Club. Keeping a straight face, Scoffer responded, 'No, I think he liked it. There was no backlash. I don't think anyone said anything about it. They probably didn't read it!' Ann says, 'Billy didn't see it, but he doesn't mind Scoff calling him Victor, Billy calls Scoff that too. They are quite alike, both a pair of grumpy buggers!'

Gavin Bland gives his thoughts on the Borrowdale club. 'Billy and Dave Wilkinson thought Keswick wasn't what they thought it should be. I didn't fall out with anybody. It was just, "do we all join Borrowdale, and yes we do", and that was that really. It was not about developing the young athletes. It was not being as competitive a club [Keswick] as they could be. I said last year we should just fold now. Keswick are the up and coming club now. It has gone full circle.'

Billy's first race of the year was at Kentmere on 7 April, coming fourth Vet and being identified for the first time as a Borrowdale runner. A week later he was eleventh, and first Vet, at the Grisedale Grind, with Borrowdale unable to count in team events. They would have just beaten Keswick AC if they had.

In May Billy came third at Coniston and was in the strange position of awarding himself the prize, as he had been asked to present the prizes. There seems to have been still been some confusion as strangely he was shown as a Keswick runner, yet James Bulman one place ahead was shown as a Borrowdale athlete. Also in May Billy came ninth at Fairfield (first Vet) and eighth at the shortened Isle of Jura Race (third Vet).

On 1 June Billy Bland won the Duddon race, ten years after setting the course record there. This was also his last win at a Lakeland Classic race. Running pretty much every weekend, he came third at Blencathra, and third at the Coledale Horseshoe, before winning at Royal Dockray. *Up and Down* magazine noted that this was his hundreth race win in its short report on the race.

> On 15th June at the Royal Dockray 17 miler that highly regarded – almost legendary – fell runner Billy Bland scored his 100th career victory. The 43-year-old veteran's winning streak dates back to 1967 when as a 19-year-old guides racer he won the Patterdale race. Billy repeated this the following year but then had to wait another ten years before crossing the finish line first again. Aptly that was at Billy's most local race, the Borrowdale, which he has since won 10 times. The self-employed builder has won every classic except Snowdon, and 9 Wasdales, 8 Mountain Trials, 6

> Duddons and 5 Ennerdales show his prowess in the sport. What's the secret? 'Hard work, training and racing' he says. 'Some of these runners today pamper themselves when it comes to racing.'

So, already in the 1990s Billy was railing against his rivals for their lifestyle choices and for not training hard enough, in his eyes.

Modestly, Billy comments that, 'some [of these wins] might have been in local races that may have not got in *Fellrunner*'. It has been difficult to quantify the exact number of wins he finally had, but nonetheless it is a mightily impressive achievement. He admits it was him that came up with the figure, and that some of them would be races that never got reported. For example, there was the 'Jaws of Borrowdale' race that Billy set up. That race was in February when the weather could be bad. Billy reckons those types of local race were as hard to win as British Championship races at the time.

There followed two low-key races at the Mell Fell Dash and Fellside, where he came third and second respectively, and then an eighth place in his local Borrowdale race, which was both an English and British Championships counter. Billy says he and Bob Whitfield ran together. When they came to the stile near the stepping stones on the run-in together Billy got cramp and, 'he did me by ten seconds', recalls Billy. The report in *Up and Down* magazine noted another member of the Bland family consistently doing their bit for fell running. 'Gavin Bland was untroubled around Green Gable, Brandreth and Dale Head, to be first to take a welcome drink from his grandma. Billy's mum always enjoys aiding the thirsty finishers and has done so ever since the race came about.'

Races now came thick and fast, with a tenth at Sedbergh Hills, and a ninth at Dufton Pike to close off August. In September the Mountain Trial was held from David Bland's farm at the south end of Thirlmere. Billy Bland had his ninth and last win at the Trial, on a course that was (deliberately) notably shorter than previously. Billy's nephew Gavin was becoming a force to be reckoned with and placed fifth that day.

Billy Bland finished his season with a win at the Grisedale Horseshoe, and then an eighth place at the Langdale race, just two behind Gavin Bland. Gavin reads his diary entry for the race and adds a comment on their rivalry in the years he and Billy overlapped. 'Langdale – fast time. Going second. Missed the top of Bow Fell and lost a lot of time. Ran with Billy from the Crinkles, so I was in front of him then. Even then some races he would beat me and some I would win.'

As a footnote the Borrowdale club were eligible for team competitions by now, and they had come third (to Bingley and Ambleside) in the Ian Hodgson Mountain Relay the week beforehand, and incidentally two places ahead of Keswick. The report noted that, 'Borrowdale made a highly creditable debut in the event to take third place with their young "stars" Gavin Bland and James Bulman breaking the 1987 first leg record of Billy Bland and Rod Pilbeam by fifty-six seconds. This was probably the outstanding performance of the day'. According to Billy they could only just raise a team of eight at that time.

Having not done enough counting races in both series, Billy came eighth Vet in the British and fourth Vet in the English championships.

The 1992 season was a bit of quiet one for Billy Bland, in that he entered only one British Champs race, and four from the English Champs. He ran twelve races and won just one. He started the year with a fourteenth place at Benson Knott, a fourth at Black Combe, and seventh at the Edale Skyline, all three times as first Vet. The next two races didn't go that well, with a thirteenth at the Grisedale Grind (and third Vet) and eighteenth at Coniston, which had an especially strong field as it was a championships counter.

In two races in May the Borrowdale Fellrunners team strength was beginning to really show. At Buttermere Sailbeck Ian Holmes won, but Gavin, Jonny and Billy Bland finished in second, fifth and sixth places for an emphatic Borrowdale team win. Three weeks later at Duddon it was even more impressive. Gavin Bland turned Ian Holmes over to win, with Jonny Bland fourth and Billy Bland fifth. On 6 June Billy Bland was fifth Vet at Dollar.

The Borrowdale domination continued throughout June, with James Bulman joining in the fun, coming second to Gavin Bland at Coledale. Billy Bland closed the team in fourth, with CFR's Donald Lee being the only intruder. On 20 June at Royal Dockray it was Gavin first again, with Billy third and Jonny Bland fourth. Kendal's Mark Roberts split them in second. Four days later at Tebay Gavin Bland set a new record, with James Bulman third and Billy Bland fourth. Again, one interloper, Ambleside's Hooson. Being reminded of this Borrowdale team strength Billy commented that, 'there was a picture at Duddon when I was a Vet and there was myself, James Bulman, Gavin Bland and Jonny Bland like mother duck and her ducklings going by'.

Another three days on and Billy partnered Scoffer in the two-man Old County Tops fell race, a tough 35-miler which they won in 6 hours 49 minutes. Billy reckoned they both suffered on a really hot day. 'Scoffer asked me to do it, so I did', recalls Billy. 'I was beating him every time in them days, even though I was getting on a bit. I said, "do you realise what you are taking on" [*to run with me*]. I can only remember the bad bits really. We crossed at Cockley Beck there, and I was picking the lines and he was following. Anyway, climbing up Grey Friar I wasn't going like I wanted to. We got to Coniston Old Man and were coming back and I went legless as we came into the Three Shire Stone. I was walking down the road before you branch off to Blea Tarn. I remember Scoff saying, "are you going to run or not?" We were in the lead with quite a nice cushion. I got summat to eat and by the time we got to the far side of the tarn I was going well and then Scoff bonked, and I had to wait for him a bit. We had a laugh about it as we won. What I had thought would be fairly easy going with Scoff didn't turn out like that.'

The season finished with an eighth place at the Grisedale Horseshoe, now in the V45 category and winning that one handsomely (he was fastest of all the Vets). Finally came the Mountain Trial, this year from the Glaramara Hostel, in Borrowdale. Guessing where the checkpoints will be is what most serious competitors will do once the venue is known. Apparently, Ken Ledward had mentioned to Billy that Greenhole was a favourite campsite of Bill Hunter, one of the planners, and Billy guessed one of the controls would be there. It was. Despite this 'knowledge' and his phenomenal memory for routes and lines in his local area, Billy Bland was bested by his nephew Gavin on this occasion, by some three minutes. This was something of a changing of the guard, as Gavin won the Mountain Trial for the next two years, and Billy competed in it only one more time (without winning). Billy adds, 'well to be honest I expected to be beaten by Gavin that day. He had beaten me before I think. I almost didn't go to that event.' He then listed all the checkpoints on that particular course, showing a facility for remembering the routes of these Mountain Trials in surprising detail.

By 1993 Billy Bland had really lost interest in the championship races as such. But he was still racing regularly, although his positions were beginning to slide down. He started with a fifth Vets placing at Long Mynd. Missing his usual early season testers, he then raced the Buttermere Sailbeck race on 9 May, winning the Vets category, but having four clubmates ahead of him, so not contributing to the team results so strongly now. A week later Billy was third Vet at Moel Eilio.

One month later it was the Coledale Horseshoe which went rather better for him. He managed fourth place, just behind Jonny Bland. Three days later it was the Ennerdale race, which was a championships race, and he won the V45 category but was outside the top ten overall.

Three races in June produced a fourth at Duddon, fifth at Tebay and fourth at Langstrath. Then there was a poor result at Whittle Pike, where he was twenty-seventh and first V45, before moving on to the Wasdale race on 10 July. Here Borrowdale Fellrunners showed complete domination, taking the first four places. Jonny and Billy Bland swapped the lead up until Esk Hause, then Jonny strode home to win in 3:57:31. Mike Fanning came through for second, with Billy third in 4:01:38, ten minutes ahead of Scoffer.

On 17 July Billy Bland went for his last race in Scotland, in a British Champs race at Melantee. He finished second Vet to Ambleside's Hoffe. Back to Borrowdale on 7 August and a crushing Borrowdale Fellrunners team win in their local race, with six out of the first seven finishers. Gavin

Bland won, followed by Simon Booth, Jonny Bland, Billy Bland, Colin Valentine (from Keswick in fifth), Scoffer Schofield and Dave Wilkinson. Billy was running for his team mostly by now (Borrowdale Fellrunners). He says, 'I think I was running between Esk Hause and the top of the Pike and I was catching Jonny and the others. I was just telling Scoffer this as he called in today for a cuppa. I got about a minute and a half off them on the Pike, but then they went away and left us after that, but I'd be 46 years old then, wouldn't I?'

At the end of August Billy Bland came twenty-eighth at Pendleton (and only fourth Vet), then sixth at the Grisedale Horseshoe a week later, before competing in his last Mountain Trial, which happened to be the last sponsored by the Ordnance Survey. It was held from Threlkeld using a course at the Back o'Skiddaw. The race report (for some reason feeling ages were important) noted: 'The first eight included five Borrowdale runners, three of them Blands: Gavin, 21, the winner in 3:55:24; Billy, 46, third; Jonny, 20, eighth. Phil Clark came second in 4:01:31. Gavin's win was the more remarkable as it followed a victory in the Three Shires race the day before.' So, Gavin was not scared of trying tough doubles like his uncle. Billy gives a forthright assessment of Gavin trying that double. 'Yeh and why not. If you think you can't do it then you won't. Gavin was well capable of winning any race at that time.'

Gavin Bland thinks that Three Shires/Mountain Trial double win was possibly as good as it got for him. Again, reading from his diary. 'Three Shires: Won easy. Best run since Ennerdale. Beat a good field. Mountain Trial: back of Skiddaw. Won by six minutes. 3:55.' He then puts it in perspective by adding that on the Saturday before he was fourth at Ben Nevis. 'I was crap. I've never ran as badly.

I was first under 23. But the difference in a week. You don't realise at the time how up and down your results are. When Billy went to run a race you could say Billy will run that time, and the same next year and so on. Whereas a lot of my stuff it was very variable.'

Gavin also says he can remember quite a lot about that Trial, concluding with a thought about a fell legend. 'When I was doing Mountain Trials, I was guaranteed to pass Joss [Naylor] whether he had set out an hour or an hour and a half earlier than me. He was doing them for doing them by then.'

The season finished for Billy at the Black Mountains race on 25 September, the last British Champs race. Reportedly, Billy who was the first veteran, 'jogged around to finish fourteenth overall.' Billy argues that they wanted to field a team and that was why he was there. 'We all went down in a minibus together. On the way back some of them were peeing in bottles because they had been on the beer. I was limping before I set off (in the race). I had pulled a muscle and thought I might not get around. It was tussocky and heathery ground which was awkward. Mike Fanning and Dave Wilkinson were in front of me at a certain point, but the buggers were dropping out so I had to carry on. I was the last counter. I remember Scoffer saying, "come on you old bugger" [*having finished three places ahead of Billy*]. I wasn't jogging, I was doing my best. But I would have happily dropped out if they hadn't.'

Despite a casual approach Billy had garnered enough points throughout the season to finish eighteenth in the British Champs (and second Vet); and third Vet in the English Championships.

Billy Bland was beginning to really wind down and only competed in four races in 1994, the first two both on the same day according to *The Fellrunner* results section (surely an error!). They were Two Riggs, where Billy came fifth, and the Royal Dockray Fell Race, where he was fifth again. Billy has no particular memories of these two, so can't resolve the issue. This last race was part one of a three race Royal Dockray race series. On 2 July Billy was twenty-fifth in the Culter Fell Horseshoe, and then on 17 September sixteenth in the Merrick Hill race.

In 1995 Billy went back to the Two Riggs race in May, coming second Vet, before a gap in the summer and another four races towards the back end of the season. On 13 August he was fifth (first Vet) at Gatesgarth, the race reporter commenting that it was, 'good to see Billy back, look out if he starts training'.

A week later Billy finished third at the Langdale Gala fell race. A month after that he competed in his local race at Dale Head, seeming to want to stay local, coming seventeenth in what turned out to be a loaded field. Billy finished his short season with an excellent second place in the orienteering-style Copeland Chase. Despite hardly racing he was twelth Vet in the British Champs and fifteenth Vet in the English Champs when the points were added up.

Billy competed in no races at in 1996. It has proved difficult to identify Billy Bland's last ever fell race. He says he thinks it was a race he did when he was 50, which would have been 1997. 'It was just a local thing up Fleetwith Pike. A real steep one with about 60 runners in it.' I can find no result for this one. However, Billy ran seven more races in 1998, which are recorded in *The Fellrunner*.

It was a very late start for him, as he came first V50 at the Coledale Horseshoe on 10 June, one place ahead of cousin Anthony Bland. Two weeks later Billy finished second overall in another local race at Langstrath.

Despite doing well in these other races, Billy says he competed in the twenth-fifth running of the Borrowdale race, with himself and Bob Whitfield both running, 'just for old time's sake. I was over 50 years old and knew I wasn't fit and purposely set off slowly, knowing I couldn't last to the end of it well. I found myself too far up at Esk Hause, even when holding back. I think I was about seventeenth.' Finding the results sheets in his folder it confirms he was first V50, with the younger Whitfield nine minutes ahead.

Running well now, Billy came fourth overall at the short Grisedale Grind, behind three other Borrowdale Fellrunners teammates – Gavin Bland, Jonny Bland and Scoffer.

One of his last races was at Buttermere where Billy was attacked by an old bloke. 'A Labrador dog was worrying me, and his owner tried to hit me', he says with a laugh. Somehow it would have seemed an appropriate end to his competitive career. It was just a country fair with a small race attached, held from Gatesgarth Farm. It went up Fleetwith Pike and around by Blackbeck Tarn, Innominate Tarn, round the back of Haystacks, then down Scarth Gap, then cut into Warnscale and finished at the farm. Ann adds that there was a policeman there and he gave the dog owner a telling off. If this is the Gatesgarth fell race on 16 August, then he is being modest by not mentioning that he was outright winner, from Boff Whalley. The report notes that, 'the conditions were atrocious with high winds and driving rain, but these did not deter evergreen Billy Bland who won by over six minutes.' I suspect that is the race that Billy had already mentioned to me as his last ever, only a year later than he thought.

However, there were in fact two more races after

that. On 29 August Billy came third in the Arnison Crag Horseshoe race, part of the Patterdale Dog Day. Finally, on 4 October 1998 there was one last hurrah. Running the third leg in the Hodgson Relay he helped Borrowdale Fellrunners to their fourth successive win in the event. He was 51 years old.

Billy thought that relay was the best event of the year. 'I used to love it, and I told the Hodgson family that. I had my differences with some of them, but I wanted them to know that. It is a great team event.' Fine words to bookend a fabulous running career.

Billy Bland loved the sport. He stopped competing when that love waned.

ACROSS THE BORDER

Billy Bland has always lived in Borrowdale, and loved to race locally throughout his career. However, he frequently ventured afar to take on new, and repeated, race challenges. Some of the races abroad were certainly ones that have gone under the radar when people have talked or written about him. However, the overriding impression is that deep down he remains just a Borrowdale lad.

Billy has lived in three different houses during his lifetime, all of which are within one kilometre of Borrowdale primary school, which he attended as a youngster. This strong attachment to his geographical roots and feeling of locational permanence seems to parallel that which is natural for the local Herdwick sheep. In hill farming parlance they are hefted to the locations they graze, meaning they hold to a place because of a learned sense of belonging.

This attitude carried over into several aspects of Billy Bland's life. He rarely went on holidays, preferred racing in the Lakes to anywhere further abroad, and chose not to get involved in the international mountain racing scene as it opened up in the latter part of his career. Billy Bland is hefted to Borrowdale. But we do need to explore occasions when Billy went abroad, both literally and metaphorically.

His attitude to international running was contrary to an earlier statement he made about the future of fell running. Interviewed after his British Fell Champs win of 1980, Billy was asked what ambitions he then had, and he gave a mixed message in response. He intimated that he'd really like to see some representative honours for fell running, and the possibility of going into Europe to race. He said, 'I'd like it to come, but it'll probably be too late for me anyway. It must come though, and that's something else to aim for. For those who win the Fell Runner of the Year there's nothing further to offer. Generally, though, I just want to take it as it comes and try to improve.'

Having advocated representative honours for fell running, including international competition, he was subsequently selected for his country a few times.

His first international race (at the age of 38) came in the autumn of 1985, on the weekend of the 21 and 22 September, when the first ever World Cup in Mountain Running was held in San Vigilio di Marebbe, Italy. It consisted of a ladies' race, a junior race and long and short races for senior men. England, Scotland and Wales were all represented, with the hosts the strong favourites. In these early days the home nations had varying levels of financial support, with some of the Welsh athletes paying their own way. The weather was searingly hot, with some athletes suffering badly. The senior long race was held on the Sunday, with the other three the day beforehand, allowing some athletes to double up.

The short men's race was an 8.5 kilometre up and down event, which Kenny Stuart won, with England teammates Ray Owen eighth and Shaun Livesey ninth. Scotland's Colin Donnelly was eleventh, with Jack Maitland sixteenth and Jon Broxap seventeenth. The next day Stuart, Maitland, and Donnelly were among those that ran the 'long' course, which was an uphill only 14.6 kilometre race. Running only in this race, Hugh Symonds came fifteenth and Billy Bland a disappointing third England scorer in twenty-fifth. This may seem a poor effort from Billy, but Jon Broxap explains it from his perspective. 'Mountain running and fell running are two different things. But Billy still put his all into it. I don't think Kenny Stuart won a long World Mountain race. The Europeans were long distance mountain race specialists.'

Jack Maitland and Colin Donnelly fared slightly better that day, finishing sixteenth and twenty-fourth respectively. Kenny Stuart recalls, 'yeh, that [*short one*] is the race I trained for and the one I wanted to win really. Being up and down, it was my type of race. I did the long one the following day, which was up only, and my legs were quite stiff and tired. But I ran quite well, actually. No-one else doubled up for England. I don't know why I got that opportunity.' Kenny's wife Pauline chips in, 'it was because you were better than the others! You were the first Englishman by a long way, in fifth place.'

On being reminded of this event, and his result, Billy Bland gave some background in explanation. 'At the

Welsh 1000m Peaks Race two years earlier in 1983, Andy Styan (who was on the selection committee) gave me an envelope at breakfast in the Victoria Hotel to say I had been picked as reserve for an international race as I was 'out of form'. I told him what to do with it. I'd never been a reserve for anything in my life and was not starting now. They weren't happy!' Two years later Billy was 38 and he agreed to go to that 1985 event. 'I looked at the course and it was just up a forest road, not even straight up. To be honest I didn't have the best attitude in the race, though I didn't purposefully run badly. That was as good as I was then, on that course. But I reckon I might have gone well in these Sky races they have now at my best though.'

Having reflected back on it further, Billy adds that after being told in 1983 that he was reserve he told the selectors that they could pick someone else. 'I think Jon Broxap got picked, I hope I have got this right, and I had the hump about him because he was telling them I was not fit. I had maybe had a little bit of time out, but I was pretty fit. They were picking others in front of me and I knew I could beat them anyway.' Jon Broxap says that he has no recollection of that, adding that he wouldn't have been actively working against Billy in the way he suggests.

Billy takes up that Welsh 1000m Peaks Race description, in 1983. 'We were on the first climb in that 1000m race and I saw Mike Short go to one side and take one way up. I was sitting at the back of Broxap and two or three others, and this envelope situation from the morning was in my head! Shorty went off and they didn't follow him. We were going somewhere else and they weren't going fast enough for me. I knew we would nail Shorty somewhere along the line. I remember distinctly saying, "is this a bloody race or what?", to Broxap mostly. Nobody responded. Anyway, I think I won the race. And that was me supposedly not fit. That of course put the selectors against me, and I didn't get picked again till I was 38.' Looking back at the results, Billy was in fact third that day, behind Kenny Stuart and John Wild, but significantly three places ahead of Jon Broxap.

Explaining why he never really ran abroad at other times, Billy had issues with the whole setup. 'I am not a member of the FRA and haven't been for years. I was never happy with the international scene because they weren't real fell races. Apart from that, it was splitting the fell running fraternity up and some of the good 'uns started concentrating on getting picked for the England teams. That is why I like Rob Jebb, as he has supported the local scene, as I did, as well as the international scene. I could see that coming – with athletes I considered not to be fell runners being picked for the team. What I would have liked to see happen was that you only got picked if you followed the fell scene. I had a go at Pete Bland once, calling him a Judas (I get on all right with him now by the way). It was because he was picking non-fell runners. To be fair they were probably better at those types of races abroad. But I think we should have been rewarding our own.'

Dave Hall gives his take on Billy, the FRA and international selection. 'I know he had a massive conflab with the FRA as I was on the committee at one point and we had a heated discussion about him. We used to have really lengthy discussions about selection. Do you select horses for courses, or do you select the best fell runners? I always maintained you selected the best fell runners, that is those running in the championships. But Billy rarely did 'B' or 'C' category races, which were often much more like the

25. At the Three Shires race, 1987

26. Billy Bland and Rod Pilbeam – finishing leg 1 at the Ian Hodgson Relay, 1987

27. Andy 'Scoffer' Schofield at the 3 Peaks race, 1988

28. Billy Bland at the Langdale race, 1990

29. Gavin Bland at the Ian Hodgson Relay, 1991

30. Near the start of the Langdale race in 1991, Billy Bland in eighth place

31. Borrowdale Fellrunners – FRA Team Gold, 1993
[l. to r. Gavin Bland, Billy, Scoffer, Steve Hicks, Simon Booth, Jonny Bland]

32. Billy Bland
– Ian Hodgson Relay, 1995

33. A Mackeson at Wasdale on the BGR record, 1982

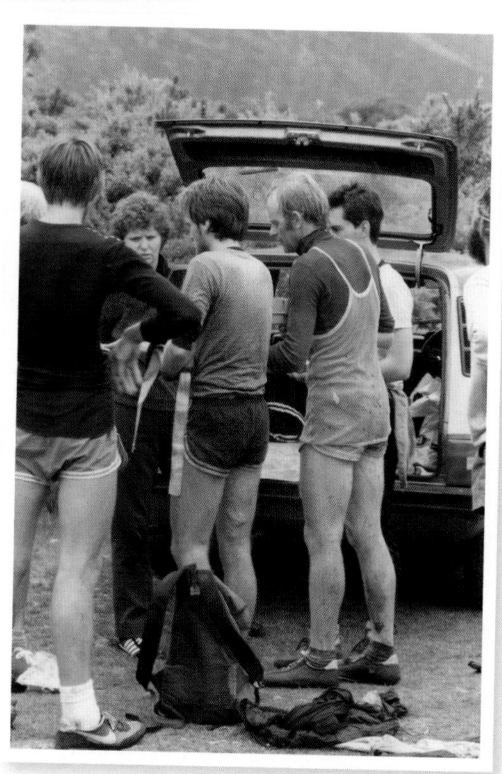

34. Support at Wasdale, BGR record

35. Record Bob Graham Round, 1982, setting off up Kirk Fell with Joss Naylor

36. The run-in, on the road in Newlands Valley on the BGR record

37. Celebrations at the Moot Hall steps on beating the BGR record
[From left: Fred Rogerson, Chris Bland, Pete Barron, Jon Broxap, Stuart Bland, Martin Stone, Billy, David Bland, Joss Naylor]

38. Reflecting on his new BGR record, at the Moot Hall

THE BOB GRAHAM 24 HOUR CLUB

APPLICATION FOR THE RATIFICATION OF A CLOCKWISE CIRCUIT ATTEMPT

BY:- NAME William Bland AGE 34 CLUB Keswick A.C.

ADDRESS 7, Mountain View, Borrowdale, Keswick

DATE OF ATTEMPT 19th June 82

1st SECTION KESWICK - THRELKELD

Assisted by:- Ken Stuart

	KESWICK	DEPART	5.00 A.M
1	SKIDDAW	ARRIVE	5.53
2	GREAT CALVA	ARRIVE	6.20
3	BLENCATHRA	ARRIVE	6.59
	THRELKELD	ARRIVE	7.13

2nd SECTION THRELKELD - DUNMAIL

Assisted on the fells by:- Pete Barron & Ian Charlton.

	THRELKELD	DEPART	7.16
4	CLOUGH HEAD	ARRIVE	7.53
5	GREAT DODD	ARRIVE	8.13
6	WATSON DODD	ARRIVE	8.18
7	STYBARROW DODD	ARRIVE	8.26
8	RAISE	ARRIVE	8.37
9	WHITE SIDE	ARRIVE	8.43
10	HELVELLYN LOW MAN	ARRIVE	8.52
	HELVELLYN	ARRIVE	8.55
12	NETHERMOST PIKE	ARRIVE	9.00
13	DOLLYWAGGON PIKE	ARRIVE	9.08
14	FAIRFIELD	ARRIVE	9.32
15	SEAT SANDAL	ARRIVE	9.46
	DUNMAIL	ARRIVE	9.57

3rd SECTION DUNMAIL - WASDALE

Assisted on the fells by:- Jon Broxap & Stuart Bland

	DUNMAIL	DEPART	10.00
16	STEEL FELL	ARRIVE	10.17
17	CALF CRAG	ARRIVE	10.27
18	HIGH RAISE	ARRIVE	11.01
19	SERGEANT MAN	ARRIVE	10.55
20	THUNACAR KNOTT	ARRIVE	11.10
21	HARRISON STICKLE	ARRIVE	11.14
22	PIKE O' STICKLE	ARRIVE	11.24
23	ROSSETT CRAG	ARRIVE	11.49
24	BOWFELL	ARRIVE	12.13
25	ESK PIKE	ARRIVE	12.26
26	GREAT END	ARRIVE	12.43
27	ILL CRAG	ARRIVE	12.53
28	BROAD CRAG	ARRIVE	12.58
29	SCAFELL PIKE	ARRIVE	1.06
30	SCAFELL	ARRIVE	1.24
	WASDALE	ARRIVE	1.43

4th SECTION WASDALE - HONISTER

Assisted on the fells by:- Joss Naylor. Pete Parkin Martin Stone

	WASDALE	DEPART	1.46
31	YEWBARROW	ARRIVE	2.17
32	RED PIKE	ARRIVE	2.56
33	STEEPLE	ARRIVE	3.06
34	PILLAR	ARRIVE	3.25
35	KIRKFELL	ARRIVE	3.58
36	GREAT GABLE	ARRIVE	4.23
37	GREEN GABLE	ARRIVE	4.30
38	BRANDRETH	ARRIVE	4.38
39	GREY KNOTTS	ARRIVE	4.43
	HONISTER	ARRIVE	4.54

5th SECTION HONISTER - KESWICK

Assisted on the fells by:- S Bland D Bland J Naylor P Barron J Broxap M Stone

	HONISTER	DEPART	5.07
40	DALE HEAD	ARRIVE	5.30
41	HINDSCARTH	ARRIVE	5.41
42	ROBINSON	ARRIVE	5.57
	KESWICK	ARRIVE	6.53

OFFICIAL USE ONLY. TOTALS

SUMMITS:-

REST TIME:-

RUNNING TIME:-

ELAPSED TIME:-

Assisted on the road access points by:-

Chris Bland

An article of up to 500 words on the attempt would be welcome for inclusion in the records.

39. Billy's ratification sheet, with pacers and timings, for the BGR record, 1982

40. Moffat Chase, 1987

41. Ian Hodgson Relay – Billy Bland & Pete Barron, 1988

42. Climbing out from Honister, supporting Boff Whalley's BGR [l. to r. Boff, Mark Whittaker, Billy, Gavin Bland]

43. On his multiple cycle trips up and down Honister Pass in 2014

44. Kenny Stuart, Joss Naylor and Billy Bland share a stage, and a laugh, Brathay 2016

45. Susan Paterson and Billy, bike racing for GB, 2017

46. Encouraging Kilian Jornet on his new record BGR, as he passes through Dunmail Raise, 2018

47. Previous and new BGR record holders on the Moot Hall steps, 2018

continental races, and many other top runners did them for practice. They were often uphill mainly on tracks and had much less descending. Billy didn't help himself there, but I still maintained that he should be selected as he was the best distance runner. They often used to discuss selecting people like Dave Lewis, Nigel Gates or Bob Treadwell. But those guys were never out running the Wasdale race against Billy.'

Danny Hughes was an advocate of international racing and was instrumental in organising some of the events that preceded the formal establishment of an international mountain racing scene. One of these was a three-race event that took place in the Lake District in 1985. In that May there were three races held within one week: the Northern Counties, Butter Crag, and the Fairfield. Billy's memory of the events seemed a little vague when we discussed it.

'I got an England vest for it. The Italians were over, and I had a bad Northern Counties. I was interviewed before that first race, and I said Kenny will win it, but I expected to be higher than the teens. I didn't really want to run Fairfield, and I think Butter Crag was a special one in midweek. Did I run Fairfield? [*He didn't in fact*] I said to Danny Hughes I wasn't gonna run the other ones and went and ran a pro race at the Buttermere Show and won that on the very day I should have been running for England. I couldn't give a toss. I was third counter in one of them anyway.'

The Fellrunner has a short report on the event, reading which makes it sound as if it wasn't as successful as had been hoped. 'The absence of overseas teams for the first two races was disappointing, but the Italians showed their potential in the Fairfield race until the mist put paid to any slim chance they had of winning.' In the first race

(Buttermere/Northern Counties) Kenny Stuart won from Jack Maitland and Mike Short, with Billy Bland in fourteenth. For the second race at Grasmere (Butter Crag) Kenny Stuart won again from Jack Maitland, with Shaun Livesey third, and Billy in sixth. Finally, at Fairfield Kenny completed the triple, from Jack Maitland (second for the third time in a week to him), and Pezzoli of Italy third. Billy Bland doesn't appear in the Fairfield results, so this was presumably when he ran the 'pro' Buttermere race.

As the international scene developed the World Cup became more established, and the fourth version came to England in 1988. The races were held from Keswick, and again organised by Danny Hughes. At one level it was a successful event, with good participation levels in the races: junior, women's, long, and short for the World Cup, together with the Open and Vets races held as part of the event. The editor of *The Fellrunner* noted that, 'the atmosphere and ambience was more in keeping with racing in Switzerland than a genuine fell race but even those sceptical of this sort of event were seen to be watching and enjoying themselves'.

Billy Bland was certainly someone who had reservations, as he didn't like the World Cup being on marked courses, and he fell out with Danny Hughes over that. He also gave his forthright analysis of the event. 'I was a Vet by then. They had put this Vet race on and called it a World thing, which it wasn't. We had to pay way over the odds to run. I remember saying to Danny Hughes that we are just providing money for other international runners, so you can stick your race up your arse, and I didn't run. John Nixon won the race and I would have expected to beat John. I am not saying I would have, because he ran very well that day.' It won't come as much of a surprise to hear that Billy Bland, who was now 41, was out watching that World Cup race in 1988.

He backs up that assessment of his form by adding proudly, 'by then I was just a Vet 40, and in August 1987 I did 2:41:18 at Borrowdale which will be the Vets record for the race. [*Race winner in 2018 – Ricky Lightfoot 2:51*] And then the next year [*the year of the World Trophy*] at 41 I did 2:42:50.'

When that World Cup was held at Keswick, Dave Hall had been all for having it at Coniston as it has everything, including climbing up Wetherlam, ridge running and the great descents. 'They said it was far too rough. The Italians won't do it. Very few foreigners will come. At the time we weren't allowed to flag it but could use human markers. I think the markers were asked to try to get the runners to run slightly different lines.' Chris Brasher was co-opted on to the organising committee for that World Cup, but Dave points out that he could never get on to the FRA committee. 'This was because in those days you had to have done two 'A' category races in a calendar year to be eligible. Brasher had never done that. It didn't matter where you finished or what races, they just had to be 'A' categories.'

Billy argued with Mark Rigby on behalf of the club (Borrowdale) on another occasion. This was at the FRA relays in Scotland one time. Mark Rigby ran for both Westerlands and Ambleside in the same relay. Billy had a real go at Hughes about that. Billy does concede though that Hughes did a lot of good for the sport, and that he was a damn good organiser.

After Billy Bland's period of seeming local invincibility was over, his nephew Gavin Bland was the top man on the fells for a while. Gavin had a much keener interest in international running than his uncle Billy. After his 1990 junior Word Cup success, Gavin Bland also represented England in senior races at the World Mountain Running Trophy in 1991 and 1992. He cites these as possible his finest achievements, commenting that, 'continental races are certainly different. They are flatter and faster and not rough enough really, but I like them. You need to be a good road runner, which is why I often struggle in them.' On hearing this, Billy Bland gave his final word on why he didn't compete in continental hill races. Billy snapped: 'Because I am a fell runner, not a bloody road runner.'

I originally thought that Billy Bland knew the terrain and race routes so well for his local Lakes fell races that it meant he won many of his races there but had rarely done so outside of the Lake District. I thought that he 'didn't travel well', which was how some people saw it. Looking at the results and talking to him, it isn't as simple as that. Of his many race wins throughout his career many were in the Lake District, but about one fifth have been 'abroad' from the Lake District. This was in no small part due to him having a penchant for raids over the Scottish border, for instance four times doing the weekend double of the Melantee race and the Half Nevis. He seemed to relish these double weekend challenges, often attempting a Borrowdale/Latrigg double on a weekend as well.

Billy seemed less enamoured with the racing scene in Lancashire, Yorkshire, the Peak District and Wales though. When we talked about this, he said there was no particular reason for this, and confirmed some of the great performances which he did have across all the normal fell race locations.

One that didn't go so well was what Billy originally said was his first attempt at the Three Peaks Race, in 1977.

The results from that day show Billy finishing in thirty-fourth position in a time of 3:09:20, some 18 minutes behind winner John Calvert. He says that he, 'didn't like the experience, but maybe did go back once. I was just no good at it, it was too runnable in between the peaks for me to do well. Maybe I should have persevered a bit more. I doubt if I would ever have won it. But it was nowt to do with travel.'

Now here is a thing. Billy Bland's recall of detail from specific races has been pretty amazing as we have gone through his career. But here he had something of a blip. His memory of maybe going back, possibly in 1978 or 1979 as he recalled it, is not correct. Some enquiries on social media uncovered the fact that he had in fact run the Three Peaks race the year before that, i.e. in 1976. This was a surprise as he was only just getting into his stride in long races by then, and Ann Bland noted that, 'he didn't win Borrowdale till 1976 and I don't think he would even think of doing Three Peaks till after that.' Then, on being told he had done it earlier, she mischievously added, 'he must have thought he was better than he was!' But run he did in 1976, coming a lowly ninety-first in 3:17:10.

Psychologists describe 'thinking you are better than you are' as being an illusory superiority. Matthew Syed, in his book *The Greatest*, when talking about it, concludes that it, 'is not by any means all bad. When we rate ourselves highly, we tend to become more positive, optimistic and resilient'. As he progressed through his career, Billy Bland certainly developed those three characteristics, and his superiority was anything but illusory when at his peak. People were convinced that they could not beat him.

Eventually we sorted the dates out and it prompted a story from that very first attempt in 1976. 'There is

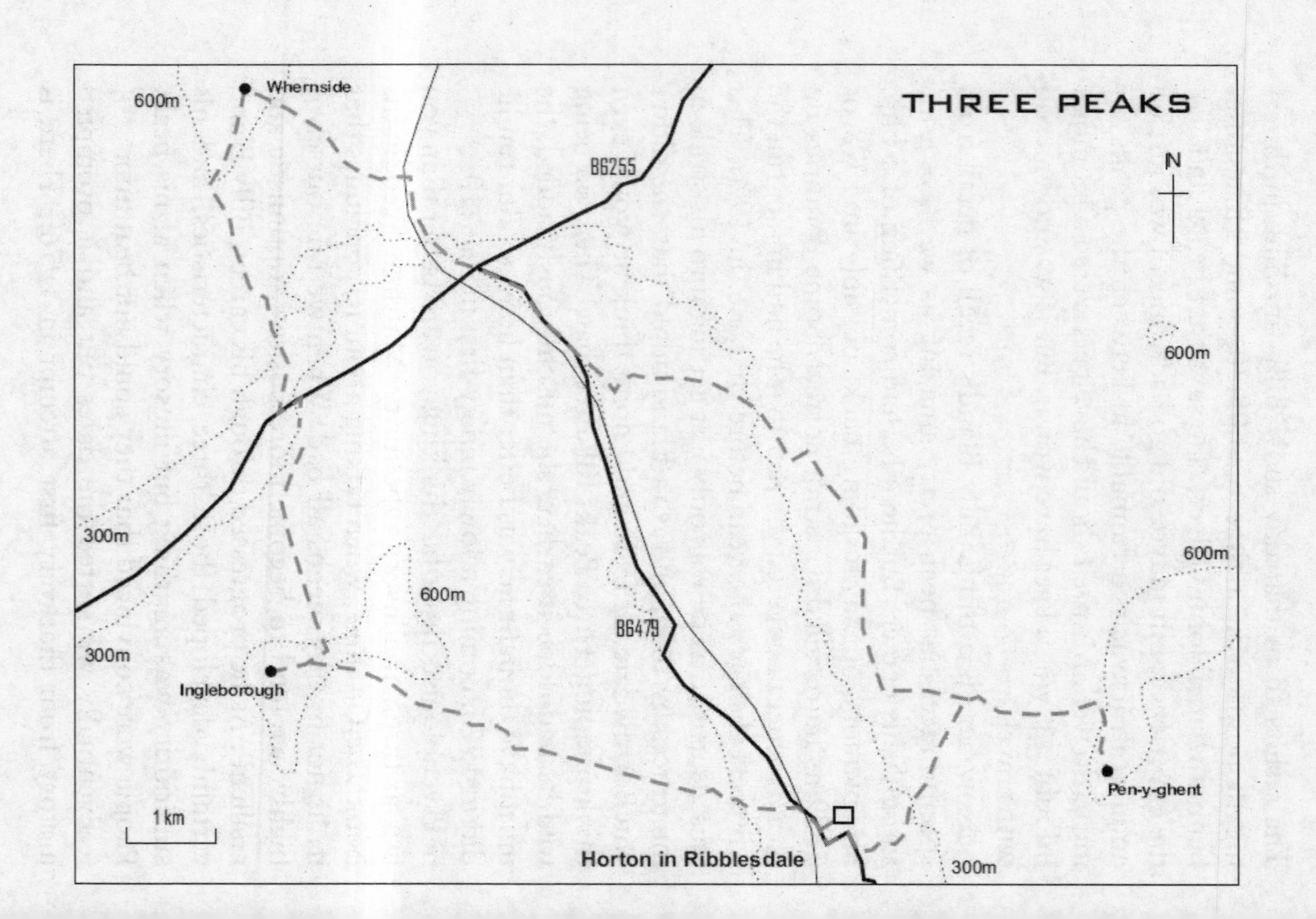
THREE PEAKS
N
Whernside
600m
B6255
600m
300m
600m
300m
600m
Ingleborough
B6479
Pen-y-ghent
1 km
Horton in Ribblesdale
300m

a tale there. I ran myself legless and I was coming off Ingleborough and I tried to cadge some food off walkers but didn't manage it. Then I saw this full orange lying on the ground, slightly split as though someone may have sat on it in a rucksack, or something, and thus wouldn't eat it. I picked it up and ate it all and didn't even peel it. I ate the skin as well! The race distance was fine, but it was too runnable a course at that time. I became a lot better runner after that.'

But this was in April 1976, before he had won a race as an amateur. He was in some sort of liminal space between being a competitor and a winner. This milestone of his first amateur race win didn't come until the Borrowdale race on 9 August 1976.

Billy Bland also had limited success at the Ben Nevis race. He did win the race once, but struggled to repeat the feat, as he explained. 'The Ben should have suited me down to the ground really, apart from the start and finish. It wasn't the flat that beat me it was being legless from what had gone before. Putting too much into getting to the top. When I did win it, I missed Dave Cannon's record by one second. If I had known as I was going around the field, I am sure I would have found a couple of seconds. Despite becoming a lot better runner after that I never ran it in the same time again. This was quite simply because I had become a better runner and thought I could win it, so I was far more competitive going up. I was spending too much petrol going up.'

Billy also ran the Edale, Pendle and Chew Valley races (among others), so made quite a few trips out from Lakes. He adds, 'I went to a Show race at Newcastleton too. I was going to run that and then go back to run Burnsall, just as a bit of an experiment to see how it was to run two races in a day. They were faffing about so much at the first race that I went off to run Burnsall instead.'

He did the Chew Valley race a few times, as he used to try to get in 1,000 miles of running between the first of January and the third week in March each year. 'I knew that Chew Valley would finish that mileage off for me. I remember once going down for the Chew and it was snowy and icy, and the reservoir was all frozen over. We went up the first top, Saddleworth Moor I think it was, and Bob Ashworth had gone clear. Bob could have run me to Manchester that day and I wouldn't have known where I was. I made a habit of using that race as a marker for the season, as it was in March. If I ran well in that I knew I was absolutely setup for the Lakes races because I knew I was fit. You still had to train more, but you knew that the base was in place.'

Billy Bland is rightly proud of some of his race achievement outside of the Lake District. 'I won the Welsh 1000m Peaks, maybe two times I think, it doesn't matter. Winning Ben Nevis, I was pleased with that, as I didn't think I would win. That became a bit of a millstone round my neck as I thought I should have won more [*Bens*] than I did, but that was my fault. Winning the Edale Skyline, because it wasn't my kind of running really being too flat, so I was pleased that I won that.'

Going back to racing abroad, or out of his comfort zone, Billy Bland had three excursions that surprised me when I came across them.

Firstly, in 1989 he ran the Mount Cameroon Race of Hope, coming fourteenth in an event won by Jack Maitland. Billy, by now a Vet, was paid to go, with Guinness sponsoring him. Ironic for a non-drinker, perhaps. Because he had set the Bob Graham record time there was a bit of fuss in the media about him. He says he knew Mike Short had been out to race there, and secretly it hurt that he wasn't getting invited. 'Mike had won the race and he was a god out there. It was certainly an experience.' But Billy had had a hernia operation 11 weeks before he went out there. Not wanting to break an agreement he had gone anyway, knowing that he would be nowhere near his best, and tried his hardest when he got there. Ann points out how much he had got his eyes opened, to see how people lived. Billy remembers landing in Douala and the smell and heat hit just hitting him. 'I couldn't believe the shanty towns. It was a real culture shock. I thought, "what am I doing here?" I was 42 then so I should have been invited long before! Anyway, we stayed in the university and it didn't have any warm water. There were millipedes in the bed, which didn't bother me greatly.' Ann chuckles as she recalls that he spent no money while he was there, apart from buying some oranges. Everything else was paid for.

Secondly, there was the Three Peaks Yacht Race in 1990, where his team was third fastest on the fells, which he calls 'another bloody escapade'. For this event the running distances are massive: 24 miles for Caernarvon to Snowdon, 32 miles Ravenglass to Scafell Pike, 17.5 miles to the summit of Ben Nevis and back, all after spending a good deal of time in a small boat. Billy sets the scene. 'The Derwentwater Boat Club had a fellow called Chris Bownes and he had a yacht that he wanted to enter for the event. He was a Sellafield man, I think. I was working for someone who knew him, so I got asked to be a runner. I offered to get another runner, and I was thinking of Bob Whitfield. We would have been good enough to have won the thing, running-wise. They had a second runner, and he was a road runner, capable of running 51 minutes for

10 miles, like. I said, "I will be no good on the boat. I will be spewing in no time". We went down to Maryport for a go in the boat out in Solway. It got quite choppy and I was over the side right away trying to save my two false front teeth.' He wanted to forget it, but they went anyway. Billy tells of the frustrating time he had with his running partner doing the actual event:

'We went down to Barmouth to the start and it was flat calm within an hour, so we had to get the oars out straight away. Then it turned out our boat wasn't really that good when the wind got up. We got to Caernarvon and you had to run a lot of road before you reach the backside of Snowdon. I had never been up from that way. It soon became clear that this guy wasn't the runner he might be, even on the road. Halfway up Snowdon I said, "give us your bag", and on we went. We came down and made our way back. I felt sorry for him at first but that soon went out the window when he brings out his camomile tea and whatever. After the boat ride to the Lakes, we were running up from Ravenglass and by then we were hardly speaking to each other. We got back down from Scafell Pike and were supposed to stay together, but he wouldn't talk to me. So, I just ran away down the road and waited for him on the way into Ravenglass. The tide was wrong and we couldn't get out for a bit. It got a bit interesting going up to Scotland, hairy in fact. The fence [*as Billy puts it*] on the side of the boat was practically in the water. I looked across at some other faces and thought if they are not panicking I won't. I went below and tried to sleep for a while. There is a village called Caol just outside Fort William and you run an old railway track into Fort William. Climbing up I offered to carry his rucksack but he wouldn't let me. We got to the top of the Ben and there were a couple of ramps of snow there. I said, "we will come down that snow when we come back". He wouldn't go near it. I ran back to Caol and laid down to wait for him, maybe 50 yards from the finish. He comes along and instead of running in together he sprinted ahead. I gave him a serious bollocking. The boat lot said, "we will go out for a dinner at night", and I said, "no, I am staying on the boat", so I could catch the first train out of there. I am happy that I did it though. It is another tale to tell. Happy days!'

Naturally enough fell runners dominated the fastest times on the fell sections that year. Mark Rigby and Adrian Belton were fastest, and second were Martin Stone and Jack Maitland, with Billy's pair third.

They used to have all sailors doing it in the early days. Then it got very competitive and they realised they could get three sailors and two fell runners. The sailing wins it really. For Scafell you are trying to turn the boat around on the same tide. Joss Naylor did it once with Mike Walford for an ITV team. Joss got seasick something rotten and said, "never again".

Thirdly, in August 1991, a week after the Borrowdale race Billy ran the Sierre-Zinal race for the one and only time, coming forty-seventh and fifth Vet. Billy thinks that Dave Wilkinson wrote to the organisers saying that the Borrowdale club would like an invite, which they got, partly on the back of Billy's name. 'So myself, Dave, James Bulman and Gavin Bland went, with accommodation being provided. Young James had the best race he ever ran in his life, finishing fourteenth. Gavin was sixty-sixth. We hired a car and had a few days over there. We also went up the first bit of the Matterhorn, and then we were hit by a thunderstorm, so we sat it out in the car in our underpants, soaking wet.' Billy may have been a fair way down the field, being 44 years old by then, but he showed his old resolve in facing up to a rival who he wouldn't let beat him. 'Three quarters of the way into the race I could see John Blair-Fish and he should never be beating me. There must have been about 50 runners between me and him. I fought him on the last bit of downhill and did beat him but had to work for it. At one point I told him to get out of the road because he was one for sticking his elbows out at yer.'

In discussing Billy's career, Pete Bland concluded that you might say that he didn't travel well. He added, 'I have been surprised to see that he has been going abroad for these cycle trips now. He has changed. He was much better running on home soil. He knew those routes like the back of his hand, he knew the best lines.' Having surveyed the evidence I am now thinking that he did travel pretty well (in terms of the results he did have), but often chose not to go to distant races and concentrated more on the local race scene.

Billy's cycling friend Mark Wilson reckons that whenever Billy is asked where he is from when they are abroad, he always answers 'Borrowdale' first, followed by 'the Lake District' second, and if pressed 'the north of England' last.

Billy himself has said that his greatest pleasure has been in 'getting there'. He would rather win the Borrowdale than any other race because, in his words, 'if you're nowt at home, you're nowt anywhere'.

NO SURRENDER

For all the worthy exhortations that it is the taking part that counts, it is rivalries that define sport to me. Just look at the passions a local derby between the 'Old Firm' football clubs from Glasgow can raise. Those with a deep interest in their sport are still talking about the rivalry between Seb Coe and Steve Ovett in the golden era of athletics in the 1980s, and that between Bernard Hinault and Greg Le Mond in cycling. It is no different in the sport of fell running. As Billy Bland has said when asked about motivation, 'there were a couple of athletes that I thought I would never be as good as. Eventually I got them though.'

Runners use their immediate rivals as a yardstick to measure their relative and absolute positions in the sport by. It has been quite instructive to find out Billy Bland's thoughts on his rivals, and their reflections on him.

Billy Bland didn't have to wait till he was a champion runner to experience his first rivalries. Like many families, sibling rivalry was rampant in the Bland family. Billy retells a story that illustrates that the ruthlessness amongst themselves knew no bounds. 'Brotherly love wasn't in it', he says, with a laugh. 'My brother Stuart overtook me once on Crag Fell. He asked me if I needed something to eat. "Aye", I said. "I'm clean out of petrol. What have you got?" He said he could give me a Mars bar. But instead of handing it to me he threw it on the ground, so I had to stop and pick it up.'

David Bland also mentioned family rivalry when interviewed towards the end of the 1970s. He said it was something he relished and also used to his advantage. 'It gives me a boost in a race to know either my brothers or cousins are going badly one mile behind! Having members of the family up ahead spurs me on to possibly help win a team prize.'

Jonny Bland, when asked about rivalry, replied, 'I like to beat anyone I can in any race. Obviously, I like to beat Gavin [Bland, his cousin] if I can, but mainly I just like to do well, and probably try a bit harder when we have got a good team out at a race.' He also observed, unsurprisingly, that Stuart and Billy Bland had been a significant positive influence on him.

When Gavin Bland was asked the same question, he replied slightly differently, admittedly from his slightly higher position in the fell running firmament. 'The chief rivals over a steep rough course are cousin Jonny in long races and John Atkinson in short ones. Kenny Stuart and Colin Donnelly are runners I admire particularly, while uncle Billy has been the biggest influence.'

Gavin also had big ambitions, which in 1993 included a wish to be, 'winner at the British Championship and eventually to break Billy's record for the Bob Graham Round.' As we have seen, he achieved the first but has (yet) to do the second, being past his physical peak, even though he was racing at a high level still when 40 years old.

Different motivations from three different members of the same family, but they all have in common some kind of familial rivalry.

Billy Bland had a clear idea of the people whom he looked up to in the sport when he was younger and gave a hard-hitting assessment of two of them. 'Well, Mike Short was a fantastic uphill runner, but useless downhill. Harry Walker, a big feller, another good uphiller but crap downhill.'

Later, Kenny Stuart and John Wild came on the scene and Billy rather surprisingly says he was never as good a runner as they were, being happy that he achieved the best he could from the natural ability he had been gifted. 'But I did get them occasionally', he says. 'But no, I never wished I was anybody else. I wanted to get the best out of myself, and I was enjoying what I did, which is why I did it.'

Billy Bland goes on to give a harsh assessment of other members of his family and their abilities and achievements. 'Well David, my younger brother and Gavin's father, he was a lazy sod. Of the three brothers David probably had the most ability, but it is no wonder Gavin turned out like he did. Stuart had less ability than me, but was a real good downhiller, but he had pleurisy as a 20-odd-year-old and

I think that held him back. It may have been the reason he wasn't even better. If there had been downhill races Stuart would have been a superstar.'

I have had several discussions with Billy Bland about his rivals and at one point he said, 'I see bad in somebody before I see good. What that says about me I am not sure!' In one long session, Billy and I talked about the top runners he had raced against and he laid out a few thoughts on some of the others that had won the British Fell Championship either side of his 1980 title. As always, he tells it like he sees it.

Dave Cannon was the first British Champion, in 1972, which was before Billy moved to amateur racing from the pros. Cannon also ran 2:11 for the marathon. Billy didn't race against Cannon much really, as he was on the fell scene just before his time, but with a strange shift to partially speaking in the third person gives his analysis. 'Whether he made himself into what he was I don't know, but he must have had more speed than I had. What he did on the roads Billy Bland could never have done. You could never have made Billy Bland fast enough to do a good marathon time.'

Harry Walker was the next Champion (in 1973) and was an early marker for Billy in races. 'His strength was climbing. He was a big lad, which isn't ideal. He was a builder, so knew what hard work was. When I started, I thought I would never beat Harry to the top of Ben Nevis, or at climbing at all.'

Jeff Norman was the next champion and is still running at a decent level many years on, having been an Olympian at the marathon as well as his exploits on the fells. He won the only marathon Billy ever competed in, at Barnsley in 1980. 'Again, Jeff did great times in the marathon. I didn't bump into him a lot except that Skiddaw was one race he would come to and that absolutely suited him. I remember being in front of him going up the side of Latrigg and here comes Jeff pitter-pattering away. Not exactly a clock in his head but he was racing a very sensible race, and not getting dragged into anything. He knew what he could do and knew how to race. I liked him as a person, very unassuming.'

Mike Short was the first person to win the Championship twice (in 1975 and 1978) and was someone Billy crossed swords with as he progressed in the sport. Short was a very frequent racer, whom Billy couldn't beat early on, but eventually got the drop on, a metaphor for both their careers and the way races between them tended to pan out. 'I feel very sorry for Mike because he was a tremendous uphill runner, but the poor feller could not run downhill, which must have been demoralising.'

Andy Styan won the title the year before Billy did, and Billy says he has a lot of respect for Styan, particularly for his outstanding record for the Langdale race which has lasted since 1977. 'He kind of told me what sort of training he did, and it became quite obvious to me that he was a good downhill runner and I wasn't going to get anything out of him on a downhill. He must have complained about me talking to him in races because as soon as I knew that then I would be wanting to talk to him, like! He had the Wasdale record till I knocked 5 minutes off it. He still has the Langdale record. I think I was 14 seconds behind him that day. There was four of us coming off Blisco together. I definitely became a better runner after that and yet I still couldn't beat that Langdale time.'

I reminded Colin Donnelly of Billy's talking tactic and

he gave a different perspective on this gambit. 'I wouldn't mind if he talked to me in a race. But I do remember something funny happening to Billy. We were doing the Moffat Chase one year, with Billy having done it before. There was an electric fence as you came off Saddle Yoke, half-way down. I approached it very cautiously, with Billy just in front of me. He ran at it and grabbed it with both hands, swung his legs over at the same time, and got this tremendous shock going through him. He turned to me and said, "why didn't you warn me, you must have known about the electric fence?" I said, "I thought you had done it before, Billy?" He was certainly talking to me then (with added expletives too), but he was normally silent with me.' The swearing was not aimed at Colin, Billy was just railing at himself.

John Wild and Kenny Stuart won the next five titles between then after Billy won in 1980, and I have already described that era in depth in *Running Hard: The Story of a Rivalry*. Partly in explanation of why he thought they were both better all-round runners than he was, Billy gave his thoughts on the two of them before the 1983 season. 'I knew from the year before that they [Wild and Stuart] could beat me quite easily, so I knew they were going to do it again in the champs that year.'

Knowing that they were two of his strongest rivals, I asked Billy for further impressions of both Wild and Stuart, and he started with Wild, whom he acknowledged that he hadn't known as well as Stuart, with him not being a local.

'John Wild was a class runner. He could push himself until he was sick, which I could never do. He was a hard man in that respect. If Kenny hadn't been about then John would have been way out there, and maybe no-one else could have pushed him like that. I think I am right in saying he won the Inter-Counties cross country championships [*he did, twice*]. Put me in the Inter-Counties and I couldn't have finished in the first half.' Billy also thought that, 'in a way coming to run in a fell race was a bit of an adventure for John.'

Moving on to Kenny Stuart, Bland thought that Kenny didn't push himself as hard as John did. 'I think he would accept defeat before John would, that is my personal view. But Kenny was a really fast runner.'

Billy concluded that in his view both John Wild and Kenny Stuart were not proper fellsmen, and that, 'for one of those two to win the championship, then it would come down to maybe what the weather did on the long 'uns that were counters. On flagged courses, to the top and back again, then they were very similar and unbeatable. But in mist anything can happen.' This was not so much of a put down as it may seem, more an acknowledgement of the difference between these three great runners, who all won the fell championship title (Billy once, John twice and Kenny three times).

Jack Maitland won the title in 1986, and like Kenny Stuart and John Wild was of the generation that looked up to Billy Bland but were determined to take him down if they could. Billy chuckles as he launches into a critique of Maitland's running and a long story about dealing with rivals. 'The look of Jack going along with his wings down like a hen. You would never have picked him out by his form in the early part of a race as a winner, but he could run. He was a bit cocky in his own way in his early career. I expect he was thinking to knock me off my perch. In an Ennerdale race once we had just left the top of Red Pike and it was misty and I was going along, and he was behind us with one or two others. Jack just said to me, "can you not find any more rough stuff, Billy?". I remember turning to him and saying, "well I don't think we are tied together Jack, you just piss off anywhere you want to go". Anyway, later in the race I left him and that was it. I don't know if it was the following year or not when I stood on the start line for 5 minutes. He was part of the reason that I did that. I didn't think I was fit enough and had travelled across with Chris, and others, and told them what I was going to do. I said, "I am sick of being followed". I don't mind being followed if I am fit enough to win but I didn't think I was at that time. I didn't want to give myself a hard time. It wasn't being big-headed – thinking I can beat them all. I caught Jack that day and I can still remember it. It was going along by Iron Crag and I just went past him like he was standing still. He won't know what that meant to me. It must have been what he said the year before that made me rub his snout in it. Folk say things like, and I didn't mind Jack at all. I had tried to knock old Joss off his perch earlier. We were going along at the Borrowdale race where I did him, maybe the first time I beat him. He said to me as we started to climb Gable, "How you going, Billy?". I says, "aye well all right so far, Joss". It wasn't long after that that I went away from him. He was likely asking to see how I was going, being as I was also a cocky youngish bugger. It is part of the game though. You are in a race together and you don't dislike anybody.'

Billy finished with a few thoughts on those who won the title as his career was winding down a bit. Colin Donnelly was the first to get a hat-trick of wins (1987 to 1989) and is still running well today. 'A good runner was Colin, and all. He is still going well, so he must have a good engine.'

Billy likes a motoring motif, often talking about running out of petrol in races.

Gary Devine won in 1990. 'He was in the punk scene wasn't he. Crazy hair and all that. A grand lad. It is that kind of sport.' Then Keith Anderson, who was coming into it when Billy was almost 40. Anderson won the title in 1991. 'I always remember saying to Gavin before a Borrowdale, "I don't think you will beat me, never mind Keith Anderson". He finished second to Keith, and maybe should have won that day. I think I was fourth in that race.'

Having heard Billy's thoughts on his major competitors, it is only right to hear some thoughts on Billy from a range people who have run against him and tried to beat him over the years.

Pete Bland competed against Billy Bland as both a professional and an amateur and is probably a good person to start with. Here is his recent assessment of Billy's strengths and weaknesses, in response to my question to him about the best ever fell runner. 'Obviously, Joss Naylor comes into it, but Joss was great at long stuff like Ennerdale and Wasdale, but he never won the Ben race. Ben Nevis is not short, but he never won it, and never won many short races at all. The other one is Kenny Stuart. Kenny was brilliant, and he could run any distance, but then his career wasn't that long in the amateur fell running side, as he went to run marathons of course. We don't really know how good he might have been had he continued, and then of course he got ill and had to retire.'

Pete then gave his rationale for Billy as being the best ever. 'As a competitor he was second to none. He was absolutely blinkered. He was tough, and his training regime was excellent. I know the amount of hours he spent every week running. A lot of people disagree with me, but I have always said that I think, and it is quite a rash statement, that he is the best fell runner of all time. This is because of his all-round ability. He could win a 15-minute race or one that would take 3 or 4 hours. His records speak for themselves. To my mind that makes Billy Bland the best all-round fell runner ever. He could win Borrowdale and Latrigg on the same weekend, and he used to say that he always felt better on the second day. I have done races back-to-back and I have been awful. I would avoid them if possible as I could never cope the next day.'

A runner who trained at times with Billy when he worked at Honister YHA, and was a pacer on the BGR record, is Pete Barron. He recently gave me his thoughts on Billy's strengths and weaknesses. 'He is very driven, that has got to be a strength. Sometimes I think that if I was half as driven as Billy, I'd be doing OK. But on the other hand, there are times you can be so driven that you can be blinkered to the bigger picture. With Billy that applies to running, biking, fox hunting, or whatever. If you are that kind of person you sometimes can't see that. There is another quote I remember from Billy. It was someone saying I haven't got enough time for training, and Billy just said, "you can make time for what you want to make time for". To a certain extent he is right. Ann has supported Billy something fantastic throughout his running career. Latterly I think he has begun to really appreciate that aspect. A number of years ago he probably didn't realise. I don't think you can be as committed, as successful and as driven as that and live in the ordinary world at the same time without somebody that is really strong backing you up. He is very fortunate that he had Ann for that. Do you know he has never been in a supermarket? I often wind him up about this.'

Pete Barron concludes, 'there was no mercy if you trained with Billy. He could burn me off if he wanted to. I could climb and wasn't bad at descending, and a flat run out would get to me, same as Billy. Billy gets great power from his slight frame. I remember there was one time when I nearly beat him in a race. It only happened once, the race and me nearly beating him. The race was from Stool End (Langdale) going up Crinkle Crags and back. I beat Billy to the top and on the way down he was not going to let me beat him. He must have turned himself inside out on the flat bit at the bottom and he beat me by four seconds in the end.'

Although not a contemporary of Billy's, Jim Mann is a student of the sport and he offered this view. 'What I have heard about Billy Bland was that he had a love of the fells and was always up there, and that he got his fitness through what we would consider as over-training.'

Mann is a big believer in heavy base mileage. He ran up to 125 miles a week as he came back from an injury and worked to get fit for one of his winter Bob Graham rounds. 'If you are trying to do the really long stuff I think you need the base mileage. I thought Billy did more mileage than indicated in his training notes. I don't think what he was doing was scientific, but then I don't think anyone has broken down fell running into a science yet, not properly.'

Rob Jebb also never raced against Billy Bland at his prime, nor John Wild or Kenny Stuart. 'Those guys were born with talent. They had an ability to run well over rough terrain. If you go training every day over rough ground you will probably be good at it, and that is what Billy did.'

Interviewed in the Jul/Aug 1990 issue of *Up and Down* magazine Colin Donnelly commented: 'I admire Billy Bland. He's an excellent ambassador for our sport. He incorporates high principles and sportsmanship with athletic brilliance, a typical fell-mountain runner. Kenny Stuart and Bob Whitfield are chips off the same block.'

Billy had commented once about both himself and Donnelly being nervous before races, a point I put to Colin recently. 'I do suffer from nerves', Donnelly admitted. 'Even when I am not bothered about a race and have nothing at stake, just doing it for the craic, I find I go to the toilet three times beforehand. So, inside I am nervous. With Billy himself I don't remember him coming across as nervous. Maybe he was keeping it inside himself.'

Donnelly then shares a story which may (or may not) reflect nerves being shown by another champion fellrunner. 'I do remember Andy Styan, who was British Champion one year, he had an interesting way of trying to psyche out the competition, and maybe this was dealing with nerves for him. He liked to turn up at a race and he would puff away at a cigarette on the start line. I don't know if it was to psyche us out or calm his nerves, but it was a great technique.'

Kenny Stuart has always had fairly strong views on training and fell running, arguing that Billy's strengths were in the type of terrain he trained over. 'Every day he worked on his stamina base. It wasn't my way of training, but it worked for him and he was likely happy with that. His weaknesses – perhaps if he was getting beaten, he might back off a little earlier than he should have done. He never travelled well when it was really hot. When Joss and them, including Billy Bland, went out to do these challenges they went out and they just ran hard from the start and then just held on for grim death. The modern athlete is doing it with a stopwatch and has got it all down meticulously to time. It is more scientific now. Also, the fact of the matter is that the fells are more accessible. I mean there is a trod around the Bob Graham Round now and it is like a motorway. Someone should have broken that [*Bob Graham*] record five or six years ago.'

Tony Cresswell's view was that without doubt Billy Bland's greatest strength was his single mindedness, and his drive. 'He applied himself very well but didn't go on about it. How he ever ran so well at the doubles, like Borrowdale and Latrigg, I do not know. There were lads that saved themselves for the Latrigg and Billy just blew them away.' Tony adds that he rarely watched fell races but does remember Billy fading on the Duddon. 'Andy Styan caught him. I was with Ann Bland at the Three Shires Stone and he came through in the lead. Andy getting him was unusual. Billy barely had a weakness. If I was going to be harsh, I would say he got a little agitated at times if he was not happy with himself. He would get short tempered and get miffed.'

Cresswell also reckons that Billy was often being brought out before races to show his gear to prove that he had all that was required. 'That used to annoy Billy. He is all or nothing. There are no grey areas with him. He is a man on a mission', concludes Cresswell.

John Wild never trained with Billy Bland. As noted, Billy was a bit of loner in that aspect. 'That was always my impression', says John Wild now. 'Billy always used to run the fells. I don't think he ever did what I would call 'efforts'. He was a tough competitor though, especially in the long Lakeland events. He was an Ennerdale, Borrowdale and Wasdale man, wasn't he? Had he turned his mind to other disciplines I am sure he would have succeeded.'

It is Wild's view that Billy Bland's strength was his staying power, and that on the long races he was the best, being something of a specialist. 'His weakness was his lack of speed, though', he concludes. 'He wouldn't have beaten Kenny or myself in a sprint finish. Billy had good climbing ability, and he could certainly descend. He was probably the best all-round fell runner in my humble opinion. I take my hat off to him for his Bob Graham Round, that is such an arduous thing to do. He had a very good eye for rough ground. Some have that and some haven't. He did.'

John Wild is not alone in noting one characteristic of Billy Bland that stands out when looking back on the earlier days. 'I don't ever remember socialising with Billy, apart from at the Borrowdale race, in the marquee. All his family and friends were there for that. The Borrowdale clan.' Saying that about BIand is not a criticism, says Wild, who finishes with a measured tribute to him. 'Billy always seemed a fair guy. I have got no bad feelings or anything towards him. He was a genuinely nice guy.'

Hugh Symonds feels that he saw Billy as continuing on from Joss Naylor. 'Joss had been invincible at the Lake District classics, and then Billy became invincible at them. You go face to face with someone like that in a race and they have an aura about them. It is hard to deal with that. Rumour has it that Ann did everything for him. Ann would be on the course with a drink and whatever.'

Symonds also added that counter-intuitively Billy Bland wasn't a terribly fast runner. 'He wouldn't be first up something like the Blisco Dash, but the descent is tricky, and he was fantastic coming down that. Some courses suited him more than others. The finish at Ennerdale was quite runnable which didn't suit Billy, whereas Wasdale was straight off the mountain. He wouldn't be someone you would see at a road race or a cross country race. Also, Billy never won the Three Peaks, which some people call a marathon with three hills in it.'

Hugh Symonds tells a story about when one of his sons [Andrew or Joe] was running a Junior International race at Keswick once, on the low fells around Latrigg and Billy was there watching. 'For some reason we got chatting about Joss, who was still running. Billy said, "hey he should stop this running you know".'

Symonds adds, 'I helped Joss on a long stage of his 60 at 60. We were on Scafell somewhere, possibly Lord's Rake, and Billy just came in from nowhere and appeared. The first thing he said to Joss was, "you are going far too fast, you need to slow down if you are going to do the whole lot". He was quite forceful about it. Joss looked comfortable to me.'

Dave Hall feels that Billy Bland's strength and weakness are the same thing – his stubbornness. 'He was certainly very good over the rough stuff. A very good navigator, particularly by accumulating prior knowledge of recced routes. Like Joss he could remember places stone by stone almost. He was a talented climber and brilliant descender. His legacy? He was one of the best if not THE best distance fell runners, over the longer races like Wasdale and Duddon.'

Howard Pattinson goes as far as to say that Billy was an inspiration to him. For a profile in his own athletic club magazine, Howard wrote: Favourite athlete? Billy Bland. He explains, 'It was not Cram or Coe, it was Bland, on what he has achieved. That was on the back of a full-time physical job. If you want to achieve anything, you have to put the work in, and that was what he did. I have nothing but admiration for him. There are little things where we have a difference of opinion, but I can live with that. That is him.'

As evidence Pattinson adds, 'The Four Peaks [*the two Scafells, Skiddaw and Helvellyn*] would be the weekend before the Ennerdale, and it didn't bother Billy to do both. He didn't believe in resting. He could do that you see. He was a beautiful mover over the ground, and he would see the Four Peaks as a training run. He was a racer.'

Jon Broxap was racing well at Billy Bland's peak. It is Broxap's considered view that Billy's strength as a runner was his capacity to train, the sheer volume and dedication he put in. 'He was certainly very focussed. His strength came from being from the Lakes and knowing the Lakes so well. His ability to run over rocks and rough ground was unbelievable. He was also very strong mentally. If you were at his house and he wanted to go to bed, off he would go, no matter who you were. Billy had to get up to go to work and that was it, bedtime.'

Jon Broxap also mentions that Kenny Stuart trained differently, not really doing big mileage, and not going on the high fells as much as others. People have asked Broxap who the best fell racer was and he says Kenny Stuart, with John Wild very close behind. But he adds that, 'the best fell or mountain runner was Billy Bland, without doubt. Billy was very driven and very focussed. If it came to mountain craft, particularly in bad weather he would find his way round, Billy was untouchable. Kenny too could run downhill mind. Kenny still holds the Ben record, whilst I still hold the record for the slowest winning time at Kentmere!'

Jon Broxap can't remember beating Billy in any

particular races, except maybe on the road. 'But I can distinctly remember a few occasions when I didn't beat Billy. One day I got within a minute and a half of him at Ennerdale because he got lost. That was the big back-to-back double, as the next day was Muncaster Luck, which was a ten miler. It finished with an uphill stretch onto the lawn of the castle. I was leading Billy across the flat to there and he took me at the bottom of that last little hill, literally in the last 100 yards. I was spent, and he was very stubborn.'

Scoffer Schofield also gave his thoughts on Billy Bland's strengths and weaknesses. 'As to a weakness you could point to the fact that he wasn't fast enough. He might have liked to have been able to run uphill a little quicker. He was just hard. He would run until he fell over. He didn't often do that, but he did once or twice. There are loads of races where he has felt rubbish and ended up winning. If someone beat him Billy would always say that he had beaten him fair and square. No excuses, like.'

Jon Broxap had suggested that Billy and Ann were very much a team, and that she supported him wholeheartedly. 'I think it was before an Ennerdale race once I went to stay with them, as I must have been living away at the time. His breakfast was cooked, she was totally supportive. She gave him the time to go and do what he did. She was also a runner in her time, often just for the pleasure of it.'

There is very much a feeling that Ann Bland was the strong woman behind her successful man. Billy Bland took the time to acknowledge the support he got from his wife at his peak, when he commented in an interview after he had won the British Championship. It comes across now as an old-fashioned outlook on life but is certainly extremely deserved credit. 'Support at home. No bother.

It's essential really isn't it? It's a struggle enough without a struggle at home. I can get out when I want, and I am glad I have that support.'

Scoffer also knows Billy and Ann well, and explained their relationship as he saw it. 'I think her support was [*searches for correct word*] invaluable. The wind beneath his wings, mebbe.' [*There was then a discussion of who recorded that song. We decided it was Bette Midler. Scoffer reckoned Jack Duckworth did a good version!*] Scoffer continued, 'Ann would do all his cooking and everything. But they are always falling out or disagreeing over things. She deserves a medal, for being married to Billy, like.' Billy responds to this last comment by saying, 'talk about the kettle calling the pan!'

Then Scoffer mentioned one of Billy's habits that really frustrated him. 'What used to annoy me was we would go to a race and we had to get there like three hours beforehand. He would just sit and read *The Racing Post* and we would be hanging about. I like to get there 10 minutes before the start.' [*Gavin Bland, who was with us at the time, laughed, 'That is a Bland thing though!'*] 'He is like that at work', Scoffer added. 'He gets there at 7:15 and sits and reads his paper on the drive for half an hour. Even for a bike ride he will say meet you at 10 and by twenty to he is there.'

On a lighter note Scoffer mentioned that if Billy ever wants anything off the internet he often orders it for him. 'Wheels, or anything else for his bike. He can't do a gas canister on his bike. He won't take it in. You can't tell him owt! He is just not technical.' Surprising perhaps for someone so skilled with his hands in other ways. Scoffer did add that there were two bits of advice that Billy did give him. 'Never, ever, follow a Cumberland Fell Runner [*the club*], as they haven't a clue where they are going; and never, ever, buy a trail hound.' When asked whether he had followed that advice, he replied, 'Well, I have never bought a trail hound!'

Scoffer finished with a story that I had read in a profile of him once. 'It was my 21st birthday party in Rochdale and Billy came. For a present he gave me one of his tankards from the Mountain Trial wins. I thought that was really tight. He couldn't be bothered, like.' Despite all the above, Billy and Scoffer are really good friends. Interestingly, a cabinet in Billy's front room with some Mountain Trial tankards in it is one of the very few signs that you can see in his house of his amazing success as a runner.

When I talked with David Bland and his son Gavin, David posited that the family sporting prowess was all down to Gavin's grandfather Joe Bland. 'His heart rate was never above forty, often mid-thirties and he was the father of Billy, Stuart and I.' Gavin then proceeded to compare himself and Billy, with their similarities and differences. 'I would suggest that me and Billy are very similar and that if you put us on a treadmill we would be like a very good woman. By that I mean that our VO2 max would be very ordinary (for men). But I could run races and have lads running beside me who would be puffing their guts out. Ian Holmes is an example. If you were running with Holmesy and he was gonna beat yer you could tell by how hard he was working. If I was gonna beat him I would just cruise away. But Billy had a better recovery than I had. I would be tired. That is how he could do the training that he did.'

Gavin ventured a theory that really Billy was far too single minded. 'That was his weakness. But to win nine

Wasdales or ten Borrowdales, or whatever he did, you have to be single minded. One of my first memories of a fell race is Billy coming to the finish at Borrowdale, up the lonning towards Rosthwaite, in probably 1988. I was standing watching and he was beating Mike Fanning but only just by a very small margin. It wasn't a sprint, but he only just gapped him. Mike was just two years older than me, just a lad really. For a year or two he nearly had Billy but not quite. My point is that Billy was not eyeballs out, but just running strong.'

It is right that Billy has the last word here. I asked him who was the most naturally talented youngster he can remember coming into the sport. The reply came without much hesitation. 'Gavin Bland, absolutely. He was the best fell runner I have ever come across. Folk will say he is just bunging his nephew there, but I wouldn't do that. Gavin had the full range of ability, except what was between his lugs. A good job for everybody else! He could have won an awful lot more than he did and set more records. Kilian Jornet would have been coming over to chase rather more than he had to timewise.'

I then asked Billy who was the least talented runner, yet who had made the most out of themselves. He replied immediately, 'you are looking at him', to roars of laughter from Ann and I. 'Genuinely. I don't think anyone got any more out of themselves than I got out from what I was playing with. Yeh. I had a talent for running downhill and covering rough ground, and a bit of confidence in my own ability to look at the ground and see which the best line was to take. I didn't make many mistakes that way. My route choosing was good. Call it a gift or what you like. Certainly, hard work got me to be a winner. In lots of ways the later you achieve your targets, and the more years you have gone through, the more rewarding it is when you do so.'

Billy Bland has massive strengths and some weaknesses, but all the above accords with my own view that he is the greatest fell runner of all time. A unique one too, as a look at his life choices shows.

IT'S MY LIFE

Billy Bland is very much his own man. He has his own ethos and ways of responding to situations and dealing with things. He has rarely compromised throughout his life and will probably continue that way until his death. Someone said of him, 'he is a firecracker'. More like a dormant volcano, I would say. His lifestyle over the years fits the 'all or nothing at all' characterisation.

Drink, for instance, is a simple black and white choice for Billy. He is a non-drinker, and has been for a long time, despite dabbling when he was younger, possibly under peer pressure. 'I have been drunk twice in my life, like really drunk', he says now. 'I learned as a teenager that drinking cider and stuff when playing darts, it went to your head really fast. It might be good for your confidence like, but it spoiled the next day. Like I say I was drunk twice and after the second time I stuck to not drinking, and that was at nineteen years old. It wasn't for me, and it didn't like me. Its tea and water for me.'

As for food, he claims that he does not have strong likes and dislikes, and just likes good plain food. Talking to him about it though, he does reveal that he does have some quite strong opinions, which reflect his personality and also his upbringing. 'If Ann put something on the table and I didn't like I would say, and we wouldn't have it again. I don't like spicy foods. If I was out somewhere as a guest, I would eat anything like. When we were younger you cleaned your plate out, as there was nowt else.'

Even when he was running 70 to 100 miles a week Billy didn't have anything fancy as far as his diet was concerned. 'I just ate sensible food, basically whatever was put in front of me. I didn't ask for anything in particular, but there is one thing when you are training hard you can eat what you want really, because you are burning off what you put in.' Drinking water from streams and carrying simple sugary foods was how he was when he was running. 'When I am cycling now I know these gels work, but there wasn't any gels in my day. You might take out a Mars bar or a fudge or something like that, but half the time you only took them because you had to take them', he concludes.

That his training and racing kit requirements were suitably simple comes as no surprise. 'I can't remember having a bum bag, it was just like a money pouch really. You could get a Mars bar and a map in, and a compass. It was just like a belt and your cagoule would be tied round your waist and knotted, not stuffed in a bum bag. I remember running round, the day Bob English died I think, in the Ennerdale race with just a Lifa top on, and Tecwyn Davies said to me "you are a hard man". I just looked at him and said, "well as long as you are making body heat, you are fine". I might have put me cagoule on if I was cold.'

Taking holidays hasn't really figured in Billy and Ann's life over the years, as Billy explains. 'A holiday to do nowt, which is what a lot of people want, is not for me. We once went with the local pub for four days in Majorca, which was the only time Ann has ever flown, and she didn't reckon much of it. Holidays might be a few days up at Fort William.' They used to go with the children to the Lochaber race weekend and used to really like that, as they found a place that they used to stay at each year. He recalls that they also went with Pete Barron once to Snowdon and stayed at the Royal Victoria Hotel.

This all prompted a memory they both had of a visit to Morecambe. 'That was a day trip, when we were quite young. It seemed like the end of the world at that time, was Morecambe.' The topic was closed by a smiling comment from Ann. 'When Billy goes off on a bike trip that is my holiday!'

Many people have hobbies that consume much of their spare time during their working life, and often are given full reign to in retirement. Billy Bland doesn't really fit that mould, as he was a classic sleep-run-eat person throughout his running career. But dig a little deeper and you come across two passions, one of which was fleeting and one which has lasted a lifetime.

The first might surprise you. Billy Bland took up golf for a while, but eventually the things that you might expect about the sport to get to him finally did. He illustrates his whole golf career in one short story.

'I quite fancied it because up [*at work*] at Honister we would have a get together on a Friday night and go down to the miniature golf course at Keswick. Just a nine-hole pitch and putt like. We would have a competition and throw a quid in apiece, and winner got it all. It was usually me or Mick Taylor that won. Then I started playing proper golf and that was a real challenge. Great game, very well behaved. There won't be a better-behaved sport, apart from possibly fell running. I would go [*up to Threlkeld*] and do a competition on a Sunday morning. First hole or two might be poor and then you can't walk off a golf course, so you carry on. But I would be thinking about going running in the afternoon. There was one time I was playing for Keswick Golf Club in a match and I went down in a pair of shorts. Going into the clubhouse and I got a tap on my shoulder and was told no shorts in here. So, I just walked out. Nonsense, as you get some arsehole who has been in the club for years who is an absolute alcoholic who makes a complete fool of himself. He is the one that should have been thrown out. I played for five or six years though. I have still got my clubs and used to go out in the field and hit some balls about.'

So, he had a brief encounter with golf in the late 1980s but didn't care much for the general atmosphere surrounding the game, the handicap system, or the interference which the time to play the game placed on his running. After four and a half hours of golf, he still had to go on a 10 to 15-mile training run. He says he just played because some of his mates were playing golf.

Billy's cousin Chris was into orienteering. Billy admits that he also went orienteering sometimes to practice his navigation. 'Being competitive I wanted to do as well as I could, then found I wasn't as good as I should be. You can get really found out at that game. No matter how fast you are running if it is in the wrong direction you are stuffed. So, the second day at Duddon, which was a long orienteering event, never really appealed to me. I did get better at it, when I started to use my compass and my head a bit more. What I was a fair hand at was once I knew the two points, one that I was leaving and one where I was heading to, then I was good at finding the best lines.'

I asked Billy once whether he was ever into rock climbing, to which he said no. But Scoffer revealed that was a time when the two of them had a dabble at it. 'We went to the climbing wall and that a few times. None of us were any good though.' One day they were climbing at the Binka Stone, as Scoffer recalled. 'It is down by Gavin Bland's place, just before you get to Harrop. It is just a little flat crag. It is vertical though. It is too wet to rock climb on really. It is only 20 feet high and is black and greasy. It is only 10 yards off the road, that is why we were there! It was Billy [*the expert, as he calls him, with deep irony in his voice*], Gavin and me. Ann was there and was chipping away at Billy, criticising him. Billy just turned to her and says, "will you just shurrup yow bossy laal cow". I just burst out laughing.' Scoffer says he has adopted the expression and jokingly says that to her sometimes when she is having a go at him about something, when they are organising a race or whatever.

Another spare-time passion developed whilst working at Honister. That was an interest in a further sport – horse racing – which continues today. It has involved part-ownership of a few horses along the way, rarely to the financial benefit of Billy and his co-owners. The manager at Honister took bets for folk. It is something which Billy still enjoys to the extent that should he ever come up on the lottery, he would invest in a racehorse but train it himself.

He explained about the part-ownership of a horse. Since the 1980s he has been a member of the Racegoers Club and has had shares in horses. They lease horses from breeders for a couple of seasons. You pay a couple of hundred pounds a year to be part of the scheme. 'It is you and quite a lot more people. You stump your money up and you are given a telephone line to ring and they will tell you where it is running and what its chances are. I must have had shares in 8 or 10 horses over time, some were even winners. You get a share of the prize money, after trainers and jockeys and fees are taken out. Any left-over is divided at the end of the year amongst the syndicate. Just interest really. There is a lot of bullshit in the sport mind.'

As a member of the Racegoers Club you get a concession of £5 off entry at Carlisle. 'Now I am a pensioner it doesn't make any difference really!' chuckles Billy. 'There are also a few free days at Carlisle, which makes it worthwhile as it is only about £27 to join. Occasionally I go to Catterick as well, as there are free days there too. Me and Stuart used to go all over North England to races. We have had some good days. It is a game of opinions, and I am not short opinions, as you know!'

Billy then tells another story which illustrates his attitude to both possessions, and making and keeping promises. 'Back in 1984 I backed Burrough Hill Lad to win the Cheltenham Gold Cup at 50-1, which was a very early price in October. Well the price came right down by the race [*in March*] and it won as a favourite. My £20 each way got me £1200. The kids wanted a colour TV, and I had said there is nowt wrong with that telly. Till it goes wrong we are stopping with black and white. Anyway, I had promised the kids that if Burrough Hill Lad won the Gold Cup then you can have your colour TV. So, I had to stick to what I had said.'

Nowadays he goes to the occasional horse race, saying that he doesn't miss many meetings at Carlisle. One time when we were doing an interview I turned up at the house and Billy asked me to bear with him whilst he finished watching a horse race that he had been watching on the television. It was the St Leger from Doncaster, and he quietly mentioned as we started talking that he 'had won a few bob' that day.

There was laughter all round when I asked Billy about doing DIY and stuff around the house. Ann very grudgingly admitted that he does it if he has to. Things lightened up as we moved on to Billy's artistic skills. 'I got a prize for art at school as well as for woodwork. I was also quite a good copy drawer. I used to like drawing things.' A softer side of Billy was emerging, as Ann added that he used to make earrings out of little bits of slate. Taking up the topic, Billy explained he had some practical skills but not others that might be useful to him. 'I also used to fashion letters out of slate, just with a drill and a hacksaw. I made the Nook Farm sign as individual letters, but they are painted white now and you can't tell they are slate. But I am mechanically absolutely bloody useless. Andrea got me a course to go to, on bike maintenance. It was a nice day and that, but unfortunately none of it stopped in there.'

Ann Bland remembers a local artist called Dick Jackson, who did wood carving and also made clocks, and made a well in his garden. She laughs as she recalls that she was petrified of him and used to run away. 'I was about 7 or 8 at the time. He used to come around selling calor gas, and want to buy me for half a crown! Then we came to live next door but one to him. He was quite talented in a lot of ways. He could hear music and then just play it. It was just a gift that he had got.'

One aspect of Billy's early lifestyle turned into a passion and another into an obsession.

Ann Bland's grandad, Ben Pattinson, was behind the first. He had trained trail hounds and taught her mother all she knew about hounds. Ann's father died in 1973 and her grandad (her mother's father) died a fortnight later. Her mother was only in her late forties, and she was very low for a while after that. Ann explains. 'Then she got this dog called Buacail, and that sort of got her going again. Really that was the only dog that she trained herself. She helped at all the hound trail events. She had also walked the dogs with my grandad, and he had plenty of champions. He had a wooden leg, believe it or not. At the age of fourteen he was playing football and broke his leg. He didn't get it set properly, it went bad and he got gangrene. Bear in mind that it was 30 miles to the nearest hospital, and I don't know how they would even get there. He had a stump, as he wouldn't have a false foot. He would still go on the fells and get sheep out of crags. There were no quad bikes in them days.' Ann's mum, Peggy Horsley, became a fixture on the hound trailing scene. She was noted for always wearing red, thinking that dogs would recognise the colour. Billy mused on whether dogs actually recognised colours or not.

Billy got involved and eventually he too trained a hound. He says, 'Ann would know what her mother had done and what her grandfather had done before.

This particular dog we had was a good dog, but he got towards the finish of trails and he wasn't bothered, like.' Ann points out that he was good in the rain, and that he won a few races then. It made him hurry up, apparently. 'If it was thundering, I would bet my life he would win as he didn't like it. He would go around as fast as he could to get back and get in out of it', laughs Billy.

The basics of training a hound were fairly simple, as the Blands explained to me. You start them when they are young, maybe a year old. You go for a walk around a field and then let someone else hold it. Then you let it see you go. It is following your footing, which leaves a scent. Next, you go out of sight and come back and it is let off before you get back and it follows your trail. Then you dip your feet in aniseed and paraffin and get them to follow that, until it gets used to following the scent rather than the person. Then you try it with another person that is not connected at all, and that is how it learns. When the hound trail courses are set out there are two trailers who set the course. They meet in the middle and one walks to the finish and one walks back to the start. It can be a ten-mile course altogether, and the course will be a loop, back to the start. Ann adds, 'at the time Billy was doing races I would go and set a trail sometimes, and we would run Pisces. It was a pup that my mother had, and nobody wanted. He was a big dog. We called him Pisces because that is my star sign.' According to Billy, 'he had bags of ability, what they called a driving hound. He would be the one in front, not like Kenny Stuart! He was just not so good at finishing and wouldn't put it all in on the run-in. Attitude in a dog makes a winner.' Notwithstanding Billy's harsh assessment of his attitudinal failings, Pisces was three times runner-up at Grasmere (in 1974 to Shannon;

in 1975 to Rose and Crown: and in 1977 to Buacail itself).

The hounds looked really thin, often looking like it a malnutrition case, but they were fed well. Ann Bland explains. 'There was a balance between keeping them hungry 24 hours before a race and them not having any energy. If they are fat though they are not going to keep up.' Ann's mother used to make a loaf which they used to call cock loaf and her grandma used to make it before that.

One recipe for cock loaf (found on the internet) comprised: 4 lb of white flour, 12 whites and 4 yolks of eggs, ¼ oz aniseed, ¼ oz glove gillyflower [*a fragrant flower*], 1 oz sugar candy, ½ oz coriander seed, ½ oz caraway seed and a small amount of balm.

It may sound an amusing name but there is a reason for it. It was originally a recipe to feed champion cocks when cockfighting was popular, before it was declared illegal in the early 1800s, according to William Rollinson's *Cumbrian Dictionary of Dialect, Tradition and Folklore*.

The Bland's recipe had big raisins, bran flour and loads of eggs. You just cooked it like a fruit loaf. Billy Bland questions the trust put in its efficacy. 'It may have been the key, but it is like running. There is no good eating a big meal and then towing the line ten minutes after.' There is a small amount of food at the finish line, and they get a substantial feed when they are taken back to the owner's vehicle where they are towelled down. The hounds will go back to the barn and be towelled down and get a bit more of a meal. They run races from one year old, but they only do five miles at that age. Trails have to be between 15 and 25 minutes for a pup or it is a void trail. When the dogs are older it is between 25 and 45 minutes.

This talk of homemade loaves prompted a story from

Ann Bland. 'My grandma took in guests at the farm and people would come every year at about the same time, staying for a week. There were a group of men who came from Burnley who were keen walkers. One night after coming back from the pub they'd gone into the dairy and helped themselves to some cake. Next morning they said to my grandma, "that was good cake we had last night". They'd eaten the dog loaf! I bet they bounded over the fells that day!'

According to Billy hound trailing was just a thing that they were brought up with locally. I found out (through Billy initially) that hound trailing apparently had a lot of dubious behaviour. Owners were showing their dogs round the trails beforehand, which is against the ethos of the sport. Billy then made a rather surprising admission, that as he put it he, 'got in among all that'. He claims that the people who were cheating were some of the so-called big wheels in trail hound training. So, he thought he'd do it that way, and be like them, and then beat them that way. He was banned, for being caught showing a dog round a course. He says, 'they were all doing it. They got me instead of the main culprits. Later, I was told I could go back but I said up yours.'

This brings to mind something that Adharanand Finn says in *The Rise of the Ultra Runners* when discussing cheating in ultras. 'Cheating, psychologists say, is especially easy to justify when you frame situations to cast yourself as a victim of some kind of unfairness. Then it becomes a matter of evening the score; you're not cheating, you're restoring fairness.'

The situation, as explained by Billy, worried me so much that I went back and asked if we could discuss it further. I asked Billy to try to explain more fully the circumstances behind him stepping out of line in the way he did.

He gave quite a long response. 'I could name names, but I won't. I had been living with Ann's mother and father and they had a lot of champion hounds. There were several people from surrounding areas who were rogues and also on the committee, not a healthy situation. So, it was a case of if you can't beat them, join them. They would be doing what they called flogging a trail, that is showing the hound round a known course. They then know where they are going. Some of the trails were fixed courses so you knew were they went. My wrongdoing was to show my dog around. These people were known for it, and I had heard our family members talking about it all, as they were getting beaten by these people. It will still be going on. I believe that is what is killing it or has killed it. The family were moaning and doing nowt about it. When these others were doing it to me, I thought I would get them back.' Ann chips in: 'most people would do it when everything is quiet, and nobody is around. Not him. He did it in broad daylight!' 'Well, I wanted them to know', retorts Billy. 'I knew what they were doing. I was calling them out. They would have to accept it because the ones at the top had been doing it.' I asked if he regretted it now. 'Nope. I have given the reason. Yes, it was cheating. I wasn't doing it to cheat anyone who was playing fair. I was trying to get it dealt with officially. These people were big in the Hound Trailing Association so I reckon if they were caught they would have covered it up. There is a parallel with what has happened in the cycling world. That was my way of dealing with it.' Billy says he was just standing up for himself, but I was still surprised by this behaviour from someone who had shown such a sense of fairness to others in the rest of his life.

Ann recalls that looking after the dogs used to take quite a lot of their time. Billy admits it was nice to see your dog doing well, and you could have a bet on them. In fact, you had to bet on them to make any money. Billy confirms that, 'the first six in a race got prizes and that was from a fiver downwards from first place. By the time you had paid your petrol there was nothing in it. The sport is dying a death now actually, because of the very thing I have talked about. There are nowhere near as many dogs being run as there used to be. In them days there might have been 30 dogs in an average event.'

The second aspect of life that just happened around Billy Bland was hunting. Jon Broxap points out that Billy's experiences came from his background. As Jon says, 'Billy was not part of the hunting and shooting set, but it was just him being a farmer's son. Billy was a product of where he was from and he was very much a part of the Lakes and part of the countryside. People often don't see that side of him. For instance, I did know about his interest in wildlife and landscape, but it was not something we ever chatted about much.'

Billy also says he was brought up with the hunt being part of Borrowdale life. 'Taking it even further back than me, then the huntsman would be someone like Johnny Richardson of Blencathra, and he would actually walk his dogs to Borrowdale. He would walk then on a Monday from Threlkeld to a farm, of which Nook Farm was one, and they would stay there for a week, the huntsman and the dogs. He would feed his hounds in the stable or whatever. They would hunt in Borrowdale for three days and then return to their kennels and go to another valley the following week.'

This was in winter, starting at the end of August and

right through till May time. Billy liked being out on the fells, so he would go hunting when they were up in Borrowdale. 'Not always cos I was working. I couldn't see owt wrong with it at that time. They were supposedly doing a good job for the farmers. But I am afraid I know different now. It doesn't add up anymore. They said it was pest control, well it isn't. It was sport to them.' Billy started keeping hounds for a pack and saw a lot of things he didn't like in the way they treated them. For instance, they just used to shoot them when they had finished with them. Ann adds that they had a couple they looked after and they were far too thin in the winter when they were in the kennels. As Billy says 'we just boarded them through the summer. But I saw what was happening in the kennels. They had a 10-foot trough and there was 50 hounds coming to feed. Well if you had a shy feeder which was a bit nervous of other dogs then they would be standing back and got nowt. They should have had them out first and fed them separately.' He says he started bringing this up and making a noise about it. He then went on a Countryside Alliance march in London and listened to the speakers there and leant a thing or two. 'They were saying a hound kills a fox with a single bite to the neck. Why should a fox die when it has had one bite in its neck? We have seen a kill and it is not like that.'

Howard Pattinson maintains that he doesn't know what made Billy change his mind on hunting. 'I have been hunting with him, mind I am going back a long way, the late seventies or thereabouts. We would go to the New Year's Day meet. He was really keen, but today he seems to be set against it. One day recently I bumped into him at the bottom of Skiddaw on his bike. I said, "what are you doing here?" He said, "I am going to see what the hunt are doing". I can't remember, but I think he was hoping to film them. I said "what?". He said, "the buggers are hunting, when they bloody shouldn't be". I was surprised and slightly taken a back, I sensed he was quite serious, so I just left it.'

A court case that the Blands got involved with was part of what made Billy change his mind about hunting. The Blands had been walking two dogs since they were six months old. They had an agreement that the hounds were to be returned to them and live with them out of the hunting season and that, when their working lives were over, they would live with the Blands permanently. But the dogs were not returned to the Blands at the end of the hunt season, and they launched a legal bid to get them back.

Billy says that it is part of his life he should never have gone down. Commitment to justice took them to court. With no real satisfaction Billy concludes that they were proved right. 'We looked after the dogs for nowt and thought the world of them. Them lot thought nothing of them. They would put a bullet through them as soon as look at them. We got one dog back.'

Billy is now working with hunt monitoring groups. He maintains that the problem is that the police are not policing the hunting law. He maintains that he is not a saboteur, he is just in their faces to make his point. Ann adds, 'they don't like it. He is a monitor really. He wants to make people aware of the situation. He doesn't like liars and doesn't like people breaking the law.'

I was also interested in finding out how Billy and his family fit into the community, both now and in earlier days. We have already seen how Billy's family have worked various farms in Borrowdale and the surrounding area. Also, how Billy has always lived in a very small patch of the valley, and worked widely right across the valley, and into the wider county of Cumbria.

Howard Pattinson comments that Billy never talked to him about his interest in wildlife, it just never came up. 'I do know that for stone walling, he sometimes gets the stones that have rolled down from the mountains when it floods, and he fishes stones out of the edge of the beck at the back of his house to use.'

Billy Bland has obviously become an iconic figure both locally and further afield because of his outstanding performances as a fell runner. Since retiring from the sport, he has been heavily involved in the life of the valley, as has Ann. For instance, Billy attends parish council meetings, seeing that as a forum for trying to influence local decisions.

At one point when we were looking at possible photographs for this book Ann showed me one of Billy up on a fell side kneeling and holding a long metal tube. It illustrates another aspect of their community spirit which perhaps not many people will know about. In the photograph Billy is taking a reading from a rain gauge, as Ann explains, laughing at the thought that it was probably the first time a fellrunner was on the front page of the *Times* (where the photo originally appeared). 'Peter Edmondson was the farmer at Seathwaite Farm. He took the readings, from a series of rain gauges, which went to the Met Office in Bracknell, in Berkshire. He did it for ages and then got fed up of doing it and we agreed to take over. The first day of every month you had to read them. We used to do six gauges between us. One near Stockley Bridge, one at Sprinkling Tarn, then Styhead Tarn, then two on Seathwaite Fell, and one at Seathwaite Farm. We did the rain gauge reading for a long time. I have a cutting from the paper but cannot remember for how long we did it, about 17 years I think – we used to get £52 a year for doing it.' If you know the area, you will know what a commitment it would be to visit those six rainwater recording stations.

It is generally accepted that Seathwaite is the wettest inhabited place in England. It receives around 3.5 metres (140 inches) of rain per year. Ann Bland summed up the weather there that day in one of our recent conversations saying, 'today its nobbut watter'.

Ann explained how she became the Race Organiser of the Borrowdale Race. 'It was because nobody would take the Borrowdale race on. I have helped at every Borrowdale race there has ever been. I started doing teas and making cakes. Then Keswick AC took it over when we were in the Keswick club. Nobody would do it, so I did it with Pete Barron helping me. I did it for about 20 years, I think. Basically, Borrowdale Fellrunners took it off Keswick AC.' Ann organised it for Keswick then for Borrowdale. She quite enjoyed doing it, until it got to be that all the Health and Safety rules and regulations became a real burden. 'Billy asked me to stop then. Then Scoffer took it on. Scoffer is organiser in name now, but we have all got our jobs. I do my part still.' She adds that Miles Jessop (at the Scafell Hotel) plays a big part still with his generosity with money and feeding people like the Mountain Rescue with breakfast, for instance.

The 2001 fell season was disrupted by the foot and mouth crisis, but Ann and Billy spear-headed a huge effort to make the Borrowdale race the first to be run after the all clear. They had opened up the high fells on 9 June, and all the fells again on 1 August. Ann picks up the story.

'We put a bit of pressure on the farmers, because we had to keep off for so long. The man that helped a lot was the Park Ranger, who went round the farmers and asked them to agree to access.' They had about four days to make the arrangements, with the race being on the first Saturday in August. The race hadn't been cancelled because there had also been a hope that it could run. 'We took entries on the day. Some were against having the race, including the tenant of Yew Tree Farm. I was running round and I bumped into him. I said thanks for letting us use the land. "It shouldn't be happening." "Why not?" "Shouldn't be allowed." I said, "isn't it one of your best days in the café?" He never said any more.'

Prince Philip was coming to Honister to visit the mine at Honister for a second time that weekend. Miles Jessop got on the bandwagon and said he'll ask him to come to the Borrowdale race. Billy Bland and Pete Barron (another of the organising team) met the Prince, but Billy says he is no royalist and doesn't really remember it. The Prince drove down from Honister in his own Range Rover. He went into the front of the Scafell Hotel and parked there. Ann adds that they, 'had already presented the prizes, but we held a few back and did the three main ones with him.'

Scoffer had come fourth in the race that day and also met Prince Philip. He remembers well what Prince Philip said to him. It was that Scoffer was, 'fat and too big for running'.

Ann also recalls that on the Borrowdale race certificates in the 1980s there was a Wainwright drawing. 'There was a publisher called Alan Hill who had a house up behind the Scafell Hotel. He used to give us the certificates as Chris Bland did a bit of work for him. It stopped when he died though. He would do the printing for nowt.'

She went on to describe the amount of her time it used up after the race. 'I spent night after night after a Borrowdale race working all the intermediate times out from the checkpoint data. You used to have tags like the fasteners for a loaf of bread and you dropped a tag at every checkpoint. We had a board here and when you felt like it you used to sort the tags back into order and hook them up again.' It worked but she says it was a right pain.

Ann Bland reckons that every fell runner should be made to help at a fell race to see what actually goes into organising one. It is in no small part due to her efforts over the years that the Borrowdale race has remained one of the most consistently popular events.

Ann Bland is still helping organise the Borrowdale race, but Billy has long stopped running. He has taken up a new sport, which he applies himself to pretty seriously. He is having considerable success at it, and also derives great pleasure from it.

REAL WORLD

Billy Bland ran his last fell race in 1998, so he has been retired from running competitively for a considerable length of time now. What he hasn't done is retire from work, which he still enjoys doing on a part-time basis.

He stopped running because he wasn't enjoying training anymore and was beginning to consistently get aches and pains in his body. Billy did win a race when he was 50, but he says it was just a minor race at a local show which he happened to win. It was from Gatesgarth, where there was a small show and shepherds' meet. 'I had kinda packed in by then anyway. I ran really well up till I was 43 I think, and not bad at 45. To be honest I was losing interest, and I had taken it as far as I could. The training was less good, but once you build an engine up over a period of years that engine will still do you good, and it is doing me good even now as a cyclist. It will keep me in good stead for the rest of my life, which might finish tomorrow [*laughter*]. I don't run any more as my ankles ache too much. But my legs are strong enough, and my knees are all right .'

Having been heavily involved in starting Borrowdale Fellrunners in 1991, he turned out for them in relays in those early years. But Billy says his own efforts were only half-hearted by then. 'The fire was going out', he says. But, as one fell runner said, 'it had been an almighty conflagration'.

Colin Donnelly recently gave me his thoughts on Billy Bland retiring from running, after meeting him a few years ago. He started by describing Billy is a legend, before adding, 'I was down at a race in the Lake District, I think a championship race, and Billy was there spectating. So, I was chatting to him after and I said, "Billy, you are quite young yet. Why don't you go for the Vets?" I think he did for a year or two quite seriously and then dropped off. I made a comment at that time that he was still near the front, to which he replied, "First is first, second is nowhere." I think with Billy, if he wasn't winning a race it wasn't good enough. He didn't like to be chasing the win. He wasn't AT the front, and that is the crux of it. To get around that you must deal with it in your head, and people like Rob Jebb and Holmesy they will be dealing with that as well now. They were winning races, and maybe they are not winning now. They are not far off and are probably in a chasing group. But they must get their heads around that, but not leading. Going for the V40 or V50, they are new challenges, mind. You must accept you were right up there, but that is finished.'

At one of his recent public talks someone asked Billy Bland if he had ever done a park run. His reply illustrated how massively things have changed since he started running. 'There weren't any [*park runs*]. But it something new, and gets people out running. Anyone who is out running, cycling, anything, that is fantastic. There are more and more females, which is great. Back in the 1980s even we men used to be out running some places and they looked at you as if you were an alien. There were no women, hardly, running then. How times have changed.'

Strangely, Billy doesn't even get out on the fells much at all these days, even to go walking. 'A doctor mate of mine who I ride my bike with asked if I would walk the first leg of the Bob Graham Round with him. I said, "go on then", and we did'. They set out from Market Square, as Billy insisted he was, 'not bothering with the bit by Moot Hall' [*Can you imagine the scene?*]. So, he did that for his friend. That story is continued elsewhere, in the context of a new BGR record time being set. Billy adds, 'I sometimes help a farmer with a sheep that is crag fast if I am asked. No. I am on the bike all the time now.'

This is not just going out for a spin on his bike now and again, as it has included some big routes. In some ways Billy has transferred his running obsession across to a cycling obsession, as he gets out pretty much every day for a ride. He also mentions doing the Fred Whitton Challenge – an event that likes to call itself Britain's premier cycle sportive. It is a 114-mile ride around the Lake District, starting at Grasmere and taking in climbs of the Kirkstone, Honister, Newlands, Whinlatter, Hardknott and Wrynose passes, with fastest times usually around six hours. He has done four Fred Whittons and dropped out of a couple as well. Billy also goes on long rides abroad frequently, having done Geneva-Nice three or four years ago, and also some long climbs across the Pyrenees, such as Perpignan to Biarritz.

Mark Wilson is a friend who often does cycling rides and trips with Billy. Ann Bland once asked Mark what is was like being on holiday with Billy. Mark replied that it was just like taking another kid along with you. On hearing of this, Billy's passive aggressive response was, 'I would ride my bike, eat supper and go to bed. I can never get Mark out of bed. We have gone on holiday to ride the bike.' He does admit that none of these trips would happen unless Mark organised them.

I recently met Mark Wilson to hear his side of their biking partnership, which he explained in a quiet and measured way that probably comes from his background working in medicine. He was born in St Albans in 1970, with a mother from Thirlmere and a father who was from Cork. He moved up to the Lakes when he was six and a half, and lived at Thirlmere, where his parents had a guest house. He was at secondary school with Billy's daughter, being in the same year as Andrea. He is a doctor, in cardiology, at Carlisle Hospital, and is the friend that Billy told the story about doing the first leg of the BGR with.

Mark Wilson met Billy when he was 18 years old and took a year off to go travelling. That year he spent three months labouring on his parent's barn conversion. Billy Bland was the stonemason on that job. Mark adds that they had a place called Brackenrigg [*just north of Thirlmere*]. At the time Billy was working with Chris [his cousin].

Mark explains how Billy Bland got into biking. 'I have always ridden a bike. My wife Rachel and I were abroad, and we came back and brought the place we are in now [*in Embleton*]. In about 2005 I was doing a barn conversion here and I hadn't seen Billy for years. I phoned him to say, "could I have a hand knocking a window out". He turned up and ended up project managing the whole job for a year. I asked him if he was into biking.' Billy replied to Mark that he didn't have a bike. Billy couldn't run by then because of his ankles. He watched the fell races but seemed a little lost in the world to some. Mark says they also had a walk or two, also with Raymond Paterson who got Billy into biking. But Billy says he would never describe myself as having been lost. 'I have always filled my days with whatever comes along. Biking has given me a new focus for competing though. When you are riding with young 'uns and can keep up that gives you a buzz too.'

Mark continues the story. 'Raymond Paterson got him into biking first by suggesting a coast to coast ride. This was in 2005. Raymond lent him a hybrid bike with flat pedals, straight handlebars and Billy rode in his own trainers. They did it in about eight and a half hours. Every time they stopped for a drink Billy kept going, till he bonked.' Billy recalls the occasion. 'I said how far is it. It was from Workington to a place called Blackhall Rocks. It was about 120 miles, although we hadn't a route yet.' Billy said if they can't do that in 10 hours then he'd be eating hay with a horse again. So, he did it on that old bike with Raymond. 'I had never biked any distance before.' Billy adds. 'We took well under ten hours and my back really hurt. That was the start of biking for me.'

Back to Mark Wilson who takes up what happened next. 'So, when we talked about it again, in 2006, I got him a bike and he hasn't stopped since. We said then [in the November] how about doing the Whitton the next

May.' Billy had initially said he was not paying £500 for a bike. But Mark helped him get one from the Bike Bank in Workington at a good price. The first ride they had together was from Keswick to Ambleside then up The Struggle. Billy made it up and down Kirkstone Pass and got to Threlkeld and completely ran out of juice.

'He was grumpy and bored at the time,' adds Mark. 'I think cycling saved him really. We did the Whitton that May in something over seven hours, and we both found it hard. Although it was hard, he would still tell me what the birds were that we saw, and what flowers too. He told me that the oak trees on the Whitton route never lose their leaves in winter. I never knew that.'

Things went on from there. 'We trained harder the next year and went out to Spain. Down in Granada, which he absolutely loved.'

Hugh Symonds is another fell runner who took to biking when his competitive running days were done, and now cycle tours extensively with wife Pauline. He soon noticed the way Billy challenged himself at cycling events. 'At the end of the 2000s we used to do cycle Sportives. We did the Etape du Dales in 2006 and Billy Bland was in it. It is about 100 miles. He did it with Bob Whitfield and they did it as a two-up, alternately taking the wind. They did a really fast time between them.' Sportives are mass participation cycling events, but for many they are treated as time trials.

'Knowing Raymond and Mark, we started a club,' recalls Billy. 'The Blue Moon Club, because we got together every blue moon. That is how this Clive's Cumbrian Way bike ride started. You may never have heard of it, but you bike round Cumbria in two days [*it is 266 miles, about 150 first day, 120 the next*]. It is the best value in bike riding. Raymond set it up in memory of a schoolmate who died of Motor Neurone Disease. We had been talking about a ride around the county, which is pretty big, and that is how this came about. It is going to be the tenth one this year.' In a turn that may not surprise readers, Billy then announced that he was finished with doing it. 'A lot of the club I was in (Honister 92) were good lads for biking but they started dropping their pants and dancing about after having a few drinks. They got into trouble at the overnight stop which bothered me, and caused problems for the organisers. I do a bit of support now on the course.' He adds that, 'later on I bought a bike from Wheelbase in Staveley, it is upstairs.' Having seen two in the yard that is at least three bikes he has, then. 'It is five actually', says Ann.

Billy Bland has indeed become a very good biker, as talking to Mark Wilson revealed [*and Billy didn't, until pressed on the matter*]. He got a good time of 6:50 on the Fred Whitton when he was 63 years old. Billy is particularly proud of that ride. 'When I took to biking, each year went by and I tried to break 7 hours. After several years I eventually got it. I got a huge buzz out of that at 63, when I hadn't got it at 57. That was down to learning how to ride the event properly.'

Mark explains that Billy has also learnt about fuelling on the bike. 'Originally, he wouldn't eat on the bike, which you have to do if you go long. Nowadays he likes a bit of cake and has plain water.' Mark is not above getting one over on Billy competitively. 'There was a year that Raymond and I dropped him and got a much better time at the Whitton. Billy said to me, "have you been in the medicine cupboard, doctor. I can't believe that change in form". He needed an explanation'.

That comment mirrors something Hugh Symonds recently told me. 'I know there was one race when I ran away from everyone and Billy Bland turned to Jon Broxap and said, "has Hugh been on the diet?" Billy had to have a reason for that happening.'

What Billy hasn't learned is bike maintenance, despite having been on a course. 'He just doesn't do much bike maintenance,' says Mark. 'He does about 10,000 miles a year on his bike, and his cogs are just worn out.' Mark reckons that Billy has good bike handling skills though. 'He had an accident when his bike stem (that Scoffer gave him) sheared off, and he broke his collar-bone. But he is not a reckless downhill cyclist. He is very nice to ride with because he keeps a nice pace.'

Billy Bland is a perfectionist in many ways, and Mark Wilson and I discussed this in relation to his cycling, an area where Mark doesn't think he is coachable. 'He likes to do things his own way. He doesn't like the cycling aspect of getting dragged into a race. So, he always says "set off as you mean to finish". He has his pace, but cycling is about nipping behind people and resting for a bit. Billy didn't get that at first. So, he thought you had to find a pace to the whole ride at. He has come around to it now though.'

I wondered what Billy was like to ride and tour with. Peter Barron had told me about when he and Billy crossed the Alps and the Pyrenees, which was one long trip he shared with him. Pete recalled the end of the trip. 'On this trip I was doing all the cycle navigating and speaking in French (because he wouldn't speak to anybody) and we talked a lot about the environment, and at the end of the trip he says to me, "there's more to you than I thought, and I wouldn't say that to many". I more or less agree with Billy on the environment, except that I don't just blame farmers *per se*.'

The communication aspect struck a chord with Mark Wilson too. 'Although Billy is a very nice person to go away with, he just won't try to communicate abroad. Once we were doing something different and we met up after 5 or 6 hours and Billy says to me, "will you buy me a sandwich, I didn't like to ask". He would rather starve than face that task.' These are both pretty harsh assessments. Billy just doesn't speak any French, and isn't confident in those situations.

He must be pretty frustrating in other ways to be with too, as this story from Mark shows. 'I am quite easy going. Once we went to Italy, out in Aprica. The day before a race we went for a training ride. We parked at a small cemetery. We finished the ride and I was driving back to the chalet. It was about an hour and a half drive on a beautiful day. Nearly back home he said, "Mark, my bag is back at the cemetery". I didn't say a word. I just turned around drove an hour and a half back and we got the bag. His first comment was, "well if it was in England, they would have stolen it". We drove back, still not speaking much. We got back to the home and he says, "hey Mark, I can't believe WE left it there". He is never wrong.' Billy admitted eventually that they were both at fault. 'We had sat there for about 20 minutes having a sandwich or summat. We piled in the car and drove away leaving the bag there. Mark's passport was in it, not mine. We bombed back and there it was.'

Billy also doesn't fit the normal men in Lycra mould, as another of Mark's stories illustrates. 'We did a race in Nice and he turned up there with his rucksack on. He says, "I have seen them clouds and I am taking my jacket." We did well and got a prize. He always wears his bandana and an old pair of glasses.'

Billy doesn't get nervous riding a bike. He suggests that, 'you would never go down Honister on a bike if you thought of all that could happen to you, like your handlebars come to bits (and it has happened, but not to me). My stem broke one day, but I wasn't on Honister fortunately. After I broke my collarbone, it didn't stop me going over Honister, but it is in your head for quite a while.'

When he had that accident it was a frosty day and he was coming from Lorton to Buttermere. It happened near Rannerdale car park. 'There is a sign that says "tek care on t'road, there are lambs about". All of a sudden the stem snapped, and I am over the handlebars like a sack of tatties. I landed on my back and jeez that hurt. I got up and thought I had got away with it. It could have happened at a much worse spot. I put my arm up and popped my collarbone. I got taken to a mate's at Buttermere and they got the ambulance. It gets into your head after something like that. After that I was thinking of it every time I went down Honister. Hoping nothing happens like.'

Ann Bland says she doesn't worry about the biking when Billy goes away, or even on a local ride. 'Sometimes if he is not back from biking I think well he will have gone in somewhere and he will be chatting to folk because that is what he likes doing. Some of the rides are social ones too.'

Another situation shows a sensitive and slightly insecure side to Billy Bland, which comes out in something that Mark Wilson says next. 'I was out in Nice with him and a friend, and we were standing on the promenade. There were loads of people walking and rollerblading. Billy looked at my friend and I and said, "I am no-one here. No-one knows Billy Bland". It was a bit of an epiphany for him to think that he was out of Borrowdale in a built-up area with thousands of people and no-one knew him.' Mark adds that it was a bizarre thing to say, but to me it speaks volumes about Billy. The man who was so big back in Cumbria, and in the wider arena of sporting excellence, seemed to be having trouble coming to terms with being a relative nobody down in the south of France.

So, how good a biker is Billy Bland? He won his age category once in a race. He also qualified to represent Great Britain when he went down to Cambridge for an 80-mile race. 'Anyone that got in the top 10 per cent could represent Great Britain in the finals which were in Denmark that year. I finished third in my age group in Cambridge. I finished first British rider in Denmark, but I gave a bad account of myself really. I was naive. I was 67 at that time.' The qualifier was the Tour of Cambridge, on 7 June 2015, which took Billy 3:35:01 to complete. On 6 September in Denmark Billy was twenty-eighth in his age group, finishing the 115 kilometre race in 3:24:48.

When he was 70 (in 2017) he qualified again in Scotland, although he was 69 when he did the qualifier. He explains, 'I was counted as a 70-year-old for age categories. I was actually 70 when I rode in the finals in France. So, I went up to Ayr and rode that race and finished second and qualified for the finals. It was a guy called Michael Holmes that beat me, an ex-pro. I was well beaten', Billy says.

Billy adds that Michael Holmes just got pipped in the final by a French rider. 'There was a group of four Frenchmen and they kinda did him. I was sixteenth, in the same group as the twelfth man, and was third Brit. My cycle sprinting is the same as my running sprinting – crap. In running you could try and get somebody out of the race in the last two miles or so, but in biking you can't do that. If you go to the front, then you are the idiot that is pulling everybody else along.' He was pleased that he gone though. It was a really hot day, and he thinks he did as well as he could. 'You had to buy your own kit. There was a good buzz about the whole thing. I don't get beat by a 65- or 70-year-old in Cumbria in Sportives, so I like testing myself at these bigger events.'

The aforementioned Italian race was La Campionissimo, on 26 June 2016 in Aprica in the Alps. It is described in the race publicity as, 'everything the international cyclist wants in an Italian Gran Fondo. Iconic climbs such as Gavia and Mortirolo, offer challenge and beauty in equal measure'. Aprica has also hosted the Giro d'Italia a few times. There were about 4,500 entrants and you all set off together. Billy describes the day. 'It was about 100 miles on a hot day and I said to Mark [Wilson], "I am not doing the 100 so did the Medium" (which was50 to 60 miles), as I knew I couldn't race all that way without fading. I hadn't a clue how I was doing until after I'd finished. But I did my best like. Going up the last pass there was no-one overtaking me, even though all the age groups were in together. After the finish I was at the ski station where you got changed and there was a meal on afterwards. All the razzmatazz was about a 4-minute walk down to the town centre. I'd finished but the longer race was still going on. There was a prize giving for the shorter course. I was just strolling about downtown and heard it all going on. I walked up to where the podium was and the guy with the microphone announced third place and I thought the bloke looked about my age. Then second place went up and then he gave my name out. I might not have been there, I just happened on it. I'd won my age category by about seven minutes I think it was. It was as much a buzz as the running had been.'

Billy is ruthless at climbing on the bike. Mark Wilson said to him that he read that Lance Armstrong didn't have a lot of lactate. 'I don't understand about lactate,' Billy replied. 'I have never had this burn in my legs. I run out of breath and that is it.' Mark suggests that maybe he has got a very special physiology. 'He has said no Blands can sprint. We went to the Worlds and he got to the final sprint and he is still sitting down. He couldn't sprint there either.'

Billy Bland says that even now that he has podium potential on the bike, his cycling training is similar to his running training – he just goes out and does it because he likes it. There are no sophisticated race tactics either, but he is very competitive. Mark Wilson adds, 'when Billy is 75 I want to see if I can get him to enter the World Masters cycling race (for the third time), as he realises the competition are slowly dying off, but he is showing no sign of slowing down.'

Despite his age, Billy Bland has unbelievable stamina. I ask Mark Wilson to summarise Billy's biking. 'He hasn't got any sprint in him. If you pass him he will draw you back, he is gonna keep coming. If he meets a stranger on the hills he starts whistling, to show he has got enough breath to do it! He will say to people that attack hills, "don't ride at it, ride up it". He spins when bike riding.' He concludes with a nugget about meeting Chris Boardman. 'Billy met a group on a trip in France, wealthy people who had won or bought a day with Boardman and got himself invited along. Afterwards he said, "I like that bloke". I said, "why?". He said, "he goes to bed at 8 o'clock".' A man after his own ways.

Billy concludes our discussions about his biking with a tale which seems to illustrate 'riding up to it'. On the group bike trip out in Gran Canaria, Martin Mikkelsen-Barron had gone ahead of the group, riding hard to the top of this hill. Billy takes up the tale. 'Then he was coming back to meet us because we were five to six minutes behind. He said, "I have just seen Ian Stannard [*a rider in Chris Froome's team, now sponsored by Ineos*] and a Tinkoff rider." He had heard Stannard say that he recognised his Fred Whitton shirt. I was biking on to the top and there were fruit sellers on top of the hill, and they step in the road to try and stop you to sell stuff. I think Stannard and them must have stopped there. They were on a training ride and just as I got to the fruit seller I could see them about a quarter of a mile ahead. I thought I will see if I can catch them, because they didn't seem to be going that fast. It took me about three miles, but I did it, even though I had a small rucksack on. When I got there no words were said and I sat on their wheels for a few hundred yards and then one of them who was at back, I think a Wiggins rider, turned round and still said nowt. I rode a while there but Stannard never turned around, unfortunately. I peeled off and waited for the others to catch up and I said to our lads, "I just caught Stannard". I will be telling that tale for a while now.'

One of the perennial problems that athletics in general faces is finding a role for top athletes in the formal, or informal, coaching structure of the sport in order to share their vast experience with the upcoming young athletes. You might assume that an athlete of Billy's calibre might have been asked to work on a formal basis with the next generation of athletes. Well, he has, but it didn't go well. When I asked him about it and what the problem was, Billy laughed, and replied. 'You know the answer to that. I was invited to go to Coniston [*Billy can't be sure which year it was*] to say a few words in support of the new coach. I said I can't do that when I don't even know him.'

Billy does have the occasional very informal advisory role now with some athletes, as he used to with nephew Gavin back in the day. He gives a blunt response to people searching him out for advice. 'If you can't be arsed to come and see me then that is all right by me.'

He explains. 'I do it now with Hannah Horsburgh, who I have had a few words with, because I know her step-father. Hannah got on to the England team, well got picked but never actually ran in the race. She was told she was not to run the Borrowdale race prior to the international. I said to her, "take no notice, you run Borrowdale if you want. You are getting picked because as a runner you do what you do. Before you worry about the international you become good enough to be picked for England on what you are doing yourself". She is going really well and has worked on her weaknesses, which myself and her stepfather have pointed out to her. She is a good worker, and ran well in the relay in Italy recently, breaking the record for one leg. She did not like being told what to do by some coach or other [*in the system*].'

Knowing that Billy has had several conversations with Carl Bell it would seem that there was another advisory partnership that might prove fruitful. Unsurprisingly, Billy gave his usual blunt assessment of the situation.

'If Carl can't see what is going on around him I will tell him, if we get into a conversation. I will tell him what he needs to learn off what Kilian [Jornet] does. Several of them were on a good pace at the Borrowdale race this year but couldn't sustain it. Why not? Because they are not fit enough. If you can run from Rosthwaite to Scafell Pike knowing that there is a second half to it and knowing that is the sort of time you need to run a record and you can't hack it in the second half there is only one thing causing that. That is your fitness. You need to stick at it and eventually your body will adapt. I am happy to talk to anybody. They can say, "he talks a load of shite", well fair enough. If it got back to me that is what they are saying, then I wouldn't bother with them again.'

He finishes with a fine expression that I have not heard before, which he claims to be an old Cumbrian saying, referring in this instance to those with potential who turn a deaf ear to his advice: 'You can't push string.'

Howard Pattinson had an interesting take on Billy's current status. 'I would see Ann Bland in Keswick and would have to stop myself from just saying "how is Billy?" and ask her about herself. Recently Kathy and I got the bus to Bassenthwaite to walk back to Keswick. Billy was working on a house there with Ken Hebson. I retired at 60 and keep busy walking, gardening, and travelling. I don't think Billy will retire. You have to do something, and that is what he does. If he is not doing that, he is out on his bike. With regard to fell running achievements, I have no regrets and I don't think Billy can have either.'

Work always came first for Billy though. Biking is part of his life now. In 2013 he rode up Honister 440 times. He then decided to set himself a target of getting to 500 Honister rides in 2014 by his birthday (28 July). He achieved that, so decided to carry on till the end of the year and reached 744. As someone said, 'that is Lakeland Grit, isn't it'. The idea was to strengthen his legs to be able to keep up with the young 'uns on the bike. He lost interest the following year.

He goes out on the bike most days and makes sure he does his 10,000 miles a year. Everything is documented. All or nothing at all.

LAND OF HOPE AND DREAMS

Having lived his whole life in Borrowdale, Billy Bland has seen many changes in the valley and in the wider area of the Lake District. Not all those changes are for the better, as Billy likes to explain to anyone who is prepared to listen.

With its narrow winding road and limited bus service Borrowdale is not that easy of access even now. It used to be even harder. William Gilpin, the champion of the picturesque, visited the valley in 1752, and wrote: 'On the 9th June we set out on horseback (which I mention, as it is the only conveyance the road will admit) on an expedition into Borrowdale; a wild country south west of Keswick.' Visiting the Lakes in 1794, the gothic novelist Ann Radcliffe described the view into Borrowdale. 'Dark caverns yawn at its entrance, terrific as the wildness of a maniac, and disclose a narrow straight running up between mountains of granite that are shook into almost every possible form of horror.'

This was all before the so-called 'Lakes Poets', including Wordsworth, started influencing more people to come to the area, and a tourism boom began. Ian Thompson, in *The English Lakes: a History*, described William Wordsworth's poetry as being about, 'the organic relationship between human beings and the natural world'.

The Borrowdale Story website describes the early settlement of the valley, and that natural world:

> Farming in Borrowdale, as we know it today, goes back at least 1,000 years to when Scandinavians came as refugees from Ireland and settled the valley. No doubt they felt at home in this mountainous environment. Picture a valley, probably wooded up to 1,500 or 2,000 feet. and imagine settling here. They made clearings or 'thwaites' to create settlements and established summer pastures or 'saetres' higher up the valley for their livestock; as at Seatoller – 'the summer pastures with alder trees'. Notice the tightly grouped hamlets in Borrowdale and how many of them end in 'thwaite'.

Since that time there has only been a limited amount of expansion of the number and size of the hamlets, but huge changes have occurred to the landscape. From medieval times land was cleared for crop growing, and ridge and furrow field patterns may still be seen in the Rosthwaite area. Over time more cattle were kept, and the level of sheep grazing also increased, which prevented the regeneration of natural woodland on the higher fells.

But Borrowdale does have more surviving woodland than many other Lakeland valleys.

In 1934 the Forestry Commission was looking to expand its acreage of commercial coniferous forestry. It planned to purchase large areas of Eskdale and Upper Dunnerdale to that end. Having seen what the Forestry Commission had done in Ennerdale and Whinlatter, there was much opposition from amenity groups to this plan. Cousins notes that, 'The National Trust negotiated with the Forestry Commission to see if some of the Lake District could be declared a 'forest free' zone. In 1935 there was an agreement for an exclusion zone to include Borrowdale, Newlands, the Langdales, and Eskdale head, while the Forestry Commission was prepared to consult before planting in Wasdale or between Ullswater and Windermere.' This may be partially responsible for the valley retaining so much of its wooded landscape.

The most important industries in Borrowdale have been farming, mining and more recently tourism. Billy Bland, and members of his extended family, have been involved in all three of these and are in an excellent position to comment on changes they have seen over the years.

The landscape of Borrowdale has evolved over millions of years, and at the simplest level is a result of being sculptured by ice thousands of years ago. Nature and human habitation have slowly changed it in more recent times.

Millenia ago the seabed erupted with a staggering violence. In the course of a few million years (a heartbeat in geological time) a layer of rock was formed, comprising hard lava beds interspersed with softer bands of ash and boulders. To geologists this is known as the Borrowdale Volcanic Series. These Borrowdale Volcanics are almost as hard as granite, and tend to break down into large blocks, which are very resistant to external forces. The head of Borrowdale is composed of these rocks, while the area north of Grange is comprised of Skiddaw Slates, which tend to break down more easily, and thus tending to form fells that are smoother and sleeker. All this happened several thousand miles away in the southern hemisphere, because landmasses are constantly moving.

One other factor created the shape of the landscape that we see today. The Ice Age started a mere two million years ago, and in the geological timescale it has only just finished. The mountain building phase had concluded with a huge dome being pushed up in Central Lakeland. Huge amounts of snow built up layer upon layer on the upper levels of this dome, and formed great ice fields that eventually started to grind their way down the valleys. Under the pressure of their own massive weight, the glaciers' destructive power was awesome. Gouging and grinding, ever deeper, ever wider, scouring the fellsides, the ice sculpted the distinctive landscape, the U-shaped valleys, the dramatic crags and waterfalls, the hanging valleys, and the lakes and tarns that we see today. Wherever there was a hollow or a blockage damming the valley, perhaps created by a terminal moraine, the water collected and lakes were formed, but then they gradually silted up.

At the end of the last Ice Age (about 10,000 years ago) ancient wildwood probably covered around 80 per cent of the Borrowdale Valley. From about 6,000 years ago this woodland was beginning to be cleared, as stone axes were being perfected. Over time much of the woodland was coppiced (for charcoal, tools and pit props) and pollarded (for fuel and agricultural use). The National Trust owns nearly 2,000 acres of woodland in Borrowdale, primarily managing it for access and its landscape value.

On one of my trips up the valley to talk with Billy Bland when writing this book, I stopped off at the National Trust car park and walked into one of these wooded areas to re-visit the Bowder Stone, which is illustrated at the top of this chapter.

The Bowder Stone is either an enormous glacial erratic set down by melting glaciers, or an immense fragment that fell from the crag above, rolling and crashing down the slope before coming to rest in this unlikely position. It depends who you believe, but the evidence for the latter is pretty strong.

The stone is a quirky tourist attraction, as it gives interesting views over the valley and over to Castle Crag if you climb the ladder to gain access to the top of it. It was established as a tourist attraction by Joseph Pocklington in 1798. He'd already built a house on Derwent Island, diverted Barrow Cascade to make it more impressive, and created a tradition of armed invasions of his island as part of the Derwentwater Regatta. He also owned Barrow House, which later was a hotel run by Bob Graham (of Bob Graham Round fame). The National Trust website adds that Pocklington's:

> ... approach to the Bowder Stone was characteristically unsubtle. He set up 'a crazy ladder' for tourists to stand on the summit, built a mock hermitage nearby and erected a 'druidical' standing stone. He also built a cottage where he installed an old woman whose duty was to 'lend the place quaint atmosphere'. This tradition continued throughout the Nineteenth century.

In earlier times the Borrowdale valley cannot have been inviting with its marshes, scrubby hillsides and craggy rocks, and prior to Roman times there is very little evidence of habitation anywhere, although there is conjecture that the Romanised British fled there and built a hill fort on Castle Crag to defend themselves. David Howe, in his book *Rocks and Rain, Reason and Romance*, gives a further reason for lack of Roman influence in Borrowdale. He says their route to the coast was via, 'a road, known as the Tenth Iter, connecting Kendal, Ambleside and then over the hills to Ravenglass on the coast'. Bear in mind those hills required the negotiating of Wrynose and Hardknott passes, not your typical Roman road making tasks.

As noted above, farming in the valley began as it became more permanently settled, predominantly by invading Norsemen, who started creating more and more clearings. As family sizes increased these thwaites and saetres (both Norse words) developed into farms in their own right. David Howe also highlights other Norse words that have left their legacy. For instance, 'beck' is from *bekr* for stream; *dalr* becomes 'dale'; *fjall* for hill evolved into 'fell'; and *tjorns* for small lakes gave us 'tarns'.

After the Norman Conquest, Borrowdale was part of one of the great baronies created in northern England. Then, in the thirteenth century, much of the valley was owned by Furness Abbey and Fountains Abbey. Records of the time mention the Herdwick sheep, whose wool provided the monks with their coarse habits. For over 300 years the valley was farmed by the industrious monks, who possibly built the first field walls as they kept sheep, and cultivated rye, oats and barley. With the introduction of cattle as well, the farming would have been much more self-sufficient than it is today, whereby sheep farming is dominant, supported by tourism (through self-catering, bed and breakfast and tearooms).

The other activity that has impacted both the landscape and the lifestyle of residents of the valley has been mining and quarrying. Organised mining developed in the sixteenth century when German miners were invited in by Queen Elizabeth I, an early example of getting migrants to do the tough jobs. She established the Society of Mines Royal to encourage more mining. This resulted in the stripping of considerable amounts of woodland in order to use the wood in the mines. It also resulted in the parish register of Crosthwaite Church, Keswick, recording 176 children being born to German fathers between 1565 and 1584. There was also small-scale extraction of iron, lead and copper in the valley.

It is thought that the medieval monks may have used graphite from Seathwaite to draw lines in their books for the scribes to follow. The Seathwaite graphite deposits were the most expensive substance ever mined in Cumbria. There were many uses of graphite, including shepherds marking their sheep in the early days. Later it made cannon balls smoother and rounder, which meant they went further and straighter, and it was also the basis for the establishment of the world's first industrial pencil making factory, in Keswick. In an article in the *Guardian* in September 2018, Pete May claimed that, 'mining once accounted for 80 per cent of Cumbria's wealth'.

From the seventeenth century there was much extraction of stone and slate for building. The Honister slate mine, where Billy Bland worked for 10 years, is still in production today, although with a tourist slant to its activities. Several other prominent, but now long closed, old slate mines can be seen in the Borrowdale valley at sites including Rigg Head, Quay Foot and Castle Crag. At this latter location you can walk up through the quarry to get an awesome view back down the valley over Derwent Water to Keswick and the fells beyond.

I had thought that gold was mined once in Borrowdale, but Billy Bland corrected me on that aspect. 'Hindscarth's other name is Goldscope, but there wasn't really any gold in Borrowdale', he explained. 'There was the Goldscope mine, located on the lower slopes of Hindscarth near Low Snab Farm, over the other side of Hindscarth which is not in Borrowdale'. It operated from the sixteenth century and yielded such large amounts of lead and copper that it was called 'Gottesgab' (God's Gift) by the German miners who were brought over to develop the mine in its early days. The mine closed at the end of the 19th century.

Tourism has recently been a major influence in the Lake District. But before the late eighteenth century it was considered a wild and desolate place. In 1724 Daniel Defoe described the area as 'the wildest, most barren and frightful of any that I have passed over in England', hardly a clarion call to potential visitors. In 1778 Father Thomas West published 'A Guide to the Lakes', in which he recommended the best locations for admiring the landscape. Before long, poets such as Wordsworth, Southey and Coleridge were promoting the beauty and splendour of the landscape to a nation eager to escape the increasingly over-crowded cities. In 1820 William Wordsworth published his own guidebook 'A Guide through the District of the Lakes in the North of England' which sold well and encouraged many more visitors. As an alternative to the Grand Tours of the great cities of Europe, people were looking for opportunities to travel closer to home.

People from a working-class background were able to be more adventurous holiday makers, as improved working conditions gave them a shorter working week, increased wages and paid holidays. It was possible to reach Windermere by rail from 1847, followed by further lines to Keswick and Lakeside at the south end of Windermere. This facilitated many more people from a wide range of social classes to visit on day trips from cities like Manchester and Liverpool. Improvements in the roads, widespread car ownership and a further rise in standards of living led to ever increasing numbers of visitors to the Lakes from the 1960s onwards.

The outcome of all these interactions has produced its own issues, and many people are concerned about what the future holds for both the Lake District, and the Borrowdale valley in particular. The granting of World Heritage Site status to the Lake District may bring further dramatic changes to the area.

Billy Bland has lived in Borrowdale all his life and has seen the many changes that have occurred in the last seven decades. He has some very stringent views on what has happened, and is happening, in Cumbria and has a deep passion for the area and its landscape. At one of his talks he was asked about the Lake District being a World Heritage site. His reply was, 'I could talk for a week on that subject! Just don't talk to me about politicians and that. The Lake District is seriously going backwards, less wildflowers, no fish in the beck, and wants sorting out.' We moved swiftly on at the talk as the audience were there for running banter not a lecture.

But Billy has patiently explained his point of view to me in a number of our conversations, and we have batted the topic around till a picture emerges, a sort of personal alternative vision for the future.

Billy's starting point is how the landscape has changed, in his mind mostly for the worse. 'I could take you to a meadow down the road where I found over twenty different wildflowers in one field when I was young. They are just not there now, which I find sad. Nitrogen is the reason. It is the farming methods. I can't remember seeing deer in Borrowdale in my youth, but they have come in since. Red deer were in Thirlmere, and they have eventually encroached over here. People like to see them.'

Billy Bland has recently recorded an interview for an exhibition at Wordsworth House, in Cockermouth. It was made for the National Trust and in it Billy gives a longish explanation for one of his consistent gripes, which is with the farming community.

'Being a farmer's son, I was brought up to think that foxes were a nuisance and I have persecuted foxes myself. Looking back now, having just entered my seventies, and I now think, "what was that all about?". A fox isn't a nuisance. Yes, it can go with a lamb or two, but they have got to eat. They clean the dead 'uns up on the fells. But that is how it was. The farming community have virtually mucked the wildlife out of this valley. I find that sad. I remember my father talking about seeing pine martens or foulmarts (known for their stink), or both. That was when I was young, and I was born in 1947. There were eagles in Borrowdale, not in my time mind. I remember curlews in the fields, because of the hay meadows, and lapwings. You haven't got them now. Go to feed the hens and you would get a cloud of yellowhammer. You would struggle to find a yellowhammer in this valley now. I haven't seen one for a few years. There should be a place for everything. Farming has been a lot to do with why we haven't got variety. Anything that eats a blade of grass has to go, except sheep. A farmer's livelihood doesn't depend on that. The taxpayer gives them their livelihood now. It is time things changed. Nitrogen wants stopping from being put in the fields. You put it on just to get another flush of grass. They will say it will feed a lot of sheep, but they are supposed to be keeping less sheep. But there is a lot of non-compliance with the rules'.

In one of our conversations he expanded on this view. 'What I mean by non-compliance is that farmers have signed up to keep less sheep but keep them anyway. It is totally wrong in my view. It is bad for the valley.' I asked how he knew that nitrogen kills the wildflowers. 'I know because they started disappearing as soon as they started using it. It is simple as that. Nobody will argue with that. Then the wildlife goes with it. If we had all our fields full of wildflowers and all the wildlife back, then even more people would want to come, wouldn't they?'

Pete Barron says that recently he and Billy have had a lot of discussions about Billy's love of wildlife, although earlier Pete didn't know about that deep love. 'What I didn't realise is that he has had quite a long-term interest in what is around him. Billy is very observant and does not miss much. He is particularly interested in flowers, I think. We were cycling somewhere, and I was pointing out this and that, as it is what I did for work, and I was honestly surprised that he knew so much. He has got a passion now for highlighting the changes in the valley, which are tremendous. I might have a bigger picture than Billy through my work, but he is dead right. We do have less wildlife value in the area than before the National Park, which is ironical when you think about it. It is largely down to government policy post-war, I think. They tried to fund farming in a way to make us more productive. It is not the farmers fault really. They have just responded to government policy. It is phenomenal the decline in wildlife that we have had in the last fifty years. Billy and I are both worried about what we have lost, and none of us seem to be doing much about it. We should be shouting about this, every one of us.'

Talking of even more people wanting to come brings out a dichotomy in Billy Bland's views, illustrated by the problems that locals have in obtaining housing in the area since off-comers have moved in. Neither of his own children live in Borrowdale and would have issues if they wanted to. 'They are not far away; one is at Keswick and one is at Penrith. But plenty of people raised in this valley haven't been able to stay. It wasn't much different when Ann and I were looking for somewhere to live. If it wasn't for her grandfather, then we wouldn't have been able to stay in the valley.'

Getting into his stride he continues with this theme. 'I strongly believe that there shouldn't be any second homes allowed in the National Park. There are plenty of hotels. If there isn't plenty, then let's have some more. If people want to come and stay, come and have a holiday, everyone is welcome. But houses have been bought up because they are an investment. It shouldn't be like that. There are plenty of houses in Borrowdale for the people who want to live in Borrowdale, if there weren't second homes here, and holiday houses. I would call it common sense but there isn't much of that about.'

When it comes to housing policy, Billy feels it is too late. 'It should have happened years ago, as soon as it started. Houses for investment is also part of the problem, rather than houses to live in. There was a shop in Rosthwaite till about 4 or 5 years ago and now there isn't. That was turned into flats. The nearest shop is in Keswick now.' Dave Hall reckons that the shop used to have 'local rates' and 'tourist rates'. All well and good if you knew, Dave chuckles. Billy says it is unfair to say the shop had different rates. 'It cost more for having it up the end of the valley rather than in Keswick.'

At one point our conversation turned to some of the many agencies that are involved in managing the Cumbrian landscape. I mentioned some of the policies of these agencies as a prompt and Billy came back to give his thoughts as we went through the list. His comments did tend to be focussed on particular issues.

We started with the National Park Authority, who Billy says he is getting totally disillusioned with. 'They know what is going on. I have had meetings with them over this fox hunting carry-on. They will do nothing about it. They are the same with the farming non-compliance. In fact, they glorify the farmers. I express my view but there are an awful lot of people that won't voice their opinion.'

I took a trip to High Borrowdale, way over the east side of the Lakes, to talk with Jan Darrall and find out where the Friends of the Lake District (FLD) sit and what their policies are. Darrall is the Policy Officer for FLD, and took a break from working with some volunteers on a wildflower meadow project there to enlighten me. It was possibly the finest interview location I have ever had.

Later on, back with Billy Bland, I pointed out to him a couple of things FLD had been saying about the review of the National Park Plan. Firstly that, 'the Local Plan is too focussed on tourism business and should be more aware of conserving and enhancing the landscape; and of the needs of people who live in and work in the Lake District.' Secondly that, 'the Lake District Local Plan's Biodiversity policy is not aspirational enough to make sure that wildlife in the National Park thrives.'

Billy agreed with these sentiments from the Friends of the Lake District. 'They are on the ball. George Monbiot's book [*Feral*] is smack on target. But didn't he half get a lacing about it. I don't agree with the National Park's attitude, which encourages loads more tourists. We have got plenty of tourists now. However, I don't want to see anyone barred from coming here.'

Next, I reiterated a statement from the National Trust. They say they, 'are committed to retaining the cultural landscape which has evolved over time, improving the area's biodiversity and working with our local communities to maintain a viable living.' Billy responded that he, 'likes some things that the National Trust are saying, but it seems like a lot of PR. There are a lot of words from them and the National Park Authority. I will believe it when I see it. They are thinking of putting in lynx in Scotland, aren't they? But when they take a survey about it, they only survey those they want to get answers from. Lynx don't eat sheep; they eat deer and that is what they want them for in Scotland. Nature's picture is that there should be a place for everything.'

Billy finishes that topic with a further rant against the current farming situation, seemingly his real *bete noir*. 'There is only one thing that motivates a farmer, money.' Unfortunately, Billy's very strong views on farming have resulted in him falling out with close members of his own family that are involved in farming in the Lakes.

He continued by saying that the valley is almost wholly owned by the National Trust. 'They could make some changes. I just biked across the Pyrenees and they can have wildflowers there, why can't we. There hasn't been a field ploughed in Borrowdale for at least 40 years. It is a no-no in the agreements with various agencies.'

Another possibility raised in my discussion with Jan Darrall (of FLD) was a tourism tax. Billy was in favour, but with reservations. 'We have been cycling in Gran Canaria and they had a tax there. It was put on at about a couple of pounds a head and we thought it was a good idea. As long as it is spent wisely to improve the environment.'

There had been a suggestion of Showcase areas in the Lakes in the local plan, but it has since been dropped. Borrowdale was being mooted as one such, with the LDNPA perhaps relaxing restrictions in the valley. Billy then comes out with an extraordinary suggestion. 'If people want to come up here to walk then fine. But I would put a traffic barrier at the bottom end of Borrowdale and have said that for 15 years.'

He then outlined some thoughts on the landscape, which after all is why many come to the area. 'Get wildflowers in the fields. Get the farmers to be the ones that stay on their tenanted farms and get them to show people how it used to be done. That would be of interest to people coming in. There seem to be no ploughed fields, and no potato fields these days. Joseph Weir is showing the way locally – with using manure, brought in where necessary, and I have never seen so much grass in this valley as there was last spring. Just shows what can be done.'

Billy has more time for the John Muir Trust, who are currently managing a large part of the Helvellyn range. 'They stand for the sort of thing I am talking about. Somebody said to me "there is no void in nature". If you have the habitat then nature will fill it.'

One of the possible actions of Wild Ennerdale (WE) is reintroducing pine martens to the area. Billy surprised me by not being fully in favour of some of the WE work. 'Maybe they are trying to justify things by rewilding. It was always wild, was Ennerdale. Then they put cattle on to the ground. Them cows in some cases have been there for ten years, breaking up the ground. They should take the cows off and let it be natural. Pine martens would be good there though. But they would only get persecuted. Farmers will shoot them – it is happening in Borrowdale with deer. They [*the National Trust*] identified this year they would shoot 100 deer. There was one shot a fortnight ago and it was pregnant. The baby was left there, fully formed – and somebody saw it and put it on social media and all hell was let loose, and rightly so. Police are making out deer are being poached in Borrowdale. It is farmers asking people to come in and shoot them. There is going to be a public meeting about this and on the farmers keeping too many sheep. I'll certainly be there.'

A short diversion, if we may, to hear more from the Friends of the Lake District, whom Billy has already said he tends to agree with where they are coming from. It may be relevant to record Jan Darrall's thoughts on the future – of both Borrowdale and the Lakes in general – as it resonates with a lot of Billy Bland's observations.

Darrall describes Borrowdale as the classic Lake District landscape. 'Glacial valley, inbye, open fells, walls, but that has issues as well. How long will commoning go on, for communal grazing?' she muses. 'There is the wildlife and biodiversity issue, and the tensions that brings. There are issues of water management down through the valley, into Derwentwater and on in to Bassenthwaite. There are livelihoods and the whole tourism debate. There have been massive changes in Borrowdale if you look beneath the surface, particularly in the culture of the communities and how they are made up. Offcomers come in, take over the parish council and try to make what they want to happen take priority. There is the problem of affordable housing. There may have been less landscape change in Borrowdale because of the NT owning so much of it, but not everyone thinks they have been good landlords though.'

Darrall agrees with Billy on some of the seemingly extreme ideas he has for protecting the valley. 'Yep. I tend to agree, even with the gate across the end of Borrowdale. I am not sure how sustainable the levels of accommodation for tourists are in Borrowdale [*citing the massive extension to the Lodore Falls Hotel*]. The basic problem is we have so many businesses that depend on tourism, they don't want the word to go out that the place is full. One of the worst aspects is the travel. Until there is a realistic and viable option what can you do? We [*at FLD*] have input to the consultation the National Park are doing because it is far too tourism-led. There is not enough for the residents.'

She added, 'one of the big concerns is the never-ending push for more tourists with no proposals for how to manage the impacts they have. We have no realistic proposals for a sustainable transport network and are seeing increasing levels of traffic congestion, more pressure for car parks, and signs of erosion of the character and fabric of the landscape, not to mention contributions to climate change. There needs to be an urgent debate about how many more visitors parts of the Lake District can take, what is sustainable and how impacts can be managed and fixed if needed.'

Darrall was certainly not happy with everything the National Parks Authority were doing. 'People have been coming out very emotionally about "*National Park not Theme Park*", she added. 'It has shown to many people that things have started to go wrong. When change is slow and incremental you don't notice, but when you stand back you suddenly think hang on a minute, do we really want this. Do we really want the whole of Thirlmere and Borrowdale to be like Windermere and Bowness?'

She was more positive on possible government responses. 'The government have said that from 2021 to 2027 will be the transitional period (post-Brexit). Payments just for your land will be phased out over that time and they will bring in this pilot called Environmental Land Management Scheme (ELMS), whereby you will be paid for public benefits. That could be biodiversity in a hay meadow, landscaping (e.g. stone walls), tree for carbon, etc. But perhaps the agricultural organisations will say, where is the food in all this?'

Finally, Darrall said she was not sure how much a difference the World Heritage Site status for the Lakes will make. 'It is great in that it has got a lot more focus on the cultural heritage side of it, but it isn't as some organisations think a fight or argument between natural heritage and cultural heritage. It is all one. The chief worry that we have is that it is already bringing in more people and areas of the Lake District are suffering. There is traffic congestion, there is footpath erosion, more commercialism, and at what point do you say enough?' That is the basis of what the Friends of the Lake District are talking about with the Lake District National Park Authority now.

Back with Billy Bland, at one point in our discussions I challenged him as to what he was doing himself, and what more he could perhaps do. Ann immediately responded, 'get himself on the parish council.' Billy is not formally on the parish council, but goes to many of the meetings, saying that he has, 'raised issues with the parish council and with farmers. I got into a meeting that they didn't know I was coming to. It was a Natural England meeting with farmers. They only meet with those they want to meet. The public should have a say too.'

He then launched into an explanation of his activism on the hunting issue. 'I am taking up the hunting situation with the parish council. I have been to the National Trust and National Park asking for trailing to be suspended as it is being done illegally. The police are turning on monitors and saboteurs because they are gathering evidence of this.' Billy is not a hunt saboteur. He argues that he is a monitor, raising awareness, and just passionately following his ideals with direct action.

We leave this chapter with Billy Bland's manifesto. 'Put that barrier on the Borrowdale Road and bus people in, or let them cycle in or walk in. It would work, I am sure it would. People would still want to come up here, especially if it was different to other valleys. The locals could have a pass for the barrier. I don't mind how many come here as long as they behave themselves.'

He continues, really getting into his stride now. 'We could have the birds we used to have and going even farther back eagles and pine martens. I knew plants because I collected wildflowers as a kid. It seemed to stick in me. If there is something roundabout you each day do you not want to know its name? If I was born now would I be interested in the wildlife around me, much of which isn't there anymore? That is partly what I am on about when I have talked with the National Trust and the National Parks.'

As chronicler it is not for me to back up Billy Bland's comments, or indeed agree or disagree with him. However, reading Isabella Tree's book *Wilding* recently I couldn't help but think of Billy saying, 'you would struggle to find a yellowhammer in this valley now. I haven't seen one for a few years' in his piece to camera for the National Trust video. In her book Tree notes that the yellowhammer is, 'one of our most rapidly declining farmland birds (a drop of 60 per cent nationwide since 1960)'. *Wilding* is the story of a farm (in Sussex) that struggled to pay its way with an intensive farming regime and over the years 'handed their 3,500 acres back to nature'. It is an immensely positive book that illustrates the huge changes in biodiversity that resulted from that move, including a return of yellowhammers.

Billy Bland strongly believes we should be moving towards a different style of land management in Borrowdale, and that similar results might ensue, given time.

From looking to the future, what of the past? Billy Bland bestrode the fell running scene for many years and has worked locally all his life. What tangible, and intangible, legacy is he leaving?

LIVING PROOF

It is sometimes difficult to see what someone's legacy really is. In some ways it can be different things to different people. In Billy Bland's case there is a mismatch between what many think it is and what he himself thinks. It is very easy to think that his Bob Graham Round time of 13:53 from 1982 is his greatest achievement and that his legacy revolves around that. But it is not as simple as that.

It is possible to list Billy Bland's running achievements, of which there are many. He won the Borrowdale race ten times, and the Wasdale race nine times consecutively. He also won the Mountain Trial nine times, the Ennerdale race five times and lost his record for the Ennerdale by just a few seconds to current record holder Kenny Stuart (in 1985). Billy's record of around 7 hrs 35 mins for the Lakeland Four 3000s remains unbeaten to this day. He is still the course record holder for the Borrowdale (from 1981) and Wasdale (from 1982) races.

But there is way more to it than just statistics. Let's look at some different aspects of his legacy.

One characteristic that perhaps gets overlooked about Billy Bland is his generosity, which has already been seen with his helping others on their Bob Graham Rounds. Miles Jessop, of the Scafell Hotel, offers a prize of a weekend for two to the winner of the Borrowdale race. Billy Bland never took that prize. Instead ten folk went for dinner at the hotel each year – with different family and friends invited each time, including race organisers from the past. Ann Bland adds, 'one year we missed the do, so we combined two years and asked runners, and others, to a tattie-pot in the back bar of the Scafell – but not after the Borrowdale race – it was in February when there was an informal run. I think there was about sixty people there. I am not sure what year that was though.'

Something else he did will never happen again. He won Ben Nevis one Saturday, the Mountain Trial the following Sunday and the Langdale race the week after that. It can't happen again because they don't all tie-in together like that. 'I remember Pete Bland saying it was the only time it has ever been done', says Billy, who also has a theory about competing, training and recovery in situations like that. 'The Ben race use to do my legs in. Recovery is what I tried to preach. If you train every day, then you are not doing anything different when training/racing after a hard race.'

Billy's own view is that his Bob Graham Round time has been put on too much of a pedestal. 'Obviously people do see the Bob Graham as something special, but to me it was never as important as the Ennerdale, Wasdale, and Borrowdale races. It was where I lived, yeh. If the Bob Graham hadn't been where it is then I wouldn't have done it. But winning the Borrowdale race because I lived in Borrowdale all my life, it was my Olympics. To win Borrowdale to me was more important than to win any race anywhere else. The Borrowdale record is a good record, and so is the Wasdale.' The fact that the BGR record has been beaten now, but the two race records are still unchallenged lends weight to this view.

In addition to that, those records were achieved in a golden era when there was a great group of fell runners at the top of their form when Billy was also running at his best (in the 1980s). Billy agrees. 'Absolutely, without a doubt. If you wanted to beat somebody when there were a batch of good 'uns then that spurred you on. There were also less races, so you had to race each other, which isn't the case now.'

I put it to Billy Bland that he could have put his phenomenal endurance to other challenges and records, that he could also have left as a legacy of his talent. Two particular options I mentioned were the Paddy Buckley Round and the Charlie Ramsay Round, the Welsh and Scottish equivalents to the Bob Graham Round. Billy's reply was simple and matched his life philosophy. 'As I have said, if the Bob Graham Round wasn't in the Lakes then I wouldn't have run it. I have lived all my life in the valley I was born in. I have been around a bit in the sport, and on the continent on my bike, and I like it when I go, but there is only one place for me and that is Borrowdale. Many people go away to work and that, but many hanker back to where they were born. It is the churchyard next stop for me!'

Billy reckons that if he was able to start his running career over again, he wouldn't approach it much differently. 'Not a lot actually. Like I say, I had the enjoyment of getting better and of meeting other lads and talking about how many miles they do. Then I started doing 40 miles a week when I thought I was breaking through. I heard people talking of 100 miles a week and the penny drops, as you are not doing nearly enough, and you will never beat them. So, it is a learning process. I would always say to anybody who was a winner immediately that I was sorry for them. Because I think you need to get beaten a lot of times and serve your time. Then there is a lot more enjoyment when you get to where you want to be, or as good as you can be. I wouldn't want to change owt really.' As Michael Jordan, the leading basketball player, once put it: 'I fail. But that is why I succeed.'

Billy reflects for a moment on whether he preferred training or racing, before giving a considered response on the fleeting nature of success. 'Race day was rewards day for what you had put in. Absolutely, I liked my training though. That is what you need, because if you do not like your training, I don't think you will ever get to the top because you won't do it. Later on, the fire started to go out and it wasn't such fun anymore, and you are sort of going through the motions, and the wins don't mean so much. The first win you ever have will mean the most and after that it means less eventually.'

Billy Bland's career was not one continuous round of successes though. His only road marathon was less than spectacular. Billy ran 2:32 for fifteenth place in the Barnsley Marathon in 1980, which Jeff Norman won in 2:22. I mentioned to Billy that I had done 2:34 for the marathon, only two minutes slower than him. 'What that day? In Barnsley?'. 'No, in London'. 'Well Barnsley is a hillier marathon', came back straight away, before he expanded on the experience. 'As British Champion fell runner I was probably expected to do better than that. I think it was Pete Haworth who persuaded me to go there and run. Stuart [Bland] had probably run the Cockermouth marathon by then, and the Windermere one. It was just something to do, but we got third team (Pete, Stuart and me). I was twenty-ninth with three miles to go and I knew there were twenty prizes so I was seeing if I could get in there and I did. Within two minutes of finishing rigor mortis had set in. I seized up a treat. I knew I wouldn't be a very good marathoner all along.'

He adds that he also did the Keswick half marathon in 1 hour 14 minutes. 'I was fourth in that just after I had been diagnosed as deficient in potassium and magnesium. I had been training hard, and all of a sudden I felt I was twenty years older. My doctor came to where I was working on a building site and took a blood test from me, and you wouldn't get that now. The test showed the problem and I was given tablets and within ten days I was fine. It was sometime in the 1980s.' Billy had the potassium and magnesium deficiency in 1980, so it looks like it was in May 1980. So, he had time to knock out a half marathon early in the season that he won his only British Fell Championship. Billy adds that he, 'ran it twice actually, as the Army asked me to do it with some of their lot. They set off together then straggled out, so I was running through them to keep them going.'

He also did the Derwentwater 10 once against athletes whom he reckons were faster than him on the flat. According to his own records this was in 1981. 'I did 53:16 on what is a pretty hilly course, as you know. Dave Cannon won in forty-nine minutes. Kenny Stuart got under fifty minutes there another day and all. I did it just because it was there.' Joe Ritson showed me the results sheet, which also showed Jon Broxap running 51:57, Hugh Symonds 51:58, and John McGee 52:07 (taking eighth, ninth and tenth places respectively). Ritson had a rare victory over Billy Bland, fifteenth (in 52:53) to Bland's sixteenth. Unabashed, Billy says Ritson, 'would possibly beat us in any road race. I couldn't win that race. I hadn't the speed for it. The race was local, so I did it. That was me. I ran everything I wanted to and wouldn't save myself.'

One of the best summaries of Billy Bland the person comes from biking friend Mark Wilson. 'In Borrowdale he is a legend. Billy has been very kind to our kids. He is also very generous, and very loyal. He is unbelievably honest, to a fault. If he believes it, he will say it. That isn't really a fault, but some people think so. He falls out with people, unfortunately. To him it doesn't matter. If he thinks something is wrong, it doesn't matter who you are. He is comfortable in his own skin.'

Another aspect of Billy's legacy, that others reading this might like to ponder on, was his determination and application. His training was hard and consistent, as has already been illustrated. But the takeaway for others is that it was relentless and he was always well prepared, as a couple of stories illustrate.

Billy was once asked if he used shorter races as training. His reply debunked that suggestion. 'I just did what races there were. A race was a race and was there to be raced. I won some shorter ones, but I wasn't as good as I was in the longs. For me any race was good if it had a good downhill finish right to the line, because if it was flat at the bottom I might get caught again.'

Contrary to some people's impressions of him, he would use a map if necessary, although he was of course a naturally good navigator. He explains his thoughts on race maps. 'Well you had to take it with you. What I used to do in later years was to write bearings on the back of my hand. Maybe if we were running over Seatallan then I would have a bearing off there written on my hand, and even a compass set on that bearing, and maybe get to some other point and have another bearing and turn the compass to that. If you get lost a map is not much use and neither is a compass. If you are not where you think you are how is that going to help?'

At one of his talks someone asked if he ever took any short cuts. His reply came instantly, ending with a brilliant putdown of poor navigators. 'There is no such thing as a short cut. People used to say I knew where I was going, well I did. You all start on the line together (normally), you follow me if you can keep up, and I will show you the way. If you choose to go further than you need that is up to you.'

The choice of footwear for runners these days is bewildering but was much less so in Billy's day. Many of his contemporaries ran in Walsh trainers and racers on the fells, including myself. Billy confirmed his choice to run in Walshes but was not beholden to any company or suppliers. 'Pete Bland used to give me a pair a year, and I would maybe get through two pairs in a year. I always liked them, but not just because he gave them to me. I would have run in something else if I had liked it better. I wasn't tied to running in anyone's shoes.'

Mention of Pete Bland brings to mind something that his wife Anne said to me. 'Our youngest grandson is called Billy Bland, not because of Billy, which would have been very nice. A few months after he was born I was talking to yon Billy at the Borrowdale race and said, "we have another Billy Bland in the family, just six months old". "I hope he is not as cantankerous as this old bugger", was his response.'

Anne then gave her personal assessment of Billy Bland. 'Billy has relaxed a lot in recent years. But he is a character, definitely. One thing about Billy is that he is honest as the day is long. He never fudges anything, just says it how it is (to him).' I happened to be reading Johnny Cash's autobiography shortly after the time of my interview with Pete and Anne Bland, and I was reminded of Roseanne Cash's comment on her father: "He believes in what he says, but that doesn't make him right." There is a sense of that in Billy Bland.

Billy told one race organiser his fortune at a race once, at the prize giving. Billy had won the race when he was a Vet. The organiser comes to Billy and says, "I am going to give the first Vet prize to somebody else." Billy says, "well, I won that prize. Anyway, who do you think you are, Father Bloody Christmas." Billy adds, 'He was giving my prizes away. If he had said beforehand it *might* have been all right.'

He also has no time for race organisers who wish to make races safer by lessening the challenge of existing races. 'They talk about dangerous ground and technical ground, what a load of shite. It is what it is in front of you. I can understand as a race organiser why you wouldn't want people on edges like Crib Goch and Striding Edge because you would get slagged off for organising a dangerous race. As far as I am concerned there is no dangerous ground, you just have to show it respect, and if you are confident on that sort of ground then you are not taking risks. If you fall, get up and swear at yourself because it is your own fault. Either your legs have gone because you are tired, or you made a mistake. Stones don't jump up at you.'

Ann Bland relays a telling tale about recording part of Billy's legacy and how it affected him at the time. Billy had won a huge batch of trophies in the 1980 season, and at some point in 1981 he got them all together and asked Neil Shuttleworth to come for a photo shoot before they all were returned to the organisers for the next winners, which in some cases would be Billy again. 'Neil Shuttleworth was putting a book together for Billy – but not solely of his photos. Neil came to see Billy to take photos of trophies he had won in the last year as they had to go back. It was a lovely day and they were in here [*Billy's front room*] and he took for ever to set up and he was going on and on – and when the photo comes out Billy is looking like thunder as he was so fed up.'

For a while in the 1980s there was a series of informal winter races, local to Borrowdale. Billy Bland set one up which he called the Jaws of Borrowdale. It was up Kings How, down towards Grange but crossing the beck not as far down as the village. This was down by the Hollows campsite. It was a river scramble as there is no bridge there. Then up to Launchy Tarn, on to Seatoller Fell, out by Tarn at Leaves and down again and up to Dock Tarn, and back home. According to Billy, 'that was just one of several. That was the one when we used the Borrowdale prize for the meal at the Scafell Hotel. Winning one of these was as tough as some champs races. We had some good 'uns in Keswick. Tony Cresswell put one of the races on at Buttermere hostel when he was warden there.'

One tangible legacy is the Billy Bland Challenge, which gets full endorsement from Billy. It is a club relay based on the five legs of the Bob Graham Round, starting and finishing at the Moot Hall in Keswick. The challenge is open to all teams of ten, split into five pairs. Each of the pairs is designated one of the five legs and a baton is passed from one team to the next. The relay is to be completed at any time in the month of June. There are several categories, these include: all male; all female; open (any old mix); mixed (man and woman on each leg); male Vets over 40 (on 30 June); female Vets over 40 (on 30 June); and disabled (same range of groups).

There are records for each category, and it is interesting to see how few teams of ten have beaten Billy Bland's solo time. So far it has remained the Billy Bland Challenge and not been re-named the Kilian Jornet Challenge, another nod to the status of Billy's Bob Graham Round record.

Something else that seems to have developed as a tribute to Billy Bland is a rake on the side of Bowfell. It is mentioned in Nicky Spink's 2005 Bob Graham Round report: 'By the time I was at Rossett Crag I felt a lot better. The pull up Billy Bland's Rake was OK, but it was soon after on Bowfell that we lost Andy Plummer.' And on a website describing the route choices: 'Often known as Billy Bland's rake, this is best not described: it needs to be seen. Take note of parallel shelves from Rossett's vantage and have faith. There are a small number of small cairns.'

I mention this to Billy and he replies, 'if they are referring to this as Billy Bland's rake, then they shouldn't be. I think they are describing the Bob Graham line slanting up when you set off from Rossett. When you are on it you are thinking there must be a better way than this, but there isn't.' Although he is reluctant to claim it, it is presumably the fast line that he pioneered on his Bob Graham record round.

However, there is also a visible legacy of the work Billy has done over the years, all of which he is very proud of.

He says he could take anyone on a journey round Keswick and the surrounding areas and point out jobs he has done that he is particularly pleased with. 'I look at them with a good feeling when I ride my bike past there. For instance, there is a house in Thornthwaite that I faced but didn't build.' Ann adds that, 'you just need to go out our back door and there are three garages he built and stone-faced, as well as a bridge in our back garden.'

The discussion concluded with Billy Bland quietly saying, 'I don't know anyone that has criticised my work, ever.'

Billy added that far as stonework is concerned it is there to look at, and therefore it should look good. He then explained under what circumstances he would NOT take a walling job on. 'People ring up and say, "I have got a job". The first thing I will say is, "have you got any stone?" If they say yes, I will say, "well I want to see it". If I look at that stone I may think, "well no, I'm a waller not a bloody magician". Quite often they have been given it by somebody who had a wall built and had some left over. If I had done that previous job, I would have left the rubbish ones, not the good ones, which is kinda obvious. If that was a case, I would say I am not interested.'

A really strong legacy that Billy leaves is his race record. A closer look at his race record further illustrates just how good (and dominant) Billy Bland was at his peak.

Winning Borrowdale ten times, Billy has the record of 2:34:38, plus the third, fourth, seventh, eighth and tenth best times – six of the top ten times. Simon Booth, with 2:35:18 on a brilliant day in 1999 also got under 2:40, a mark which Billy achieved three times. Since that day at the end of the millennium no-one has run a top ten time, with it most often being won in the high 2:40s or

2:50s. We have to disallow Ben Bardsley's 2:18:29 from 2007. Race organiser, Ann Bland, points out, 'the course was shortened when Ben won, after advice given by the Mountain Rescue team who were on Scafell Pike, who concluded the weather was too bad to run the full course. We missed it out on that day, so the course was significantly shorter, thus much faster times were achieved.' Billy won the 1987 Borrowdale race by a margin of 20:48 and has an average winning margin of fourteen minutes nine seconds for his best eight wins there.

A similar picture emerges if you look at Billy Bland's nine Wasdale wins. Including his course record of 3:25:21, he has the first, third, fourth, fifth and seventh fastest times there. The second fastest is Andy Styan's previous course record of 3:30:51 from 1979. The only time in the top ten fastest since 1990 is Carl Bell's 3:40:53 from 2017, which is tenth. Billy's winning margin when he set the record in 1982 was 19:44, from Bob Whitfield.

Although his Ennerdale course record was taken, by just seven seconds by Kenny Stuart in 1985, Billy Bland's previous record of 3:21:04 was a remarkable performance – as he finished sixteen minutes nineteen seconds in front of Andy Styan, who was on top form at the time. In his five wins Billy ran under 3:25 there three times.

The Mountain Trial is a different kettle of fish as you have a staggered start and don't know how your rivals are doing. Billy Bland won that event, which changes venue and length each year, nine times – with winning times ranging from under three and a half hours to over five hours. He had a remarkable run in the 1984 event, winning by 31:54 from a really strong field, in which Jon Broxap, Jack Maitland and Joss Naylor took the second to fourth places. Let us not forget that Joss Naylor won the Mountain Trial ten times, with a best winning margin of 26:29, and three others of over twenty minutes. He and Billy dominated that event for over two decades, winning nineteen of the twenty-six events between 1966 and 1991.

My own assessment of Billy Bland is given from afar, but from having come to understand him and his place in fell running. No-one has shown the range of ability that Billy displayed. He won short races like the Blisco Dash and Latrigg, and absolutely dominated Borrowdale and Wasdale even when John Wild and Kenny Stuart were at their peak. His 13:53 for the Bob Graham Round remains an iconic and outstanding performance, as do his records for Borrowdale and Wasdale races, which no-one has come near to taking off him.

As much as his longevity at the top of the sport, and all those numbers and facts are impressive, it is the esteem that Billy Bland is held in by his contemporaries and by the current generation of fell runners that confirm him as the greatest fell runner of all time.

Billy Bland has always played down his own achievements, saying, 'Quite a lot of people in my time have said, "Oh I could never do that". And I've said, well, yes you could. One leg past t'other – that's all running is. If you get out there and train, you might be surprised what your body can do.'

To Billy winning is just business done. He admits that he was very satisfied when he first won Borrowdale, as he didn't expect to win. But there was no yelling "yeees" or big celebrations. Billy was mostly thinking he had achieved what he set out to do. 'Hit a target and that is satisfaction in itself. I have come in off training runs maybe a handful of times in my life and sat down and said, "I could have catched a pigeon tonight".' Ann adds that there was a picture of him once clenching his fist at a race finish. That is about as triumphal as he got.

I asked Billy at one point if he had ever thought of moving in his later life, or whether he wanted to stay where he was. 'So, I don't know if I will live in this house till I die. The answer to the question is "hopefully". Why would I want to go anywhere else?'

Billy Bland also replied to a question about his own legendary status by simply saying, 'I was as good as I was. So what? However good or bad Billy Bland was, that was as good as he was. That was me.'

Through his approach to his work, running, wildlife and the environment, and to his cycling, Billy Bland always has had the same attitude. He is a proper legend. On his journey through life it has been: all or nothing at all.

LONG TIME COMING

A Postscript

For 36 years Billy Bland's record time of 13:53 for the Bob Graham Round (BGR) remained without a serious challenge. But in the summer of 2018 it was finally beaten, and how.

Billy had previously rationalised why his record hadn't been beaten. It might come across as harsh, but as usual he said it like he saw it:

'You get an aura, and people put you on a pedestal that you shouldn't be on. Because I was dominant in long fell racing and did this thing [*the BGR record*], I was put on one. Then McDermott and Hartell had taken the 24-hour total on and both tried for my time. I kinda knew they wouldn't get my record. That puts it even more on a pedestal. I never saw myself as anything special. That is where they fall down, they don't train hard enough.'

Someone who does train hard is Rob Jebb, and on 16 July 2016 he had set the second fastest time of 14:30, and there was then some speculation about who might be able to actually beat Billy's time.

Billy Bland took two and a half hours or so off the Bob Graham record, which is similar to what Jasmin Paris did to the ladies' time. He was running how he felt, and yet it was a quantum leap of improvement. He was asked once if he felt that if someone came along and takes five minutes off his time it will it have been much easier for them, because they will have had a schedule and will just shave small amounts of time off, making it a completely different type of run.

He replied that he liked his way. 'You are right, it is different. I would rather be in my shoes than somebody who was having a go at it now. They think they can't stop. They just snatch at a cup of something out of somebody's hands. How horrible, I don't envy them at all. But if they knock something off then good on them. I would much rather do it in the manner I did than the way they are going about it now.'

There are those who believe that Billy himself could have gone quicker. Howard Pattinson is one, as he explains. 'I don't think his fast BGR was necessarily the limit. I think he could have gone quicker. I said to Billy the other day, in my book it is like Roger Bannister and the four-minute mile, that is what you did with the BGR.' But as Billy has pointed out he had no intention to go back to try to go faster. Neither did the barrier-breaking that he did in 1982 lead to others soon following with further faster times, like John Landy did 46 days after Bannister first beat the four-minute mile mark.

On 9 July 2017 *The Times* newspaper published a piece that attempted to whip up some controversy about a Catalan professional runner, Kilian Jornet, being the one to finally do it. It even suggested that, 'there has been speculation among fell runners that he will have to use professionals because locals may not wish to help'. Ann Bland was quoted in the article, 'confirming that she had "heard rumours that people won't help him", although she made it clear that her husband would be happy to shake Jornet's hand if he beat the record'.

An attempt by Kilian Jornet was not formally announced, but it all started with Jornet posting a picture of himself 'on Dale Head' on the internet on Friday 6 July, with the rumour-mill taking over from there. Speculation about what Kilian Jornet was doing in the Lake District was rife on social media, with one of the very first replies being, 'visiting the Pencil Museum in Keswick'. The rumour strengthened and then he was 'definitely doing it' according to some, with Sunday morning a favoured start time.

And so it turned out. Someone in the know confirmed that he had set out at 6a.m. on the Sunday from the Moot Hall, and there was a video clip showing Keswick AC's Carl Bell as pacer on his first leg. They made great strides over the Skiddaw-Blencathra section and arrived at Threlkeld already a few minutes up on Billy Bland's schedule.

Billy Bland cycled from Borrowdale over to Dunmail to see Jornet come flying through at the end of leg two. By now a confirmed pacing list had leaked out through the ether, and it was clear that he had got absolutely top runners supporting him. Jornet had gained more time over the Helvellyn range, and there was a photo of Bland shaking Jornet's hand as he started off up Steel Fell – a fine gesture from Billy.

Many people, including myself, spent a great deal of the day (Sun 8 Jul 2018) watching different social media feeds for updates on Jornet's progress. Judging by this (admittedly filtered view), it was interesting to observe how the mood of the day seem to swing from a certain amount of 'he won't do it' (and even 'I hope he doesn't do it') to one of amazement at the predicted time as the day went on, and the sense of history being made as Carl

Bell led Jornet through a Tour de France-like throng of spectators to touch the door at the Moot Hall at the end of the round. A pacer reckoned him at about 7min per mile on the road section. It would have been good to have been there to see that.

Billy Bland had been at Honister to see Jornet come through and his biking friend Mark Wilson was there with him to experience the occasion. Mark shot a short video there and on it you can hear Kilian say to Carl Bell as they waited to head off on leg 5 of the BGR, 'maybe not so fast this time', in reference to the phenomenal pace he and Carl had run on leg 1 earlier in the day.

Billy Bland was there atop the Moot Hall steps to meet Kilian, and he sat down with him for an iconic photograph of the previous and new record holders. Billy reached behind his back and produced a bottle of champagne, which Martin Stone had procured, to give to Jornet. Another fine gesture, but an ironical one – as neither Billy nor Kilian drink alcohol. Jornet had finished in a brilliant new record of twelve hours fifty-two minutes, taking one hour and one minute off Billy's record.

What was most impressive was that Kilian went off for a shower and shortly came back to talk with some of the people who had come to watch him take on the BGR challenge. For forty minutes or so he talked with individuals, signed autographs and patiently sat for photographs (on the bottom step of the Moot Hall).

As the day unfolded, and in subsequent reports, a picture emerged of how Jornet had gone about planning to take the BGR on. He decided to do it only on the Monday beforehand, having recovered well from his recent broken leg, and having tested it in winning the Marathon du Mont Blanc. Being fit, not too tired from other events (due to the layoff), and knowing the conditions were ideal seemed to seal it. Martin Stone was helping co-ordinate pacers but was having trouble getting sufficient high-quality ones. Martin Stone's report on the event gives more background to how this panned out serendipitously:

'There was one major complication. When I emailed potential pacers last Wednesday night, about who were the fastest runners (especially for legs 1 to 3), no one replied to me. By Thursday evening with an attempt looming on Sunday I was beginning to panic. I decided it was time to get on the phone and by then it was about 9:30p.m. It was fortunate that the first person I phoned was Rob Jebb, as by complete co-incidence he told me that he had been planning to do a fast BG last Saturday but had already cancelled it because of the expected heat. He hadn't cancelled because of Kilian as he wasn't aware of Kilian's attempt when he cancelled. He was in two minds about Kilian's attempt and wasn't sure if he was comfortable being involved with it. I asked him whether if Kilian phoned him, he might agree to help? As soon as I came off the phone I contacted Kilian and explained the unfortunate co-incidence. Kilian got straight on the phone to Jebby to discuss it and asked him if he would pace him. Jebby agreed and within an hour Jebby's pacers were getting in touch with me to offer their services. Jebby's decision to help Kilian had unlocked all the pacers who until then were loyal to him and didn't want to offend him. Jebby and various other pacers then spoke to Billy to see how he felt about it. By then Billy and Ann Bland had met Kilian and been completely won over by his modesty and charm. Billy told everyone to do everything possible to make the day a success. Everyone was now onside and fully supportive of Kilian's BG attempt.'

Jornet was very aware of the tradition of the BGR and is big on the history of mountain running. He planned as low-key a round as a person of his stature could achieve, with virtually no presence from his sponsor, and certainly no big advance publicity. He acknowledges that he knew about the BGR from back in 2008 when people like Ricky Lightfoot were going out to the Alps. Although he didn't recce it all he says it is 'powerful to discover the mountains'. What he did do was call on Billy Bland to have a chat, but unfortunately the first time he called Billy was out on a bike ride. But they met up on the Friday. His approach and demeanour certainly endeared him to many observers.

Between Billy finding out Kilian Jornet had a planned attempt and him actually doing the round Billy went out supporting his cycling friend Mark Wilson. Mark was wanting to do the Bob Graham Round leg by leg. He and Billy have completed the first two legs over two days many months apart. It started with them doing leg 1 in 2017. Billy sets the scene. 'Because of my hip it took ages to come off Blencathra. We came down Hall's Fell Ridge and I was looking for ramps of grass and sliding on my arse. I still left him behind! Nobody passed us, but I was zigzagging all over the place. We got to the bottom and I said I am not doing any more.' Nonetheless, that time in July 2018 they were doing leg 2. Billy takes up the story of that day. 'I was pretty certain Calfhow Pike wasn't one of the tops, which just shows how far out of it you get. But we went on to it anyway. These other fellers had seen us going on to there and so they came up on to there. We just got talking and I asked if they were doing the BGR and they said they were recceing. Somehow my name was mentioned [*by Mark*] and I said I was the Round record holder, but probably not for very long.' Mark still wants to finish the round off with him, Billy adds. 'We have also done Dunmail to Esk Hause one day and binned it after that. We have got to go and do Esk Hause onwards yet. We might go on to Honister in the same day or do it in two bits. We are doing fast walking.'

Billy Bland then takes up the story of meeting Jornet. 'Ann had a good crack with Kilian and Jordi [*his manager*] the day I wasn't there. So, he came back again which is good of him.' Billy said to Jornet, 'I am going to give you some advice. Don't take your poles (*which he uses sometimes on longer events*). Break that record without poles. It is bullshit but it will get talked about a load if you do. Jebby agreed with me.'

It seemed Jornet was going to go out on the Sunday, or the following Tuesday. Billy adds, 'Another thing I did for him was, just as a bit of background, I took him down to the [*Stonethwaite*] churchyard to show him Bob Graham's gravestone which says it was 130 miles. I am not sure if he twigged the difference [*it is more like 62 miles*] or whether he didn't want to say anything. I also said I don't know if you are going to stop or not, but they say you aren't. As a bit of banter I added "Now then, I stopped for 21 minutes, so if you don't break it by 21 minutes then I am better than you!" We even had some banter during the round.' As Jornet came in to Honister, Billy said to him, 'I am pleased to see you are suffering'.

There was some speculation about what they said to each other on the Moot Hall steps at the end. When I asked him, Billy laughed, and said, 'someone thought we were discussing who spoke the best English!' In reality, what was said speaks volumes about the bond the two had established in such a short time. On the Moot Hall steps after Kilian had finished he leaned across and said to Billy, 'I was thinking about them 21 minutes'. Billy also jokingly said to Killian, 'no wonder you did it faster, it was only half what Bob Graham did' [*see 130 miles above*].

It was great the way the fell running community embraced Jornet and the occasion. Co-ordinator Martin Stone had been a pacer on Billy Bland's record round in 1982. One of Jornet's pacers was Martin Mikkelsen-Barron, whose father Pete was also a pacer on Billy's record round, and was there to watch him come home, along with Kenny Stuart, who had paced Billy on his leg 1, which finished right near Kenny's house.

For the record, the split times for Billy Bland (first) and Kilian Jornet were:

Leg 1	2:13	2:07:04
Leg 2	2:41	2:31:13
Leg 3	3:43	3:31:05
Leg 4	3:09	2:56:04
Leg 5	1:47	1:46:56

Given that not many people have run faster than Billy's time on leg 1, even when part of a relay round, he has been challenged in the past as to whether he actually set off too fast in 1982. Billy has always denied that charge, and now uses the data from Kilian's round to re-emphasise the point. He explains, 'I did not start too fast on my BG round. Kilian was no faster on Honister to Keswick than I was, so I was going as well as he was at the end. He was 51 minutes to the top of Skiddaw and I was 53. So, I was not going too fast, and I knew that on the day.' He also points out a weird co-incidence in their two rounds, whereby they both had a bad patch coming down in to Honister, Billy sitting down for a while there before finishing the leg. Billy says that he was pressed too hard by his pacers at that point, as they thought he could get under 14 hours, which he eventually did, despite the stop. 'I had the hiccup above Honister, and he had a hiccup in the same spot, which is bizarre. Whether he had that same thing of them talking about getting under 13 hours maybe, but it is amazing how that happened. Scoffer saw me after he had paced Kilian on that leg [*into Honister*] and he said, "he's buggered". I said he won't be, he just needs refuelling.'

There was an unfortunate conclusion to the event. Martin Stone had emailed all the pacers and asked them to go to a meal on the Monday night in Keswick. Kilian was treating them all. Kilian himself had emailed Ann and Billy Bland but their email wasn't working, and they didn't get to know about it. Ann commented ruefully, 'I felt really bad as we seemed really rude not replying and not going. When we got in touch eventually Kilian said he was going to come round and say goodbye, but Jordi had scratched their hire car and had to get it fixed.'

Jon Broxap was asked to be there at the meal after Kilian's round, as he had been a pacer for Billy, but he wasn't able to as he was away. He shared his thoughts with me later. 'I do know that there was a lot of empathy when Kilian met Billy. Billy was very much a man of the mountains, and the mountains were part of him. He was very local, was his own person, and very much a Borrowdale person. I think Kilian has that empathy with the mountains as well. Billy did not seek publicity and was a very different character to Joss, for instance. Kilian being a professional athlete is just a sign of the times. But I think there was a nice mutual respect between them.'

Billy Bland gave this assessment of Kilian Jornet, the athlete. 'Your body adapts to the load you give it. Individuals who go outside the box, if you like, are needed to move things on. They are not mass produced and he is certainly at a different level. I will be saying to any of our lot – you need to change your attitude. If you want to be as good as Kilian you will have to train like him. You need another individual that strong in the head to just go and do his own thing and sod anybody else and see what you get at the end of it.'

There have been those who are talking about a foreign and British record for the BGR. One person I know has said that they, 'look at it as an amateur record and a professional record. Nobody will go for the time now. Billy's lifestyle when he did the round in 1982 and Kilian's now are just not comparable.' But Billy doesn't agree with that assessment. 'I am embarrassed by people bringing that into it. Kilian has two arms, two legs, a heart and lungs, just like Billy Bland. I know why he is better, as he trained harder. We are all beatable, even him, and it will prove to be.'

Let's leave the last words to Billy's wife Ann Bland, plus friends Tony Cresswell and Mark Wilson.

When Claire Maxted interviewed Billy, Pete Barron and Kenny Stuart outside the Moot Hall after the event she said they looked like Foggy, Compo and Clegg. Ann Bland counters this by saying, 'had Billy been younger and fitter he would have been on the fells pacing Kilian. Fell running is an amazing sport and everyone helps each other.'

Tony Cresswell says he is pleased that the record has

gone. 'Records are set to be broken. The guy did it with dignity. I was disappointed that one of the greatest fell runners there has ever been has lost his record. Things need to move on. Billy just went out with a bunch of mates. Kilian had meticulous planning behind his round.'

Mark Wilson says he wondered how Billy would feel when he lost the BGR record. 'Billy found out this lad was born in the hills he has run every day of his life and he is actually a bit like him. This is a serious athlete who loves the mountains, and who leads a simple life. He genuinely was happy for him. I thought he would be a bit of a broken man after it, but he seems almost like it is a relief. I would love to set up a bike ride with Billy, Kilian and myself. That would be great.'

APPENDIX

Definition of fell race categories *as per the FRA (Fell Runners Association) rules*

RACE CATEGORIES

A fell race is one run on fell, hill or mountain terrain and shall be categorised as follows :

Category A – Should average:

a. Not less than 50 metres climb per kilometre
b. Should not have more than 20 per cent of the race distance on road
c. Should be at least 1.5 kilometres in length

Category B

a. Should average not less than 25 metres climb per kilometre
b. Should not have more than 30 per cent of the race distance on road

Category C

a. Should average not less than 20 metres climb per kilometre
b. Should not have more than 40 per cent of the race distance on road
c. Should contain some genuine fell terrain

RACE LENGTH CATEGORIES

a. A category L (Long) race is 20 kilometres or over
b. A category M (Medium) race is over 10 kilometres but less than 20 kilometres
c. A category S (Short) race is 10 kilometres or less

NOTE: The categories can be combined, so a race might be described as an AL or BM for instance.

REFERENCES

The following sources have been consulted for background material, or just inspiration, in writing this book.

Books:
Thorneythwaite Farm, Ian Hall; *Honister Slate Mine*, Alastair Cameron and Liz Withey; *The Story of Borrowdale*, Shelagh Sutton; *Tales of a Lakeland Valley: Borrowdale*, Sheila Richardson; *Lake District Fell Farming*, Terry McCormick; *The Ben Race*, Hugh Dan MacLennan; *Slate Mining in the Lake District*, Alastair Cameron; *Stud Marks on the Summits*, Bill Smith; *Friends of the Lake District: the early years,* John Cousins; *Rocks and Rain, Reason and Romance,* David Howe; *Wilding,* Isabella Tree; *The Greatest,* Matthew Syed; *The Cumbrian Dictionary of Dialect, Tradition and Folklore*, William Rollinson

Booklets:
Fifty Years Running: *A History of the Mountain Trial*, LDMTA; *Our Traditional Lakeland Sports: Ambleside and its Sports*, Marjorie Blackburn; *History and Records of Notable Fell Walks, 1864–1972, Within the Lake District*, Fred Rogerson

Magazines:
Fellrunner magazine; *Climber and Rambler* magazine; *Up and Down* magazine

Websites:
Fell Runners Association; The Borrowdale Story; *Keswick AC; Cumberland Fell Runners Association*

INDEX

Note: under 'Bland, Billy and races' there is a listing of all races in which Billy Bland competed and which are mentioned in the text. The suffix (r) indicates that a record time was set. There are also separate references within the index for each race.

INDEX

INDEX

INDEX